PENGUIN
COMPASS

BREAKING FAITH

John Cornwell is an award-winning journalist
and author with a lifelong interest in Vatican and
Catholic affairs. He is a regular contributor to the
Sunday Times of London and to the *Tablet* and
other religious affairs publications around the
world. He is former research fellow at Jesus
College, Cambridge, where he now directs the
Science and Human Dimension Project. His other
books include *Hitler's Pope, A Thief in the Night,*
and *The Power to Harm*. He lives in England.

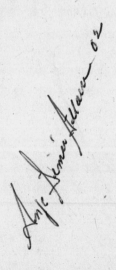

JOHN CORNWELL

BREAKING FAITH

Can the Catholic
Church Save Itself?

PENGUIN COMPASS

PENGUIN COMPASS
Published by the Penguin Group
Penguin Putnam Inc., 375 Hudson Street, New York,
New York 10014, U.S.A.
Penguin Books Ltd, 80 Strand, London WC2R 0RL, England
Penguin Books Australia Ltd, 250 Camberwell Road,
Camberwell, Victoria 3124, Australia
Penguin Books Canada Ltd, 10 Alcorn Avenue,
Toronto, Ontario, Canada M4V 3B2
Penguin Books India (P) Ltd, 11 Community Centre,
Panchsheel Park, New Delhi – 110 017, India
Penguin Books (N.Z.) Ltd, Cnr Rosedale and Airborne Roads,
Albany, Auckland, New Zealand
Penguin Books (South Africa) (Pty) Ltd, 24 Sturdee Avenue,
Rosebank, Johannesburg 2196, South Africa

Penguin Books Ltd, Registered Offices:
Harmondsworth, Middlesex, England

First published in the United States of America by Viking Compass,
a member of Penguin Putnam Inc. 2001
Published in Penguin Compass 2002

1 3 5 7 9 10 8 6 4 2

THE LIBRARY OF CONGRESS HAS CATALOGED THE HARDCOVER EDITION AS FOLLOWS:
Cornwell, John, 1940–
Breaking faith : the Pope, the people, and
the fate of Catholicism / John Cornwell.
p.   cm.
Includes bibliographical references and index.
ISBN 0-670-03002-3 (hc.)
ISBN 0 14 21.9608 8 (pbk.)
1. Catholic Church—History—1965–   2. John Paul II, Pope, 1920–   I. Title.
BX1390 .C67 2001
282'.09'045—dc 21   2001026721

Printed in the United States of America
Set in Aldus
Designed by Francesca Belanger

For my mother,
Kathleen [Egan] Cornwell,
who kept the Faith

CONTENTS

BREAKING
FAITH

CATHOLICS AND THEIR STRUGGLE TO BELIEVE

THE EVENTS OF SEPTEMBER 11, 2001 and their aftermath proved a testing time for all religious faiths, and especially the Abrahamic religions of Islam, Judaism, and Christiantity. People all over the world, but especially in the United States, have been asking as never before to what extent religion makes for a better world. How much is religion the cause of hatred and violence? Would the constraining of religion, its demise even, bring greater tolerance and peace to the world? In short, is religion a source of evil rather than good?

And yet the reactions of ordinary people, victims and relatives, and emergency service workers caught up in the consequences of that violence render the question virtually an insult. People immediately and ardently turned to their faith to find meaning and consolation in the midst of agony and despair.

Catholics were no exception. The many funerals and special services in St. Patrick's Cathedral, New York, bore testimony to the abiding stength of Catholic belief and practice, demonstrating in the eyes of the world that Catholicism remains vital and strong despite the pressures of secularism and materialism, despite the tendency to explain human history in purely rational and scientific terms. The Church proved itself to be resilient, with enormous moral and spiritual resources, an undoubted force for good.

Meanwhile, a "new" crisis threatens the Church in North America and Europe. Since the beginning of the year 2002, revelations of longstanding priestly pedophilia and other forms of sexual abuse, with evidence of official cover-ups and connivance, have dominated the news, scandalizing Catholics at every level from lay parishioners right up to the Vatican itself. The Church's reputation for holiness and integrity has been called into question. The bond of trust between parents, the young, and their pastors has been profoundly shaken, if not terminally shattered, prompting calls for radical change in the recruitment and formation of candidates for the priesthood.

As Christianity begins its third millennium, Catholics throughout the world have ample reason to scrutinize the state of their Church—to wonder, even, about its prospects for survival as a united and thriving entity in the coming century. If the Catholic community of faith can be likened to a family, it is a family in deep and widespread dysfunction. Those brought up in the Catholic faith learn early the characteristics of their Church: unity, holiness, catholicity (meaning universality), its direct descent from the first apostles. Few can doubt the universality of the billion strong Catholic Church spread across every continent and appealing to peoples of every culture and tongue; none would challenge its claims to unbroken succession from the disciples of Jesus, and in particular from St. Peter to the present Pope, John Paul II.

But the prized unity and holiness of the Church appears everywhere, and at many levels in doubt and under threat. Over the past two decades Catholics have become deeply divided between conservatives and progressives to the point of imminent schism; beyond that profound divide there are splits between men and women in the Church, between bishops and faithful, between clergy and laity, between the Curia in Rome and the diocese of the world, as well as divisions over liturgy, over theology, over questions of sexuality, marriage, and the ethics of human fertilization. Every week brings new headlines and scandalous tales of priests who sexually abuse minors, of bishops turning a blind eye to the behavior of erring pastors under their authority, of Catholics right up to the pope himself ignoring the victims' abuse. Over the past three years, moreover, historians have increasingly examined the roots of modern anti-Semitism in the Catholic Church from the late nineteenth century to the mid-twentieth century. Calls to settle specific issues relating to documentation, or to acknowledge justified criticisms, have been dealt with inadequately and inappropriately by the hierarchy in Rome.

The pontificate of John Paul II has been marked by an unassailable integrity, a single-minded dedication to duty and evident holiness of life. History will record his indisputable part in the downfall of Soviet communism in Poland and beyond. In the late years of his papacy, stricken by Parkinson's disease, he astonished the world with his fortitude; he was particularly impressive when he greeted and blessed old people, the sick, and the young.

Yet John Paul's pontificate has been assailed by a grim accumulation of woes: defections, plummeting Mass attendance, a collapsing priesthood, conflicts involving a host of moral and jurisdictional issues, the decline of Catholic marriage, and expanding Catholic divorce rates. Theologians are in conflict with bishops over academic freedom and definitions of Catholic doctrine; bishops are at odds with the Vatican over centralized authority; the faithful are battling with one another, the bishops, and the Pope over issues such as pastoral and liturgical participation, sexual morality, the status and involvement of women, the strictures that prevent divorced Catholics from full communion. In the Third World, where 70 percent of Catholics now live, the Church competes with countless sects and faces the problem of syncretism—the mixing of Christianity with pagan practices. In many parts of Africa and Latin America Catholics see their priest only once every few years. The Church is growing apace in Brazil and parts of Africa but practice and belief, according to the hierarchies of these regions, are tenuous among masses of Catholics.

In Europe, traditionally the heartland of Catholicism, practice appears to be in terminal decline. There has been a staggering drop in church attendance, especially among the young; baptisms, marriages, and ordinations to the priesthood are plummeting. At a special synod in 1999, the bishops of Europe declared that the peoples of the entire continent had decided to live "as though God did not exist."

This book, which reports on the critical condition of the institutional Church, argues that despite the persistence of faith, a thirst for spirituality, and enthusiasm for good works among the billion strong Catholic faithful, John Paul is leaving the Catholic Church in a worse state than he found it. He and leading Catholic churchmen, however, have routinely traduced the ordinary members of the faithful for the current parlous state of the Church: their selfishness, individualism, materialism, and hedonism; their headlong descent into "secularism." John Paul despairs of this generation of Catholics, placing his hope for the future in Catholic youth. He points to the mass enthusiasms, such as Youth Day in Rome during the Jubilee Year, but these passing displays are no indication of the true state of affairs: in France, for example, only 7 percent of the young ever attend church.

The Pope and the Vatican are not inclined to consider their own shortcomings and weaknesses, their own part in the plight in which the Church finds itself. In recent years, moreover, it has become increasingly difficult to write frankly of the flaws in the institutional Church without being accused of bad faith by an influential constituency of fellow Catholics.

This book argues that it is essential for Catholics, in an authentically universal Church, to examine the state of their faith honestly and boldy, to identify and quantify the trends of belief and practice, the failings and dysfunctions, and to explore the underlying reasons. The perception that the Catholic Church is fragmenting, that it is failing, that it harbors dark elements in its present and recent history, must be faced squarely by Catholics themselves if their Church is to survive another generation. The official Catholic Church, the Pope, the Vatican, and the bishops do not take kindly to lay Catholic criticism from the periphery. But Catholics now live in a world that demands transparency of its institutions, accountability of all communities and social groupings. Failure to identify the extent and the sources of dysfunction in the Catholic Church can only discourage the lapsed and partially lapsed, and further deter young Catholics who are already leaving in droves.

Accurately depicting the state of the Catholic Church and illustrating its expansion and decline in different parts of the world is no easy task, given the institution's complexity and size. I have been greatly assisted by the provision of official statistics in the second half of the twentieth century, many of them provided by the Vatican itself and by diocesan offices. Like a patient who undergoes diagnostic tests, for blood pressure and cholestorol levels, say, comparative facts and figures reveal a kaleidoscope of relevant symptoms. The decline in marriages before a priest, vocations, ordinations, baptisms, and church attendance, as well as the increase in divorces, annulments, and defections from the religious life give crucial information about the current health of the Church, and its past and potential trends.

But statistical objectivity does not of itself provide an authentic impression of faith and practice. For this reason I have grounded my report in several autobiographical accounts, confirming that the story of lived faith requires a subjective, confessional dimension of engaged personal experience. At the same time, I tell the stories of ordinary Catholics, friends, acquaintances, and family members, who give witness to the importance of religion in their lives, while struggling with the everyday problems of keeping faith in a culture that is increasingly inimical to spiritual values and belief. There is something that it is like to be a Catholic—some call it a "Catholic imagination"; it is often described as a process of routinely seeing God in the tangible things of this world, and it is shared and valued by a Church in which some 70 percent of its members live in the Third World.

My readers, Catholics and non-Catholics alike, have a right to know where I am coming from, and I have a right not to be misrepresented as I was after the publication of *Hitler's Pope*. So here, at the outset of this new work, which again contains constructive criticism of the Catholic Church, I feel it essential to state the facts unequivocally. I was born and raised a Catholic, and I spent seven years in seminaries before abandoning a vocation to the priesthood in my early twenties, and, eventually, as a matter of conscience, Christianity itself. As the years passed I became increasingly convinced that I was a happier, better person without a belief in God. I did not look back: I did not bear the slightest malice. I had reason to regret an overdisciplined youth, but I had also benefited from a privileged Catholic education—which included, ironically, the very disciplines in which the Vatican found me wanting—namely, Church history, theology, canon law.

After the seminary I started my tertiary education over again, studying for a first degree in humanities and pursuing research in philosophy and literature in Britain and Canada. Then my career took a dramatic new turn. I started to write journalism from different parts of the world, and eventually took a staff job on the foreign desk of a British national newspaper. Many of the conflicts in the world at that time—the Arab-Israeli crises, the Iran-Iraq war, the troubles in Northern Ireland—were shaped at least in part, as I saw it, by religious prejudice and fanaticism. It seemed to me that while religionists were incapable of treating their neighbors, including those of different faiths, equally as children of God, there was little to recommend their beliefs and principles. As I entered middle age I was firmly entrenched in secular humanism, believing that morality was the avoidance of actions that might bring painful consequences on our fellows and that we owed no duty beyond our obligations to family, community, and society. Nothing short of a miracle could have changed these firm convictions.

Then, about twelve years ago that miracle happened. In a moment of grace I embarked on the difficult journey back to faith. Along the way, I investigated the charge that John Paul I, the smiling Pope of thirty days, had been murdered by brother bishops in the Vatican. Published under the title *A Thief in the Night* (Penguin 1989, 2001), the book conclusively dismissed these allegations, which had been a matter of dismay for the Vatican for several years. While I was engaged on that project I met John Paul II in person after his early morning Mass and spoke with him privately. He encouraged my research, and after that I found doors opening up in the Vatican. Despite the critical tone of my report on the death of John Paul I, by the time *A Thief in the Night* was published in 1989 I had rediscovered for myself what I thought I had lost forever—that for all its wounding and self-wounding ways, the Catholic Church is a universal source of spiritual flourishing.

Many of the Church's current problems lie within the changing circumstances of contemporary cultures; the Catholic Church exists within society, and society changes inexorably, sometimes rapidly. For the first time in the Church's history, the bishops and the pope of the day acknowledged at the Second Vatican Council in the early 1960s that the Church needs to grow and change with the times: they called the process *aggionarmento*. The need to engage the modern world was acknowledged at the time, but many within the Church have forgotten or chosen to disregard that conciliar imperative. Attitudes of younger generations toward authority, the altering demographics of Catholic enclaves, and the need to live in pluralist communities that actively respect differing beliefs and value systems all have an impact on traditional Catholic attitudes. The question is whether the Church sees itself as an institution within society or standing out against it. One of the most urgent issues for the Catholic Church today is its treatment of women; still relegated to the status of second-class members, the continued disdain for women and their role within the faith is destructive and self-wounding, for these are the mothers of the priests and Catholics of tomorrow. This book reveals again and again that some Catholics are still trying to live in a Church that existed before 1960; some are even living in a Church of the nineteenth century; others are living in the Church that exists in the world of today.

At the same time, the roots of many features of the Catholic crisis lie in recent and remote history. The very meaning of the word "church" and its altering metaphors are explored in my account for their significance for today's Catholics, revealing deep contradictions in perspective. Not the least of those clashes involve powerful self-images that have become mutually exclusive. Through the early modern period the Catholic Church saw itself as a sovereign empire in antagonistic conflict with secular nation states; the Second Vatican Council, by returning to an earlier Christian-Judaic idea, encouraged images that saw the Church as a pilgrim people on the move—human, fallible, part of history, extending respect and love to people of all beliefs as well as those of none. The old metaphor of the centrist triumphalist citadel continues to exist destructively alongside the Church of the Second Vatican Council. As the Church faces, inevitably, the election and the pontificate of a new pope, the most urgent task must be to bring back the vast numbers of Catholics who have become marginalized and demoralized during a period of growing conservative intransigence. For all his evident holiness, for all that he has poured out his life in the service of his Church, the year 2002 has seen John Paul II banning general confessions (which had become popular among those discouraged by one-to-one confession), and issuing instructions forbidding Catholic lawyers to involve themselves in divorce litigation. These are just two examples of recent measures designed to exclude rather than encourage those millions of the faithful who are in greatest need of spiritual sustenance. If the Church is to survive, marginalized Catholics must seek change from within rather than abandoning the faith to conservatives, who would exclude reformers.

I am inclined—as a believer—to trust that faithful, constructive criticism may be open to the operation of providence. Writing about the condition of the Church with love and sadness is not only descriptive but creative: in other words, attempting to make sense of the state of the Church has the power to affect and to influence, however modestly, the very process one is describing. So of course it matters.

If this book seeks to influence, albeit from the periphery of my Church, it is to urge an appreciation of the Christian foundations and beneficence of pluralism—religious, political, and social. Catholics have largely disowned the virtues of pluralism in the modern era, although they have prospered and benefited under them. Catholic bishops and popes have often confused those virtues with the fallacies of relativism and indifferentism (the notion that every religion is as good or as bad as any other). In fact, there have been times when the official Church has deprecated difference in the modern period to the extent of anathematizing its exponents, excommunicating perceived "dissidents," and even depriving them of a Christian burial (as with the Jesuit Father George Tyrrell in the first decade of the twentieth century). Two popes—Pius IX and Pius X—carried their detestation of pluralism to historic extremes. Under John Paul II, we have seen—as I report in this book—the routine and "official" characterization of criticism as treachery.

Meanwhile, conservative Catholic defense groups routinely portray the Church as victim of a new wave of media persecution. These doughty apologists fail to acknowledge that the principles underpinning freedom of religious belief and practice are the same as those that underpin the legitimacy of constructive criticism. Angelo Sodano, Cardinal Secretary of State in the final years of Wojtyla, has counseled that to criticize is to fail in love: *Chi ama non critica.* Up to a point he is correct: Christian love, at its height, is utterly nonjudgmental. But there are times in any loving family, as he and John Paul would be the first to insist, when a measure of harsh truth telling ("tough love" in the parlance of the times) is essential to avoid collusion with denial and dysfunction. Freedom to practice our chosen beliefs and freedom to inquire and tell the truth are inseparable, since both are based on an equality of love due to each and every human being in the sight of God.

CHAPTER 1

A CATHOLIC DARK AGE

This is the darkest time in Catholic history . . . the collapse of religious life, the dearth of vocations, the lowering of ecclesiastical discipline, particularly vis-à-vis false teaching and moral teaching, the
general confusion, the apostasy of the Catholic universities, the loss
of the sense of the divinity of Christ, all these conspire to make this
the most difficult time in Catholic history.
—Father Benedict Groeschel, Office of Spiritual Development,
Archdiocese of New York

André Malraux was certainly right when he said that the twenty-
first century would be the century of religion or it would not be
at all.
—John Paul II, *Crossing the Threshold of Hope*

THERE IS A CHURCH I have been going to, on and off ever since I
was a boy, in the heart of London's Covent Garden. Its congregation is composed in the main of people who work locally in the
hotels, restaurants, theaters, bars, and nightclubs; there are office
workers, too, who come during their lunchtime on working days,
and occasional tourists and well-dressed guests from the nearby
Savoy Hotel. This is an area of the city dedicated to leisure and
entertainment; it is also replete with social problems: drugs,
homelessness, prostitution, pornography. I believe the parish
counts some sixty different nationalities; there are asylum seek-
ers and immigrants of every status; there are people here of most

ages, from infants to octogenarians. In a sense it is like the whole of the Catholic Church.

This Covent Garden church is dedicated to Corpus Christi—the Body of Christ—and it has a special ministry to actors. Our priest is a good man and tremendously active, but he is no longer young. He keeps his sermons short, he is good-humored, and he has preserved some of the Catholic sacramentals that have disappeared from too many of our churches: a Lady Chapel, statues of Saint Patrick, Saint Thérèse of Lisieux, and Saint Genesius, the patron saint of the stage; an offering box for candles for the Holy Souls in Purgatory (some of us Catholics still believe in companionship with our dead). There is a lunchtime Mass every day and the church, unusually for today, is kept open for locals to come in to pray.

At Mass we sing together, and pray together; we ask forgiveness, and tell God that we are unworthy to enter under his roof; we sit and stand and kneel and give each other the sign of peace with a handshake or a kiss; we take that little white bread wafer with a sip of red wine, in amnesty and mercy for the time being—which is the only time we have. Our church is no New Jerusalem, but we believe Christ is with us in the priest, in the people, in the Word, and especially in the Eucharist—that piece of bread. His presence in the bread is a kind of language; like building the New Jerusalem, it is not a language we shall manage to learn in time.

There are congregations like ours on every continent. Looking around the congregation one can see in the faces the far-flung places of our homes of origin: the jungles and pampas of South America, the frozen north of Canada, the teaming cities of Asia and the conurbations of North America, the Mediterranean regions and the industrial heartlands of Europe, the war-torn nations of the Balkans, the towns and villages of Africa, and the islands of the Caribbean. Going to a church like ours on Sundays and feast days you would think that our Catholic communities of faith are thriving. Most of our parishioners, I am sure, would be surprised to learn that the Catholic Church is in crisis.

Anyone who undertakes to traverse even a small part of the vast and complex realities of Catholicism is struck by the paradox of the persistence of flourishing local communities and the general fragmentation and decline of the Church as an organic whole. Such is the deep connectedness of Catholicism, in belief and practice, our church in Covent Garden cannot for long escape what is happening in the Church at large. It will not be long, for instance, given the graying of the priesthood and the decline in vocations in England, before the parish will have a part-time priest, or no priest at all. Within ten years, half the priests in Britain currently will have died (and we are better off than most parts of the world). Few teenagers are to be seen in the congregation, and hardly any marriages survive to flourish as Catholic families. The pews, full for the main masses on Sunday, give no impression of the countless defections of the marginalized and discouraged who have lost heart and turned away. In Britain, according to statisticians, there should now be fifteen million Catholics if all those members of the faithful who had come from Ireland, and their families, had kept the faith. Due to defections there are just over four million. Since the mid-1960s regular Mass attendance has dropped from two million to a million, now representing only a quarter of the nominally Catholic population.

Familiarity with the wider constituency of those who call themselves Catholics and those who have abandoned their Catholicism reveals a series of interconnecting fault lines and crises throughout the Church. In the United States, which boasts the fourth largest Catholic population in the world, marriages by Catholics before a priest have practically halved since the 1960s. In 1960 there were one and a half million baptisms: forty years on, and in a Catholic population almost six times greater, annual baptisms have dropped to below a million. In 1958 three-quarters of all Catholics in North America attended church regularly; by the year 2000 the figure has dropped to about a third, and ordinations to the priesthood have declined by more than two-thirds.

In Europe, the home and birthplace of Catholicism, the faith appears to be in accelerated retreat. In January 2001, reporting on the most recent surveys of Catholic worship and belief, the international Catholic weekly *The Tablet* commented that the first year of the third millennium opened with "the mainline Churches in the European countries, traditionally the heartland of Christianity, experiencing staggering declines in attendance and affiliation." Between 30 and 50 percent of parishes have no resident priest in West Europe. Even in Italy, where almost 90 percent of the nation professes Catholicism, regular Sunday attendance stands at only a quarter of the Catholic population, down 10 percent since the early 1980s, while seminary enrollments have halved during the same period. In Catholic Ireland, according to a survey conducted by Maynooth College, new vocations have dropped from 750 in 1970 to 91 in 1999 and ordinations from 259 to 43.

Nor do the indices bring great hope from East Europe and the developing world. Europe's leading statistician of religion, the Jesuit Jan Kerkhofs, declared in 1999 that "since 1987 all kinds of vocations have been decreasing in Poland." According to the *National Catholic Register*, by as early as 1993 between half and two-thirds of Catholic Poles did not assent to the Church's teachings on abortion, contraception, and premarital sex, and only a quarter of Catholic children and youth were attending church regularly. Meanwhile, in the Third World the ratio of priests to faithful continues to plummet, the worst decline in South America where in two decades the proportion of priests to people has declined from one priest for every six thousand Catholics to one priest for every seven thousand. Mass attendance in the region stands at about 15 percent of the population and, according to the National Conference of Brazilian Bishops, some 600,000 Catholics leave the Church each year to join fundamentalist and evangelical Protestant sects.

But these figures of decline and departure are merely symptomatic of deeper, structural shifts. Catholic people—bishops, priests, religious, laypeople—are asking, as never before, who they are and what is to become of their Church. They are asking not just how they can survive the current decline in practice, but how they are to relate both to God and to the world. Is it Catholic to bring down the divide between the religious and the secular? Or is it Catholic to be counter the culture and stand out against the ways of the world? Catholics are separating into rival camps, and the disagreements are increasingly marked by indignation, anger, and despair.

The Papal Cult

John Paul II is enthusiastically revered by most Catholics for his evident personal holiness and iron will. He is highly esteemed by non-Catholics the world over for his stand on moral principles, although many who praise him on this score are not bound by his strictures. But for progressive Catholics, and a vast marginalized faithful, he is a stumbling block and a contradiction.

Under John Paul II, Catholicism has become a one-man show: the Vatican's publicity machine and large sections of the Catholic media ensure that his voice and words, his opinions and verdicts, are broadcast daily and amplified throughout the world. The modern cult of papal veneration, aided by new media technology, has reached new heights and breadths during his papacy. For two decades nonstop instructions, directives, interventions, and initiatives have flowed from the Apostolic Palace ("ten whole linear feet in shelf space"), punctuated by hundreds of journeys to the ends of the earth. He is "the Sentinel" and he sees it as his task to protect the entire Church. Such is the torrent that sustains the cult of his personality, even the figure of Christ appears to be cast in the shade.

His message, invariably, is to accuse the faithful of sinfulness in the conduct of their sexual and marital relationships. In the process, countless millions of Catholics have become demoralized, discouraged, and made to think less of themselves. Not infrequently his declarations are contradictory as he tacks and veers, playing fast and loose in response to public opinion: one week he calls non-Catholic faiths "gravely deficient" and the next exhorts the people to respect other religions; one month he insists that for all time women will be denied ordination, and the next exhorts the faithful to respect them; one day he forbids AIDS sufferers the use of safe sex, and the next extols compassion for all. John Paul has taken the Church in the direction of hardline conservatism, but he has regularly exploited the media to give the opposite impression.

Yet loyalty to the Holy Father is the one issue that unites Catholics, whatever they may think of him. To criticize him is to offend the most crucial taboo; love him or loathe him, every Catholic knows that he remains our best and only option for future unity. Meanwhile, Catholic conservatives assert that Catholic progressives are destroying the Church through moral and doctrinal relativism, and Catholic progressives lament the neglected virtues of pluralism, urging a greater measure of decentralization and devolution of Catholic authority. Both sides of the divide appeal to the authority of the Second Vatican Council of the 1960s.

The Catholic Church is evidently a conservative institution. It does not pander to the latest fads and fashions: it is vigilant over its traditions of belief and practice. It does not fall into the trap of believing that, unaided by grace, human nature is perfectible. Convinced of the deep stain in our nature, Catholics believe that a better world involves the conversion of individual human hearts over and above the restructuring of society.

And yet Catholicism is nothing if not social, committed to the principles of the Sermon on the Mount, antagonistic to the status quo. Catholicism is radical, communitarian, open to all cultures and ethnicities—hence "catholic," universal. Christianity's historic message of unconditional "love," or agape, moreover, sustains a viable rationale for universal respect and hence a philosophical and theological underpinning for pluralist communities and societies. Agape, the love of all—including our enemies—is the singularly Christian commandment without which no virtue or discipline or sacrifice makes sense. Agape is sustained by the conviction that all without exception are destined toward God. It is arguable that the more or less democratic and pluralist institutions which protect Catholicism's right to exist alongside other religions owe more to the unconscious survival of Christian agape than to the principles of Locke and Jefferson, or the philosophies of ancient Greece and Rome.

So there are respectable reasons for questioning both sides of the conservative-progressive Catholic divide, respectable reasons, too, for endorsing them, although it is difficult to state their contrasting differences without betraying a bias. Witness Cardinal Joseph Ratzinger's version of the tension:

> There are the modern circles, and we all know that for them every reform is insufficient, that they set themselves against the papacy and papal teaching. But even the others, the "good Catholics," find themselves less and less comfortable in the Church . . . they suffer and grieve over the fact that now the Church is no longer a place of peace . . . but a place of constant conflicts, so that they themselves become uncertain and begin to protest.

Sociologists of religion, however, are not so pessimistic as the men in the Vatican about the decline and defections in the developed world. Recent surveys indicate that Catholics have not turned their backs on God; the faithful, say the sociologists, are accommodating the expression of their beliefs and values to the societies in which they are obliged to live. Most young practicing Catholics have little regard for the virtue of obedience. They make their own choices, especially about sexual morals. And even those who attend church regularly are relocating their sense of the holy in environmental and social concerns: the hungry, the poor, the homeless, the fragility of the planet. They have adjusted their moral imperatives so as to consider consequences and the unique pressures on individuals rather than intrinsic "absolutes."

The young generation of active Catholics nevertheless retains a voluntary attachment to sacramentals and sacraments—the visible signs of God's presence in the world that are special to Catholicism. But the old outward and inward control systems, the guilt cycle that linked regular confession to the Eucharist, no longer have any bearing on their practice or even consciousness.

The official Church, however, sees these accommodations as flights into secularism. The Pope and the Vatican read the decline in Mass attendance, the virtual disappearance of confession, the decline in marriages, the increase in divorces, the rampant "relativism" of Catholics in the north, as signs of a coming Dark Age. Contraception, homosexuality, and premarital sex are lumped together with abortion and reprotechnology as "the Culture of Death."

Progressive Catholic spokespersons who stand up for the large and growing constituencies of pro-change, marginalized, struggling, lapsed, and experimenting Catholics interpret the trends with a more open mind, with a deeper sense of trust in the strengths and advantages of pluralism and the operation of providence in the vicissitudes of history. In consequence, unbearable tensions have arisen between powerful sectors of the Church.

Dissent

Since the mid-nineteenth century theorists of modernization have argued that economic development is attended by widespread cultural change. But this does not mean that sets of beliefs and values perish inevitably and entirely. Cultural values, according to other theorists, have a continuing influence in society despite modernization and development. Data from many surveys show that despite the decline in religious practice in advanced industrialized societies at the end of the twentieth century there is a persistence and even a rise in spirituality. Released from the pressures of traditional practice imposed by ethnic immigrant communities, people in advanced and pluralist societies see their religious lives more as personal quests than familial and ethnic ritual obligation. Discovery, trial, curiosity, a willingness to mix and blend influences—as for example Eastern spirituality with Western—mark the religious journeys people make in prosperous industrial societies. Religion in everyday life is not, nor can it be, promoted or received top-down; religion in these contexts survives or dies as a result of the choices made by individuals and groups of individuals. The apparent privatization of religion appears to be a condition of its survival in a late modern environment, but to the orthodox this smacks of self-help consumerism, "cafeteria" Catholicism.

The Mother Church of Christianity, steeped in tradition and memories of holiness and suffering, insists that the Church, not the individual, must be the ultimate guide. Who could possibly propose that an individual knows better than the 2,000-year wisdom of the Catholic Church, infused, as Catholics believe, with the Holy Spirit?

But what is the Church? And where, and in whom, does the Holy Spirit dwell? Does God's presence in the Church permeate downward and outward—as nowadays it seems—exclusively from the Holy Father in Rome? Or does God dwell in all the faith communities of the world? In the early 1960s the Second Vatican Council attempted to resolve the paradox between the greater and the local Christian communities by restoring an ancient understanding of the meaning of the Church—affirming that each group of Christians gathered around its bishop is in that place, "the fullness of the church, the Spirit's temple, sacrament of Christ." Every Catholic knows instinctively that the latter is true, I certainly feel that to be true in my church in Covent Garden, and yet today it appears all too often that inspiration, guidance, and truth are supposed to flow only from the Roman center.

At the heart of the divisions and fragmentation among Catholics today are running disputes over centralization and devolution, inclusiveness and closure, pluralism and fundamentalism. The issues differ from country to country, from society to society, from culture to culture while the underlying source of conflict remains constant: is human flourishing, through spirituality and religion, better served by freedom or control?

John Paul II has made his position abundantly clear on dissent, whether it comes from individual bishops, theologians, or the voices and actions of the laity. In response to a call from Archbishop John R. Quinn of San Francisco for greater encouragement to moral theologians in September 1987, John Paul said:

> It is sometimes said that a large number of Catholics today do not adhere to the teaching of the Church on a number of questions, notably sexual and conjugal morality, divorce and remarriage. . . . It has also been noted that there is a tendency on the part of some Catholics to be selective in their adherence to the Church's moral teaching. It is sometimes claimed that dissent from the magisterium is totally compatible with being a "good Catholic" and poses no obstacle to the reception of the sacraments. This is a grave error . . . bishops should encourage assent to that which is given both to those who proclaim the message and to those to whom it is addressed.

The uncompromising terms in which dogmatic teaching on sexual morality is stated, against the background of the realities of mass "dissent," suggests a denial of the extent and power of the forces driving the spread of secularism. But the "them" and "us" dichotomy, the proclaimers and the receivers, betrays the pyramidal top-down model of centralized Church authority, with the faithful—including the bishops—as passive receptacles of teaching and guidance issuing from the Roman pinnacle, branch managers responding to the orders of the chief executive at the head office.

The faithful, however, are proving to be anything but passive; and whether the Pope likes it or not they are voting with their feet. As a recent editorial in *The Tablet* puts it, "Some authorities in the Catholic Church fear that societies in which this occurs are lost. In fact it is the Church which is lost unless it can recover and foster true Christian pluralism, while maintaining its ability to draw the lines."

The predicament presents a state of crisis for the coming papacy. Is Catholicism headed for sectarian breakup?

Much depends on the next Pope. An ultra-conservative Pope would likely move to exclude those many millions of Catholics who refuse to abide by the Church's teaching. A recklessly progressive Pope could prompt the voluntary self-exclusion of many groups of traditionalists. Meanwhile, even a neutral Pope could find himself presiding over a Church which is splintering into myriad congregationalist groups.

There are no easy solutions to the divisions within the Catholic Church. What seems clear, however, is that Catholics must rediscover the imperative of Christian love between themselves if they are to avoid breakup.

CHAPTER 2

DIVISIONS

What we see looks less like the hoped for regeneration of Catholicism than its accelerated decomposition.

—Father Louis Bouyer

I would like to think that the way pro-change Catholics deal with identity may serve as a model. . . . They demonstrate a critical trust in tradition, in community, in pluralism, in reason, and in the emancipatory power of a faith, or culture, that is public and not just private.

—Michele Dillon

ON A GRAY, damp weekend in November 1996 two groups of Catholics met at different venues in Detroit, Michigan. Both groups proclaimed themselves to be authentically Catholic, both claimed to speak in the interests of the survival of the Catholic Church; yet they disdained to recognize each other as legitimate witnesses to the faith. At COBO Conference Center in downtown Detroit, a "progressive" or "dissident" Catholic organization known as Call to Action (CTA) was holding an extraordinary annual general meeting to celebrate the twentieth anniversary of its formation in 1976. Some 5,000 priests, nuns, and members of the laity (along with four nonactive Catholic bishops) shared views on topics ranging from contraception to the need for married and women priests to Vatican oppression. They included Father Charles Curran, the moral theologian who had his teaching license at Catholic University of America revoked on the orders of the Vatican in 1989; Father Hans Küng, the noted Swiss theologian who was banned from teaching as a Catholic in 1978; María Mejía, who runs the Mexican local branch of Catholics for Free Choice; and Sister Miriam Therese Winter, author of a book entitled *Defecting in Place: Women Claiming Responsibility for Their Own Spiritual Lives.*

As well as core CTA activists there were representatives from other dissident groups in the United States and around the world: including We Are Church, Catholics Organized for Renewal, CORPUS (for former priests), Conference for Catholic Lesbians, Dignity (Catholic gays and lesbians), New Ways Ministry, Women's Ordination Conference, Association for the Rights of Catholics in the Church, Parish Renewal Consulting Services, and many more. Incorporating a wide range of single- and multiple-issue campaigners, the Call to Action group could be characterized as a movement that seeks change in the Church while remaining doggedly part of the larger tradition of Catholicism.

Meanwhile, a group titled Call to Holiness, which bluntly describes the Call to Action group as "apostates," was assembling a few miles distant at the suburban setting of the Sterling Inn Conference Center. The delegates were sponsored by Catholics United for the Faith, Roman Catholic Faithful, Knights of Columbus, the Catholic publishing house Ignatius Press, and such conservative periodicals as *Catholic Dossier, Crisis,* and *The Catholic Faith.* Their speakers included Mother Angelica of the Eternal Word Television Network; Father John Hardon, a Jesuit and Vatican theologian; Father John Harvey, director of Courage (which encourages gays to practice self-restraint and chastity); and Father Richard Welch of Human Life International.

Addressing the conference, Father John Hardon proclaimed that "the call to holiness is a call to martyrdom. . . . It is martyrdom to live under pagan former Catholics." His audience gasped when he proclaimed that his Vatican superiors had said that barring a miracle "one diocese after another in the United States will disappear."

The confrontation in Detroit that weekend was symptomatic of the clash among many polarized groups, movements, constituencies, periodicals, and websites which claim that they, and not their opponents, represent authentic Catholicism today. There are, of course, Catholics who just get on with their local parish life, experiencing a sense of harmony and joy under a unifying pastor. They are lucky. For it has become increasingly difficult for Catholic laypeople, priests, and least of all bishops, to escape the consequences of growing divisions between the Church in the United States; as was evinced by the action of Detroit's local Cardinal Archbishop. He refused to endorse either of the groups, opting for a middle way that put a curse on both their houses. "We cannot support a dialogue that publicly contradicts matters of doctrine," he told journalists, nor could he support "individuals or groups that organize counter-gatherings or protests as a response to Call to Action." His refusal to side with the traditionalists provoked instant condemnation from the conservative *Catholic World Report*, placing him squarely, as far as the periodical was concerned, in the ambit of liberal Catholicism. On the other hand the periodical approved of the action of the most Reverend Fabian Bruskewitz of Lincoln, Nebraska, who had excommunicated thirteen members of Call to Action in his diocese just a few weeks earlier.

The Progressive-Conservative Divide

The Catholic Church is on a fateful journey and the gathering momentum is astonishing. Much is at stake, and the outcome is as yet uncertain. Reminiscent of a river dividing at an estuary, the fragmentations, in a process of action and interaction, are reshaping the landscape of Catholicism. The proliferation of the divisions will certainly define the anxieties and preoccupations of the next papacy and beyond. The underlying causes are owed at least in part to a profound cultural change and the collapse of traditions, the rapid adoption of ideas under the influence of mass media, the mobility of people and money, the disappearance of "jobs for life," and the alteration and erosion of values and principles. Not least, as the Catholic population now numbers more than 700 million in the Third World, is the growing cultural disparity between the Roman center and the peripheries. The origins of the current predicament for Catholicism, however, also go back centuries and involve the attempts of successive papacies to resist the encroaching modern world. But the great single watershed was the Second Vatican Council (1962–1965).

Vatican II was a belated attempt by the Catholic Church to engage modern realities after centuries of resistance by Rome. But the Council's decisions and renewals, so optimistically (and for some, nervously) endorsed, came at a point when the Cold War threatened to erupt anew; when Robert Kennedy and Martin Luther King, Jr., were assassinated; when human-rights agendas cross-fertilized in the West with the "sexual revolution" and a host of single-issue liberations. Through the 1970s and the 1980s, as the postconciliar hurricanes blew themselves out, it became increasingly clear that the great modern narratives of sociopolitical progress were disintegrating under powerful new influences: unchecked capitalism, globalization, new information technologies, a world in which even knowledge and education were increasingly dominated not by optimism for progress but by efficiency and profit.

Catholic progressives contend that the spirit and letter of Vatican II have been betrayed. They criticize Pope Paul VI, and John Paul II, for their failure to implement the collegiality, or shared authority, endorsed by the Council fathers. They deplore the centralizing tendencies of the papacy from John Paul II's too frequent pronouncements to his tight grip on the nomination of bishops. They believe that theology is being discouraged, ecumenism and religious pluralism stifled. They believe that the climate of official intransigence on matters of sexual morality and marriage are marginalizing millions of Catholics. They believe that their centralized Church authority is failing to read the signs of the times.

Catholic conservatives, less numerous than the progressives, and themselves divided, believe that they have right on their side by sticking close to the letter and spirit of papal pronouncements. They declare that their mission is countercultural; some conservatives, following John Paul II, proclaim that they engage modernity and "transcend" it. Others, in view of the current retreat from religious "realism" and essentialist ways of looking at the world, the undermining of meaning and value, profess that their project is to restore timeless absolutes in order to combat the superficialities and deconstructions of our age. Some of them do not care that the Catholic Church might dwindle to a small remnant to achieve authentic Catholic integrity.

After the fall of Soviet communism, John Paul II and Joseph Ratzinger have seen the principal enemy, large and clear: relativism and all its works. Ever since the great "Modernist" crisis in the first decade of the twentieth century, the papacy has been in the habit of drawing an equivalence between relativism and pluralism, while viewing liberalism as a precursor to both. Nowadays the Vatican and conservative Catholics are on their guard for both internal and external pluralisms associated with liberalism.

Those who attempt to draw maps of the fault lines in Catholicism face daunting problems. There are many factions within factions, and countless splinter groups focusing on single issues, or clusters of issues. The debates are by now familiar: the reception of Vatican II, theological orthodoxy, readings of Church history, papal authority, papal infallibility, the status and nomination of bishops, the identity of the priesthood, the status of the laity, integrity of the liturgy, integrity of catechetics, the status and role of women, sexual morals, marriage and the family, calls for women and married priests, ecumenism, religious pluralism. While the larger factions make claims for their own orthodoxy over others', there are factions that consciously work for change within the Church, knowing that their views—on abortion, for example—are heterodox. Whether these pro-change groups are destined to aid the process of breakup or the process of change is as yet uncertain.

The "progressives" and "conservatives" confront each other across and within their divides on each and all of these issues. To be labeled one or the other does not grant immunity from condemnation in consequence of a suspect tone or heterodox predilection: closet progressives and conservatives are suspected and speedily sniffed out in both camps. The two sides of the divide are also characterized as liberal, pro-change, restorationist, hardliner, soft-liner, fundamentalist, separatist, traditionalist, neoconservative (or neocon), dissident, orthodox, apostate, left-wing, right-wing, professional dissenter, believing Catholic, ultra-this and ultra-that. Every appellation is subject to denial, counterdenial, and paradox. A striking illustration is the claim by a senior Catholic theologian in Britain, Professor Nicholas Lash of Cambridge University, that the supporters of "conservatism" in the Catholic Church are in fact recent and radical "innovators," and that those most often characterized as "progressives" are the "true conservationists," restoring earlier traditions of Christianity.

Writing of the 1917 Code of Canon Law, which for the first time in the history of the Catholic Church proclaimed that the Roman pontiff nominates bishops without restriction, Lash comments, "Whether it be matter for celebration or lament that, whereas most Catholics expect the Pope to pronounce almost daily on each and every subject under the sun, they rarely look to their own bishop to teach them anything: this is a thoroughly untraditional state of affairs."

Meanwhile, the conservatives have their own views about pseudoprogressivism. Here is Father Richard John Neuhaus in his column in the Catholic periodical *First Things*, commenting on a senior American Catholic theologian, Professor Richard McBrien, and the faculty of theology at the Catholic Notre Dame University. "As for Fr. McBrien and the ancien regime of theology at

Notre Dame," he writes, "they represent a generation that tends toward, to put it delicately, flabby and uncritical accommodationism. Catholicism is identified with the 'Americanist' readiness to trim Catholic distinctiveness in order not to offend cultural sensibilities. . . . But most everyone agrees that for the establishment the alignments that matter are defined by the old liberal-conservative polarities. Liberalism as an abstraction can be criticized at the edges, but never in a way that might raise doubt about one's being a liberal." In other words, liberalism is just another form of laissez-faire establishment reaction, and it is indistinguishable from old-fashioned Americanism, a term of abuse resurrected from the 1890s, when Pope Leo XIII stamped down decisively on the initiatives of Catholic churchmen who appeared to be aligning Catholicism in the United States with pluralism and democracy.

But whether one takes the terms at their face value, or turns them upside down, the antipathy and contempt are just as evident. What is unprecedented is the challenge to the papal Vatican center by cardinals, bishops, theologians, priests, religious, and laity, mainly, although not exclusively, from the progressive side of the divide, while each claiming that they speak in the name of true Catholicism.

In 1999 a group of conservative cardinals declared that the Pope was wrong to make an apology for the Church's sins of the past, including Catholic anti-Semitism and the Spanish Inquisition. A leading European churchman, Archbishop Karl Lehmann, president of the German bishops conference, publicly suggested the Pope could resign, provoking howls of repudiation from within the Vatican. A leading American archbishop, John R. Quinn, formerly head of the American bishops conference, published a book titled *The Reform of the Papacy*, calling for the pruning of papal authority. Cardinal Franz König, emeritus Archbishop of Vienna, made much the same point in an article published in 1999. Then an Italian cardinal (regarded by many as an ideal future Pope), Cardinal Carlo Martini of Milan, called for a new Vatican Council, a meeting of all the bishops of the Church, in order to allow more scope for women and the laity.

The conflict sprawls across the globe wherever Catholics find themselves in substantial numbers, from the Roman center to the peripheries of the Third World. In Germany, bishops are in conflict with brother bishops—Archbishop Meissner of Cologne refuses to compromise on his conservative definition of the Church, while Archbishop Lehmann, head of the bishops conference, seeks common ground to build bridges between the laity and the official Church. In Holland, as in Germany, the faithful are at war with their bishops, and at war with each other. The antagonism between traditionalists and progressives in the Dutch Church is mainly a result of the Vatican appointing its own favored candidates and ignoring local suggestions.

The leader of the Church in Austria, Cardinal Schönborn, is in conflict with the major part of his Church; in the United States academics are at war with the hierarchy, women against patriarchy, gays and lesbians against the Pope; in Latin America, the remnants of liberation theology, as well as certain religious orders, are in conflict with their episcopate, many of whom are members or sympathizers with Opus Dei. The disputes are on one level conducted through a war of words: a flow of papal and Vatican pronouncements, naturally, and an ever-growing torrent of media reporting, analysis, and opinion in partisan newspapers, periodicals, books, broadcasts, conferences, seminars, and Internet websites. On another level the conflict involves firings, excommunications, exclusions, denunciations: action.

The language of the factions, moreover, is getting ever more aggressive, contemptuous, and threatening. The situation is reminiscent of a comment made by Pius X when certain liberal-minded prelates pleaded with him to tone down his attacks on the so-called Modernist dissidents in the first decade of the twentieth century. "They want them to be treated with oil, soap and caresses," he said. "But they should be beaten with fists. In a duel, you don't count or measure the blows, you strike as you can. War is not made with charity; it is a struggle, a duel."

But what have moderate Catholics been doing to reconcile Catholics with one another? In 1996 the late Cardinal Bernardin of Chicago established a movement called Catholic Common Ground Initiative to facilitate discussion of doctrinal differences in the United States. He called for "a renewed spirit of civility, dialogue, generosity, and broad and serious consultation." Even before the program got under way some of Bernardin's fellow bishops were rejecting the initiative, arguing that common ground already existed in Scripture and tradition. Many avowedly progressive American participants tell me that the conservatives routinely wreck the discussions by refusing to listen and refusing to give ground. The conservatives see it differently. Citing an article by a progressive Jesuit, *Catholic World Report* has complained that the author, for all his professed preparedness to accept faults on either side, was hopelessly biased: "Excesses on the left may be regrettable or dubious, but they can be tolerated in ways 'excesses' on the right cannot be."

An unusual attempt to shed light on conservative attitudes was created in 1997 with the publication (edited by Mary Jo Weaver and R. Scott Appleby) of the collection of essays entitled *Being Right: Conservative Catholics in America* (Indiana University Press). The collection contained critiques of the right by progressives, as well as essays by conservatives on how they see themselves. Such examples of forum-making are rare indeed, and as R. Scott Appleby acknowledges in his epilogue, "Catholic intellectuals and activists often seem more comfortable with their ideological counterparts in other denominations than with their fellow Catholics."

Meanwhile, the Catholic religious media, largely dominated by the conservatives, has given the popular conservative message a daunting outreach and invective. Sister Angelica's Eternal Word television and radio operation in North America (EWTN) reaches 54 million homes and countless viewers and listeners in thirty-four countries. When she disagreed with a pastoral letter on liturgy promulgated by Roger Cardinal Mahony of Los Angeles to the parishes in his huge diocese, she trashed it as a liberal hotchpotch pedaling sociology at the expense of religious mystery and she said it virtually denied the real presence in the Eucharist. She told her audience that they should accord "zero obedience" to the Cardinal. When he objected, complaining that programs criticizing bishops threatened the unity of the Mystical Body of Christ, she apologized for inciting the faithful to disobey him, then gave him more of the same. When bishops misrepresent the faith, she told him, she is performing a service for the faith by setting them straight. The picture is completed by the redoubtable Father Richard John Neuhaus joining the fray: "It is simply not credible," he wrote in a column on the affair, "that a cardinal who is so very tolerant of theologians who call for zero obedience to the Pope wants Rome to slap an interdict on a nun who presumes to criticize him." Even great metropolitan cardinals get embroiled at their peril.

Church on the Web

Not so long ago a television producer from Brazil, home of 137 million notional Catholics, described the spread of the Internet in the teeming cities and hinterlands of her homeland: "It's everywhere, unstoppable, like the Amazonian flood waters. What it means is that everybody can ask questions, make statements, and that's precisely what they're doing."

The Internet makes for dangerous, subverting times for the Catholic Church, which has traditionally addressed the faithful from a special, timeless space at the Roman center, which claims the authority, once it has spoken on a disputed issue or principle, to discourage further debate, which expects—whatever the reality of the reception—its teachings to be accepted both in the spirit and in the letter. The Catholic Church has not, traditionally, operated on the basis of peer-group discussion. But how does such a centralized space, harboring immutable, authoritative texts, appear to the hordes of participator-voyagers surfing on multi-dimensional oceans of centerless, timeless, and real-time information: cyberspace, where every commodity, pretension, and opinion can be peddled, compared and contrasted, sampled, reshaped, interactively questioned, contradicted, bookmarked, and consigned to oblivion—including the proliferating dissidents, sects, liberal, progressive, conservative, neoconservative, restorationist, and reactionary factions of Catholicism. In the midst of these strange new oceans the website of the Vatican, with its marbled backgrounds and lapidary notice boards, its 3-D tours of St. Peter's, competes for uncentered space alongside the Internet claims of dissenting bodies, such as We Are Church, not to mention the hordes of cyberspaced sects, prophets, visionaries, aromatherapists, and psychotics.

When Father Paul Collins, an Australian Catholic priest, was denounced by the Vatican for his allegedly heterodox views on papal authority, he set up a website inviting all who had been similarly disciplined to share their experiences. When Sister Lavinia Byrne's book *Woman at the Altar* was withdrawn by its American Catholic publisher on the orders of the Vatican, the British nun started an Internet column which is visited by thousands of devotees. When the Catholic League for Civil and Religious Rights objected to the depiction of the Virgin Mary with elephant dung, its leader, Bill Donohue, summoned by website a group of Catholic loyalists armed with sick bags to protest outside the New York museum where the picture was on exhibit. The irony of the web is that it makes postmodernists of us all. Will the Catholic Church work and thrive on the Internet, or will it be altered beyond all recognition by it?

On January 13, 1995, Bishop Jacques Gaillot of Evreux in France was sacked for advocating condoms for AIDS victims and sympathizing with active homosexuals. A hugely popular firebrand, social activist, and friend of the disenfranchised, he accused the French government of racism in its immigration policies, supported Yasser Arafat, and generally defied the Vatican on every social issue. His removal, supported by his brother bishops, prompted an outcry. He remained a Bishop, however, and was granted a non-diocese called Partenia—a stretch of rocky wilderness in the middle of the Algerian desert. Partenia is a region of the world from which the Latin Church had retreated many centuries past and where Gaillot (likely unbeknownst to the Vatican) had seen action on national service as a member of the French armed forces during the 1950s. He has set up a website called www.partenia.com from which he runs a global Internet parish for disaffected and marginalized Catholics. On the first web page there is a picture of sand dunes and a few palm trees. DIOCESE WITHOUT BORDERS proclaims the headline. In the opening statement, Bishop Gaillot recalls that the last bishop of Partenia was persecuted and exiled. He goes on: "As Partenia does not exist anymore, it becomes the symbol of those who have the feeling of not existing anymore for the society or the Church. It is a vast diocese without boundaries on which the sun never sets." It remains to be seen whether Bishop Gaillot's new flock, estimated in hundreds of thousands of website hits, will create a significant Christian community for a new kind of marginalized Catholicism.

A Dysfunctional Family

Meanwhile, despite everything, the Pope remains at the very heart and center. It would be rash indeed to suggest that we are about to witness the demise of the papacy, the oldest surviving institution in the West. But the papacy has for some decades now been subject to an ever-widening gap between its teaching and the faithful's adherence. In addition to the many issues involved in the splintering structures of the global Catholic Church are questions about the Pope's power to maintain unity—a challenge John

Paul himself acknowledged in his 1995 encyclical *Ut Unum Sint* (*That They May Be One*).

The nineteenth-century British historian Lord Macaulay observed in a famous purple passage that the papacy was already in operation when "the smoke of sacrifice rose from the Pantheon," and that it has persisted through the ages while secular dynasties have crumbled all about it. Rising from the ashes of ancient imperialism, or, according to Thomas Hobbes, "no other than the Ghost of the deceased Roman Empire," the papacy is frequently characterized as the absolute authority in the interests of "conformity," the prized unity of the Church of Rome.

An alternative viewpoint would put Hobbes's reflection more benignly, but no less emphatically. "Catholicism," writes Eamon Duffy, the Cambridge church historian, "is a conversation, linking continents and cultures, and reaching backwards and forwards in time. The luxury of sectarianism, of renouncing whatever in the conversation cannot be squared with the perspective of one's own time and place, is not an option."

Great world religions do not survive when they begin to yield to sectarianism. The unifying power of the papacy still holds the warring factions together in a semblance of cohesion. But can that unifying authority be purchased by mere lip service to papal allegiance? The conservatives are right. The answer is a resounding no! Hence they stay close to papal thinking, statements, and documents, believing that this enables them to think with the Church, *sentire cum ecclesia*, even though some conservatives find difficulty with the Pope's more ecumenical and pluralist initiatives.

Through the vicissitudes of the 1990s John Paul II held the huge operation in tension. But the centrifugal forces are approaching a point where it is beyond his power, or that of a future Pope, however skillful or charismatic, to hold them together. Progressives blame John Paul II's failure to implement the decisions of the Second Vatican Council for the growing fissures in the Church (Council documents, like Holy Scripture, can be quoted in the interests of either side of the divide). But the very size and

complex scope of the Church, the unstoppable forces of secularism against the background of shifting Catholic demographics
and forces for change—not least the graying of the clergy,
coupled with priestly defections and vacant and gay-subculture
seminaries (in the developed West)—point to a structural vulner-
ability beyond the responsibility or control of the papacy, the
Curia, or the Church's hierarchy.

The Church, in its long, eventful history, has been here before,
although with different forces for destruction; the ancient self-
images of the Church as similar to a human body (with head, limbs,
and heart) tell stories of fractures and diseased organs, of survival
through severance and disciplined quarantine. Today the Church
has other images borrowed from science and psychology. They
talk, even in the Vatican, of the Church as a black hole, as a dysfunctional family. They speak of the Church as a collapsing star,
the detritus of heresy and relativism spinning in orbit around the
shrinking mass of the true if cooling remnant; some key officials
in Rome, indeed, actually take comfort from such images.

But what person of goodwill could welcome the spectacle of
the breakup and shrinkage of the Catholic Church? Even as I
write, Catholics are involved on every continent, working and in
some cases dying in order to make the world a better place. Some
thirty-one Catholics died for their faith in different parts of the
world in 1999. In the year 2000 a Dominican priest was strangled
in Albania; a Holy Cross missionary ministering to homosexuals
was shot in Mexico; a Franciscan missionary brother was beaten
to death in North India.

Catholics believe that they bring a distinctive message of love,
hope, justice, and peace, that their mission is coextensive with the
entire world. Despite their many failings, Catholics have a vision
that transcends the secular, that underpins principles of justice,
peace, and pluralism, that reacts to the greed, violence, and unbri-
dled materialism of the age.

Catholic social action, moreover, is tireless in every part of the
world; Catholic aid programs offer a wide range of professional,

financial, and technical assistance, and are in no way aimed merely at conversion or the converted. In Latin America, Catholics are struggling to mend lives broken by economic and political oppression. Voluntary workers in Africa are assisting the victims of AIDS, genocide, and hunger. In India they are working for the victims of disease, old age, famine, and flood. The task of social action is not confined to volunteers and aid workers. There can scarcely be a parish in the Northern Hemisphere where Catholics are not giving to bring relief to homelessness, poverty, hunger, and sickness of mind and body, both at home and abroad.

But what does any of this mean for the survival of the Catholic Church against the background of ebbing faith? How much longer can these wide-ranging works—socioeconomic, technical, educational, medical—be done in the name of Catholicism, and under its influence, when the Catholic faith is divided against itself and in retreat and steep decline on so many fronts? Indeed the collapse of faith throws the entire Catholic mission in doubt everywhere in the world to the detriment of us all, Catholics and non-Catholics alike.

CHAPTER 3

WHAT IS THE CHURCH?

Each of the parts brings to the others and to the whole Church the benefit of its own gifts so that the whole and each of its parts are increased by a mutual universal exchange and by a common effort towards a fullness in unity.

—*Lumen Gentium*

WHEN THE AMERICAN JESUIT scholar Father Thomas P. Rausch referred to the Catholic Church as a "big tent" in 1998, hoping thereby to offer an image of reconciliation between progressives and conservatives, he was instantly condemned by the *Catholic World Report*. "Perhaps he did not realize," wrote magazine contributor James Hitchcock, "that to Americans familiar with the country's political dialogue . . . the expression carries a great deal of negative freight." The "negative freight," according to Hitchcock, was the use of "big tent" to justify "the acceptance of legalized abortion among Republican politicians." Promoting abortion could not have been further from Father Rausch's thoughts, but softness on the issue, intended or otherwise, is a convenient stick with which to labor the "liberal" opposition. The images assigned to the meaning of "Church" are important for just as they can draw Catholics together, so they can be a source of misunderstanding and exclusion.

When I was a child, the most familiar image of the Church was not a big tent but a mother—life-giving, nourishing, protecting. Catholics in those days, moreover, saw the Church as a ship or boat, navigated by Saint Peter and his successors through the gales and dangerous shoals of human history.

To capture in the round anything so prodigious, dynamic, and mysterious as the Catholic Church, its bishops and writers have summoned powerful images down the ages, borrowing at times from our parent religion, Judaism. In the main, understanding the meaning of "Church" involves a strong identification with the nature, the person, and the mission of Jesus Christ. Ancient symbols of Christ's body, his humanity and divinity, have survived down the centuries along with, and sometimes clashing with, images and concepts that took shape following the period we call the Enlightenment. Following the breakup of Western Christendom at the Reformation, and trauma of the French Revolution, the official Church developed a new self-protective identity with accompanying new metaphors—more political and institutional, unintentionally perhaps more modern. The Church was struggling with Protestant Christianity and the emerging nation-states, both as a spiritual and temporal entity. Would the survival and unity of the Church be ensured by stronger centralization, or by devolution, allowing local bishops greater autonomy? By the middle of the nineteenth century, coinciding with the loss of the Papal States, the Pope and the bishops in council had definitively settled for centralization. As the industrialized world and modern communication and travel burgeoned and spread, the Pope and his Curia increasingly saw the Church, from the Roman center, as a body politic, "a perfect society," parallel in sovereign boundaries and integrity with great nation-states, with whom the Vatican spoke through its diplomats, the papal nuncios, while its canon lawyers negotiated concordats, agreements binding under international law. This was a Church that attempted to keep the modern world at arm's length while emulating its structures.

Through the early part of the twentieth century the Church came to resemble a latter-day spiritual empire, wielding an authority that mimicked the ideologies of modern imperial power.

Its popular theology, its Christology, focused on the Kingship of Christ; Mary the Queen of Heaven was actively involved in the course of history. But that centrist, highly bureaucratized authority was in trouble by the middle of the twentieth century. Whatever the strengths and virtues of the Church during this period (and they were many), whatever its disciplines, its unassailable unity, its loyalty to the Pope in Rome, the post–World War II era found the Church ripe for sweeping change.

From the first decade of the twentieth century Catholic theology and social teaching had been in deep freeze following the suppression of the "Modernist" movement under Pius X. Catholic social teaching leaned without embarrassment toward corporatism (selection rather than election), thus favoring the early rule of Mussolini of Italy and the entire era of Generalissimo Franco of Spain. Pius XI had influenced the withdrawal of Catholic democratic parties in the form of the Italian Partito Popolare (the People's Party) and Cardinal Secretary of State Eugenio Pacelli (the future Pius XII) had encouraged the demise of the German Zentrum, the Center Party, despite the viable challenge posed by the Popular and Center parties to Fascism and Nazism. Pius XI and the future Pius XII, as Secretary of State, were not unhappy to draw parallels between the centralized authority of the Church and the leadership principles of fascism and corporatism.

But new theological thinking was stirring. In the 1930s a group of French theologians had been at work, exploring the different meanings of Church by returning to early Christianity and the writings of the Early Fathers. In 1938 the Jesuit theologian Henri de Lubac completed his seminal thesis on the Mystical Body (*Corpus Mysticum*), the ancient view of the Church as the body of Christ; it was not published until after the war, but it achieved significant circulation and influence in manuscript. In the early years of the war Pius XII was moved to pronounce on the same theme in a major encyclical, *Mystici Corporis*, echoing de Lubac's title. But his meditation on this central symbol was profoundly different from that of the French theologian. Pius employed the image of Christ's Body to reinforce the power of the papacy. The Pope was the head of the Mystical Body on earth, he declared, and those who intentionally denied his sovereignty excluded themselves from the Mystical Body of Christ.

In the postwar era Pius shifted politically, espousing the cause of the Christian Democrats in Italy to combat the threat of communism, but he remained suspicious of democracy, believing that it meant acquiescence in the mindless will of the "masses" and was a precursor to socialism, which in turn led to communism. Despite the ideas propounded in *Mystici Corporis,* his model of the Church remained the perfect society, or sovereign empire, self-sufficient, citadel-like, counter the culture, counter the world, wholly identified with and subservient to the papal office.

Following the death of Pius XII, John XXIII saw his role as "a very humble office of shepherd." He broke the habits of centuries by visiting the sick in the hospitals of Rome and the prisoners at Regina Coeli jail. He announced a great Council of the Church on July 25, 1959, and convoked it on December 25, 1961. There were voices of warning from the old guard, but he repudiated them as "prophets of gloom, who are always forecasting disaster, as though the end of the world were at hand." Certainly, the end of the Catholic Church, as my generation and many generations previous had known it, was indeed at hand.

Vatican II

The Second Vatican Council, under the influence of de Lubac and his circle, reanimated ancient, long-forgotten symbols of the Catholic Church. In the remarkable Council document on the dogmatic constitution of the Church, known as *Lumen Gentium,* the Council fathers spoke of the Church as a sacrament, the visible sign of God's presence in the world. They also spoke of living metaphors of the Church as "taken either from the life of the shepherd or from the cultivation of the land, from the art of building or from family life and marriage." The mystery of the Church, according to this document (passed by 2,151 votes to 5), is not reducible to one image or metaphor. The Church is seen as "a sheepfold . . . the sole and necessary gateway to which is Jesus Christ," as "temple," the "dwelling place of God." At the same time the Council reaffirmed the idea of the Church as "our mother" and the "spotless spouse of Christ" to whom the Messiah will be wed at the end of time. But the Council fathers also adopted an ancient Hebrew image: the "People of God," and "stranger in a foreign land," suggesting a pilgrim people on the move; the Church as a visible symbol, across space and time, of God's gathering of humankind into his love. The implication of the dynamic, nonexclusive imagery was the readiness of the faithful to pay heed to human history, to join the rest of the human race, to respect other religions, and indeed those of no religion: to engage the world. Since the world was on the point of becoming a global village, in which the faithful in developing countries were about to outnumber those in Europe and North America, the Council encouraged a new vision of devolved and shared authority. The Council fathers committed themselves to a carefully worded advocacy of collegial authority, a sharing of authority between Pope and bishops, while acknowledging the Pope's ultimate authority as teacher and judge.

A key impetus of Vatican II, moreover, was *aggiornamento:* the Church should be prepared to develop with the passage of world history and changes in societies. The mid-1960s were thus a time of renewal, enthusiasm, and hope for most Catholics. There were programs for reform in every area of the Church's activities and a widely proclaimed sense of the presence of the Holy Spirit. The Church underwent review from top to bottom. Powerful forces for restoration and liberation were unleashed, prompting both joy and anxiety.

Images of Liberation

One of the most influential thinkers at the time of the Second Vatican Council was the German Jesuit Karl Rahner (1904–1984). He portrayed the act of human knowing as a restless process of proceeding from one question to another; of reaching one expanding horizon after another toward the infinite. His view of human nature was both liberating and expansive. In his book *Hearers of the Word*, published in Germany in 1963, he insisted that it is human to be religious: "Man is spirit . . . he lives his life in a perpetual reaching out to the Absolute, in openness to God."

Rahner argued that God's presence in the world touches nonbelievers in the secular Northern Hemisphere as well as the faithful of non-Christian religions. He made available to a new generation of Catholics a basis for respecting the beliefs and practices of other religions. Rahner liked to quote Saint Augustine as saying "many whom God has, the Church does not have; and many whom the Church has, God does not have." He coined the term "anonymous Christian" to signify that non-Christians in the act of reaching out for God their creator achieve all that is promised in Christian salvation. Rahner was too orthodox a Catholic to suggest that one religion is as complete in truth as every other. But as the anonymous Christian idea gained currency at the level of seminary teaching, pastoral preaching, and missionary work it created a theological underpinning for an aspiration already implicit in Vatican II, for a quieter, noncompetitive evangelization both at home and abroad.

Catholic theology had for generations been a timeless, abstract, unquestioned and unquestioning magisterium contained in official manuals. Vatican II also saw the unimpeded influence of the French theologians, of whom de Lubac was a member, and who formed a movement known as the New Theology. De Lubac, Yves Congar, and Marie-Dominique Chenu had been disciplined and oppressed by Pius XII and the Holy Office in the 1950s, their ideas being too strong, too disruptive and "dissident" for the times. All three became influential advisers to the Second Vatican Council.

Appealing to tradition and history, these French theologians insisted that Catholicism was nothing if not a social religion. Henri de Lubac in particular argued that Catholicism meant salvation not only for individuals but for communities. Historical research led him to believe that in the eleventh century the awareness of the "Real Presence" of Christ in Christian congregations had weakened. The consecrated bread had become the principal focus of the real presence, and the presence of Christ in communities of faith had thus become less "real." De Lubac believed that the continuity that had once existed between symbol and the real had been broken, resulting in a weakening of social Catholicism and an increase in power and control rituals, privilege, and hierarchical structures.

De Lubac and his circle were implicitly challenging the power structure of the twentieth-century Catholic Church. His work, like Rahner's, was an encouragement to Christian unity between Catholics and Christian non-Catholics and between Christians and other religions, especially Judaism.

Meanwhile, another outstanding French scholar, Father Pierre Teilhard de Chardin, was encouraging the entry of the Church into the world through a cosmic vision of Christian belief transformed by new science. His books became best-sellers, especially *The Phenomenon of Man*, originally published in 1958, followed by *Future of Man* (1964), and *Hymn of the Universe* (1970). Father Teilhard's poetic and mystical version of evolution saw Christ evolving with his creation across aeons of time through the history of the universe. On the one hand, Father Teilhard made connections between Catholic theology and Darwinian evolution; on the other, he blurred the firm margins of dogma. Like de Lubac, his theology of the real presence both enhanced and reshaped the meaning of Christ in the world. He once found himself alone in a desert in China on the Feast of the Transfiguration; unable to celebrate Mass, he had a vision of a universe consecrated to become the Body of Christ. "When Christ says, 'This is my body,' " he wrote, "these words extend beyond the morsel of bread over which they are said. They give birth to the whole Mystical Body of Christ. The effect extends beyond the consecrated host to the cosmos itself—the entire realm of matter is slowly but irresistibly affected by this great consecration."

The flowering of a new and deeper understanding of Christian community, and God's action in the world, was both exhilarating and disturbing. Vatican II taught that Christ was present in the congregation, in the person of the priest, and in the Word of liturgy, as well as in the Eucharist. This widening of the concept of "real presence" seemed to disturb the specific notion of the Eucharistic real presence that had been a focus of the conflict, and in many cases confusion, between Catholicism and Protestantism for five hundred years. Anxious lest Catholics lose a central tenet of their faith, in 1965 Pope Paul VI moved to halt what he deemed an erosion of belief in the Eucharist. He wrote an encyclical, *Mysterium Fidei* (1965), reiterating the doctrine of transubstantiation—that the bread and wine, with the words of the consecration at Mass, become the body, blood, soul, and divinity of Christ by a process of miraculous change of substance, while the appearances remain the same. At the dawn of the twenty-first century, however, few Catholics have even a remote sense of this specifically Catholic concept. Of the estimated 30 percent of Catholics who retain a devotion to the real presence in the Eucharist, few, according to most surveys, are even aware of the terms of the transubstantiation argument.

Once begun, the explosion of theological creativity seemed unstoppable. Father Edward Schillebeeckx, a Flemish priest of the Dominican order, born in 1914, wrote a three-volume account of the person of Jesus Christ, in which he pondered the neglected understanding of Jesus as prophet. This new emphasis focused on Christ as man, rather than the risen Christ as Son of God, and drew an equivalence between Jesus and Old Testament prophets as well as prophet figures in the great world religions. Schillebeeckx sees the Church as the manifestation of Jesus Christ in communities that meet for worship, rather than in the Vatican and diocesan offices. The Church is on a journey through history, he asserts, searching for solutions to the riddles and problems of human existence and engaging in dialogue with all fellow human beings. The Church is not in possession of the fullness of truth any more than it is in possession of the kingdom of God. By 1990 he would be relegating the Church below the primacy of humanity and preaching what he calls a "negative ecclesiology"—salvation, he insists, cannot be restricted to the boundaries of a hierarchically structured Church.

Hans Küng, the Swiss priest theologian, also became a best-selling author from the 1960s onward. Appealing to the documents of Vatican II, he emphasized the idea of a constantly moving, constantly changing Church. The Church is the pilgrim People of God, subordinate to the kingdom of God, to which it is the herald and servant. Each local church is the Body of Christ for that place. Küng also raised questions about the hierarchical Church and papal infallibility, analyzing the historical and theological development of papal primacy and infallibility, and critiquing the background to the First Vatican Council. In 1979 his teaching license was withdrawn by the Vatican, but this did not halt the growth of his influence. In recent years he has focused increasingly on the importance of dialogue with other religions. On every issue of disagreement in the Church, Küng is consulted by the media as their favorite dissident as if he were a one-man alternative magisterium.

Church "from Below"

Progressive as these ideas seemed during the era of Vatican II, they remained, arguably, restorationist rather than revolutionary, whereas liberation theology, which arose in Latin America in the 1960s, was profoundly innovative, with the potential to question a wide-ranging variety of orthodox Catholic models of the Church.

The key text was *A Theology of Liberation* by Gustavo Gutiérrez, a Peruvian theologian. Evil in the world comes not solely from individual hearts and souls, but derives from the oppression of particular social and political structures. Following Marx, up to a point, he insisted that the class struggle is a fact and that it is impossible to remain neutral. "As a sign of the liberation of man and history, the Church itself in its concrete existence ought to be a place of liberation," he wrote. "The break with an unjust social order and the search for new ecclesial structures . . . have their basis in this perspective."

Liberation theology proclaimed a "preferential option for the poor," indicating solidarity with the victims of oppression by joining their struggles, including armed struggles, for emancipation in a practical and committed fashion. The reality of the world, and of Christianity, is to be discovered not in metaphysical or doctrinal meditations, but in practical commitment (praxis) to the struggles of the oppressed. Jesus of Scripture is seen as Jesus the liberator, the defender of outcasts and victims of oppression.

The Brazilian Leonardo Boff, a member of the Franciscan order and also a liberation theologian, transcended the work of Gutiérrez, appealing to the idea of the Church as a Spirit-filled existence giving Jesus a "global relationship to all reality." His ideas have parallels with Teilhard de Chardin, but his principal work, *Church, Charism and Power: Liberation Theology and the Institutional Church*, called into question the institutional value of the Church, suggesting that its structures were dysfunctional and even pathological. He called for a thorough examination of every aspect of Church doctrine, liturgy, canon law, and hierarchy. He was disciplined by the Vatican in 1991 and a year later left his order and the priesthood.

Liberation theology stimulated thinking on many levels, mainly in the Third World, while marshaling a sociopolitical and intellectual following in the developed world. It has given hope to millions and the movement has had its martyrs. Its influence in recent years has declined in many parts of Latin America although its spirit continues to flourish, especially in black and feminist theologies. The Vatican issued two principal declarations on liberation theology (1984, 1986): both criticized the movement for being "insufficiently critical" and for borrowing from Marxist ideology. They warn the faithful that liberation theology reduces faith to politics, undermines Church authority, and neglects sinfulness in individual human hearts. The second Vatican statement was a little more yielding than the first, and the Pope in time assured the Brazilian bishops that aspects of liberation theology were "not only opportune but useful and necessary." But even neutral writers acknowledge that for all its virtues and authenticity, liberation theology, as Robin Nagle comments in his *Claiming the Virgin*, "did not allow room for vital and deeply held beliefs about how God, Jesus, Mary and the Church were understood to work in people's lives."

Church "from Above"

In contrast to liberation theology's model of a Church that builds "from below," no survey of post–Vatican II visions of the Church can be complete without including the impact of the Swiss theologian Hans Urs von Balthasar, who invokes the idea of the Church "from above"—the communion of saints created by the Holy Spirit. This Church in Heaven pours out its riches on the Church in the world, which he sees as the spotless Bride of Christ, a return to an early Christian metaphor. While he argues that the Church in Heaven and on earth are a unity, both spotless and yet (on earth) subject to criticism, it is difficult to see how the apparent polarities are to be resolved. He comments: "The external organization of the church at which so many take offence is really nothing other than the presentation of the vitality and capacity for life of that great organic body possessed and animated by the present Christ."

Von Balthasar had a profound influence on John Paul II. Immensely prolific, writing more than a hundred books, he is believed by his peers to be one of the outstanding theologians of the century. He insisted that the Church should be open to the world and he complained that since the Middle Ages theologians had neglected an earlier imperative to be saints as well as intellectuals. He believed in doing theology "on his knees," an ideal endorsed by John Paul II.

Feminist Theology

Parallel with liberation theology, in its championing of the oppressed, feminist theology has since Vatican II established powerful critiques of prevailing Church metaphors. Catholic feminist writers scrutinize Scripture, tradition, and liturgy to expose man-centered and patriarchal language, power symbolism, and institutionalized oppression of women.

A central Catholic figure for two decades has been Elisabeth Schüssler Fiorenza. Born in 1938, Schüssler Fiorenza is a distinguished American biblical scholar and a Harvard academic with a German and an Italian background. For Schüssler Fiorenza the Bible is man-centered, but she finds passages, particularly in Mark and John, which promote the full humanity of women as "Discipleship of Equals." Although the Church of Paul was to stifle the leadership of women, Schüssler Fiorenza asserts that this liberating aspect of the Jesus movement was never entirely eclipsed. Feminist readings of Scripture will reclaim women's discipleship and apostolic leadership, liberating Christianity from influences that prompt "violence, alienation, and oppression." Feminists are therefore called upon to renew the Church in acts of "prophetic criticism."

Meanwhile, Rosemary Radford Ruether, also American, sees the Church as a Spirit-filled community of faith in which all people—men and women—are "radically" equal with the scope and the vocation to minister to each other. Hierarchies of every kind are rejected: men over women, fathers over children, employers over employees, clergy over laity. Invoking the idea of a

"Women-Church," which is also the title of her key book, she employs the metaphor of "exodus community," by which she means conscious abandonment of the prevailing institutional Church order and its hierarchies, and the building of an alternative social order obedient only to God. The overtones of rejection, rebellion, and departure are unmistakable. Women should exercise their witness, she writes, by proclaiming themselves as Church in an act of liberation. The movement is transitional, however, rather than permanent, anticipating an "exodus" that will encourage men to become conscious of their patriarchalism and enter into real dialogue. Meanwhile, Women-Church will "reappropriate" the pastoral and education ministry from male clergy in ritual, administration, theological education, and social action.

Feminist theology has not developed a fully worked out model of the Church, or ecclesiology, although some of its exponents emphasize the virtue of Judaic tendency (endorsed by Vatican II) to employ a pluralism of metaphors eschewing a dominant model.

In 1995, however, the distinguished Catholic anthropologist Mary Douglas, author of such works as *Natural Symbols* and *Purity and Danger*, called for a new model of the Church. At the annual conference of the Catholic Theological Association of Great Britain, she said: "I am absolutely convinced that there is a real problem for the Catholic Church about women. Unless there are institutional changes no amount of apologising, or saying verbally how much we honour women, really makes any difference." She went on: "There is a real contradiction between speaking and doing that is going on now, and as an anthropologist I am very convinced there is a great deal more that could be done and should be done." Women should have "real authority," she said, in areas of sexual morality and family questions, and "when they pronounce on doctrine it should not be negated" and "nobody should proceed until some agreement has been reached."

CHAPTER 4

THE POPE FROM POLAND

The last thing the Catholic Church would want as it enters the new millennium is to appear to be just without being so.
—John Cort, *The Catholic Church in the Twentieth Century*

THE SHOCK WAVES from Vatican II, and the power of associated ideas, not necessarily part of conciliar teaching, reverberated through the Church in the 1960s and 1970s, transforming the everyday lives of religious, clergy, and laypeople alike. The effects of the Council's liberating energies were by no means everything that had been hoped for, or intended. Catholic historians will argue for centuries about the consequences of Vatican II; while none can dispute its far-reaching benefits, none can deny the resulting discord and unhappiness. Bitter quarrels broke out, marked by recrimination and counter-recrimination. From one point of view, the pride and foolishness of one group had brought the Church to the edge of calamity; from another point of view, the Church, indeed the whole of Christianity, stood on the threshold of a new era of grace and freedom.

Peter Hebblethwaite, who reported on Vatican II as editor of the Jesuit periodical *The Month*, seized on what had become a new and alarming image for the Church in the eyes of conservatives: "a runaway Church, lurching out of control."

It was patently obvious, however, that the Church was dividing between those who felt that things had gone too far and those who felt that the reforms still had a long way to go. As Hebblethwaite himself put it, speaking for the progressive view of the

Council, the movement from preconciliar to postconciliar meant a transition:

> from arrogance to humility, from unjustifiable certainty to legitimate doubt, from security to hesitation, from swagger to stammer, from triumphalism to "sharing in the joys and hopes, the griefs and the anxieties of the men of this age." Normally it would be thought superfluous to congratulate a group of human beings on admitting that they belonged to the human race, but for the Roman Catholic Church such an admission was both startling and transforming.

But there was another view. Henri de Lubac, responsible for some of the most original theology of the twentieth century, summed up the post–Vatican II aftermath from the traditionalist standpoint in a single lengthy sentence, of which this is an extracted version. The postcouncil failures, in his view, involved:

> a resentment against the abuses of yesterday producing blindness to the benefits received from the Church . . . the opening-up to the world to be evangelised turning into a mediocre and sometimes scandalous worldiness . . . the arrogance of theologians wishing to impose their own thinking on the Church . . . small pressure groups getting control of the information media and doing their best to intimidate the bishops . . . an insidious campaign against the papacy . . . a rejection of dogmatics, which is to say a rejection of the Christian faith in its original twofold character . . . a moral laxity presented as the adult man's irreversible progress which the Church must confirm . . . a politicisation of the Gospel.

This was the man who, under Pius XII, had been labeled a dissident and who, because of his "advanced" ideas, had been forbidden to teach or even to live in a house where there were students. To add to the irony and the confusion, de Lubac, fearful of the anarchy unleashed in the Church, and fast becoming a staunch conservative, continued to be widely cited in support of the progressives.

Could a new Pope act to bring together these opposing visions of the Church with what the Council had intended and created?

When on October 16, 1978, Karol Wojtyla first appeared on the balcony above St. Peter's Square, he told the Church: "Be not afraid!" Progressives believed, at first, that this was a Pope to continue the spirit of the Council, indeed to press forward with its unfinished reforms. The conservatives, on the other hand, trusted that a prelate reared in the old-fashioned Catholicism of Poland would restore many lost disciplines and values. Few suspected the extent to which he would disappoint the progressive side of the growing Church divide.

At the outset, Wojtyla indeed appeared the champion of liberation. On the eve of Whitsunday, Saturday, June 2, 1979, aged fifty-nine, and Pope for less than a year, he faced a congregation of more than a million in the heart of Communist Poland—Victory Square, Warsaw. "Come Holy Spirit," he intoned, "fill the hearts of the faithful and renew the face of the earth." He added, to the ecstatic applause of the multitude, "Of this earth," indicating with a gesture the entire country and people of Poland, and of the world.

If there was a defining moment in the pontificate of John Paul II, it was that historic liberating declaration made in the heart of his oppressed homeland. He will go down in history as the man who inspired and sustained Solidarity, the people's movement that freed Poland from atheistic communism, prompting a process that led to the eventual collapse of the Soviet system. His vision of Solidarity, a collaboration between the Church's infrastructure and Poland's Catholic workers, places him firmly in a tradition of Catholic social activism, of grassroots pluralism. And yet there were to be striking contradictions in Wojtyla's papacy from the outset. Enemy of totalitarianism, champion of social justice and religious freedom, liberator, he would nevertheless come to be viewed by a significant constituency of European Catholics, even in time within Poland, as an ecclesial authoritarian who has damaged the Catholic Church in a lasting, historic fashion.

On other continents, he would be vociferously and paradoxically challenged directly on the score of liberation: in South America by those who sought to draw a practical and inspirational equivalence between Marxism and Christianity in the battle against capitalist oppression; in North America by the liberation politics of women, lesbians, gays, sexually active unmarrieds, and divorced and remarried Catholics who were contradicting the Church's right to decide their sexual morals. When gay liberation proponents shook their banners at John Paul during his 1987 visit to the United States they were telling him that they did not regard the expression of their gender and sexuality as sinful. In Latin America, the promoters of liberation theology were insisting that evil was the result of unjust political and social structures rather than abiding individual human fallenness.

As one contemplates the papacy of John Paul II and surveys the images that represent the Catholic Church today, there are underlying, mutually exclusive, clashes of meaning and purpose. One of the most extraordinary images of body language evincing a collision of both oppression and liberation was the moment in 1983, four years after the Victory Square triumph, when John Paul II visited Managua, Nicaragua, against the background of United States–sponsored guerrillas and the split between the bishops and the junta. The junta included five priests, one of them the minister of culture—Father Ernesto Cardenal.

Cardenal had repeatedly disobeyed the order of Managua's Archbishop Miguel Obando y Bravo to quit the government, and John Paul had threatened to boycott Nicaragua on his trip through Central America until all the junta priests resigned. In the end it was agreed that the five priests would absent themselves from the official receptions and ceremonies. In the event, Cardenal placed himself in the official lineup to greet the Pope, projecting an eloquent posture. Father Cardenal, dressed in casual clothes, went down on one knee to kiss the papal ring. John Paul withdrew his hand and shook his finger at him. "You must straighten out your position with the Church," he said. From one perspective a disrespectful priest was defying the Pope in public, making a mockery of the papal visitation; from another, an authoritarian Pope was repudiating a gesture of allegiance and humility on the part of a brother priest working against neocolonialism in the Third World.

From a Far Country

Karol Wojtyla was born on May 18, 1920, in Wadowice, a small town some twenty miles southwest of Krakow, not far from the Czech border. His Polishness is a key to his character, to his vision of the Church, and to his papacy. Apart from two years' study in Rome, he was to spend the first fifty-eight years of his life in Poland. When he spoke of Poland, it was as if he had internalized his country's precarious destiny, its tragedies and triumphs under both Nazism and communism. His addresses, originally written in Polish, were punctuated with Poland's centenaries and jubilees, its cults and devotions to the Virgin Mary, as if he were constantly attempting to reinterpret and repossess its past in the light of his faith.

After the war he worked as a parish priest and seminary professor while continuing his philosophical studies. For seven years he pondered the theme of personal moral agency—what he called the "acting person." He was strongly under the influence of Max Scheler, the Catholic German founder of philosophical anthropology and the sociology of knowledge. Scheler's work involves a circuitous, ruminative, onion-peeling approach to speculation: it emphasizes an anthropological approach to understanding personhood and knowing. As Wojtyla's thinking matured, however, he drew increasingly on the absolutes of scholastic sexual morality. "The innate language that expresses the total reciprocal, self-giving of husband and wife," he wrote, typically, "is overlaid, through contraception, by an objectively contradictory language, namely, that of not giving oneself totally to the other."

In the early days of his priestly ministry in Poland, he displayed the all-round talents of pastor, sportsman, intellectual. He spent much time with young people, leading them on grueling hiking and kayaking expeditions and impressing on them the imperative of chastity as a form of physical and spiritual fitness. In the mid-1950s he came under the influence of a doctor called Wanda Poltawska, who advocated family planning by a form of self-control reminiscent of athletic training. Dr. Poltawska would emphasize an equivalence between contraception and abortion due to the loss of fertilized eggs in some forms of the contraceptive pill. Her association with Wojtyla would continue into his old age.

He received early promotion, succeeding in 1964 to the archbishopric of Krakow. He proved a shrewd opponent of Poland's repressive Communist regime, and received the red hat at the unusually youthful age of forty-seven. In the 1960s he emerged as an influential figure at the Second Vatican Council, although his initiatives involved characteristic contradictions. He provided Paul VI with sources in the writing of the famous encyclical *Humanae Vitae,* and became an enthusiastic supporter of the Pontiff's verdict on contraception. Yet on other topics he was a progressive, arguing that the Church should grant non-Catholics, even non-Christians, the same liberties of thought and speech which it claimed for itself.

Wojtyla was elected on October 16, 1978, following John Paul I's untimely death, on the eighth ballot by a clear majority (104 out of 111 votes). He was the compromise candidate following a tie between two Italian cardinals. He was the first Slav Pope in history. At fifty-eight he was the youngest Pope since Pius IX, elected almost a century and a half earlier.

His frequent journeys abroad soon established him as a Pope of the people. With his cinematic good looks and telling expressions and gestures in the presence of vast crowds, he struck an immediate appeal. He took to kissing the runway on arrival at each new destination. In the first twelve months of his pontificate he traveled to Poland and to the United States. His benign appearance before the masses, however, concealed a sterner presence behind closed doors. In Chicago, one year into his pontificate, he privately lectured the American bishops on their failure to denounce contraception, abortion, homosexuality, and divorce. As he traveled ever wider, he continued to admonish the hierarchies. He scolded the French bishops for not withstanding the drift into secularization, reminded the Germans that they should preach the strict message of the Gospel without fear of displeasing the faithful, and warned the Africans about the dangers of enculturation—the tendency to merge local cultural, even pagan, practices with Catholicism.

Ignoring the collective authority of his bishops, even at the regular synods called in Rome to discuss the problems of the Church, he also turned a deaf ear to calls for local discretion in the nomination of new bishops. Theologians who dared to dissent from papal teachings were interrogated and censured. In the first year of his papacy, Edward Schillebeeckx was summoned to the Vatican three times to be cross-examined about his interpretation of Scripture. In the mid-1980s, Charles Curran of Catholic University in Washington, D.C., had his teaching license revoked because of his moderate views on secularity, and Archbishop Raymond Hunthausen of Seattle, a well-known opponent of nuclear arms, was required to accept a monitor to scrutinize his comments on marriage annulments and his dealings with the local homosexual community.

In Latin America, the Pope confronted Marxist-inspired liberation theology, the notion that sin was not so much a refusal to listen to the Word of God as the outcome of unjust social and political structures. Four years into his reign, he shook with indignation on a trip to Nicaragua when he faced a heckling mob of left-wing faithful and priests at an open-air Mass. They should adhere to the teaching of Rome, he told them, and reject "ideological compromises."

But if many of Latin America's Catholics were seeking freedom from economic and social oppression, many North American Catholics were demanding liberation from papal authority no less than original sin itself. In the United States single-issue interest groups—gays, lesbians, feminists, pro-choicers—sought individualistic expression of their faith. Meanwhile, in Europe the followers of Marcel Lefebvre, the Swiss-based traditionalist Archbishop, believed that too much had been abandoned of their old Church. They wanted the Mass in Latin, frequent confession, a concise catechism, acknowledgment of the reality of mortal sin and Hell. As it used to be. John Paul excommunicated him in 1988. From the opposite extreme, however, there were calls in Europe for greater participation of the laity in pastoral and liturgical affairs, new thinking on divorce and contraception, a greater role for women. And all the while there was a mounting crisis over priestly morals, in particular, of widespread pedophile abuse by clergy.

As his pontificate matured, his determination to hold the line grew stronger. From San Francisco to Warsaw Wojtyla grappled on a daily basis with moral and social dissensions within the Catholic Church. Should priests be allowed to marry? Should women be ordained priests? Should he sanction the use of condoms in the worldwide battle against AIDS, or turn a blind eye to abortion for rape victims in Bosnia?

As early as the mid-1980s, there were growing rifts in Rome itself. The Curia—the home-based bureaucratic cardinals and monsignori—were weary of his global style and independent administration. And there were internal problems, too, not least a scandal within the Vatican Bank, run by the Chicago-born Archbishop Paul Casimir Marcinkus. In 1984 an international commission found the Vatican Bank jointly liable for the crash of the Banco Ambrosiano, a Milan finance house, amidst accusations of serious malfeasance. The Vatican, under pressure, contributed

$250 million to the losses sustained by the Ambrosiano's credi-
tors, confirming an impression of culpability. John Paul continued
to support Marcinkus for at least six more years before replacing him.

The Curia longed for an Italian Pope whom they could control
within the traditional politics of the Vatican. Meanwhile, the "foreign" pastoral cardinals who led their national flocks pined for a
more liberal Pope who would implement at last the crucial decision of the Second Vatican Council of the 1960s to create a more
devolved, less centralized Church. Cardinal Bernardin of Chicago
complained with exasperation: "He treats us like altar boys."

The progressives had gotten into the habit of blaming Wojtyla
(and Paul VI before him) for failing to implement the decisions of
Vatican II. But the conservatives were calling for greater control
from the center, greater papal allegiance. And there were other
forces at work which had little to do with the Pope, the Curia, the
bishops, or Catholic responsibilities of any kind on either side of
the ecclesial divide.

The Church in a Late Modern World

Vatican II occurred at a time when many institutions and values
of the West were under assault—traditional sexual morality, family values, respect for authority and commitment. Hence the
Council, or elements of it, became identified in the minds of even
men of de Lubac's stature with the dubious liberations of the day.
And here, or so it was perceived by many who are now described
as traditionalists, were the seeds of the devastation that would
occur in subsequent decades. The loss of some 100,000 priests and
a quarter of a million nuns, the anything-goes expression of
liturgy, the mixing of paganism and orthodox worship, ecumenism and religious pluralism that implied an equivalence
among all denominations and all religions, the irresponsible flir-
tations with Marxism, the challenges to papal authority and bish-

ops, the adoption of the morals of sexual permissiveness that underpinned the contemporary "Culture of Death," as John Paul termed the contemporary climate—abortion, contraception, sex before marriage, divorce, homosexuality, reprotechnology. In a word, the freedoms that have degenerated, according to the traditionalist view, into license and wholesale relativism.

Under John Paul II the image of the "pilgrim church" has been dropped in official quarters, and one rarely hears references to the Church as "Mother." John Paul, despite his huge flow of writing and thinking, has not proclaimed a strong view of the Church during his pontificate. Strong on sexual morals, he is remarkably weak on ecclesiology, the theology of the Church itself. One has been more aware during his papacy of a proliferation of jaundiced images indicating the deepening of antipathy, internal strife, and fragmentation. The progressives are in the habit of assigning derogatory images to their opponents, as in a "citadel" or "fortress" Catholicism; by contrast, the traditionalists speak of "smorgasbord," "cafeteria," and "salad bar" Catholics who pick and chose from a variety of "wilting" options to suit themselves.

Archbishop Rembert Weakland of Milwaukee, thirty years on from the end of the Council, has called for a renewed and holistic concept of the Church. He has stressed the need to see the Church's mission as a communion that is inward-looking as well as outward-looking; his recommendation is accompanied by a grotesquely unflattering evocation of the current American "model." "The grand model of the Church in the United States today," he comments, "is McDonald's: self-service, broad selection, cheap prices, eat fast, and get out quick. There is no need for community." He also inveighs against the "therapeutic model": "The Church and its ministers are reduced to being psychological healers only. . . . Far too many priests are turning themselves into amateur psychologists—the world's most dangerous profession."

Metaphors that encapsulate the internecine struggles everywhere abound. *The Tablet*'s editor, John Wilkins, in a notable comment, has likened the Church to a "dysfunctional family": sibling rivals squabbling about an abusing father. No less negative is the image used by the journalist Peter Seewald in his interview with Joseph Ratzinger in his book *Salt of the Earth*. He put it to the Cardinal that the Church was like a black hole in space, then went on: "In other words, to a collapsing star whose centre has long become invisible and gradually shrinks to dwarflike proportions." Developing the metaphor, he writes: "Small fragments of the old mass, that aren't able to escape the attraction of the mother-body, fly helplessly around in small new units, collide, or destroy one another." Images of stars and mothers take on a remarkable new significance informed by popularized cosmology.

Ratzinger did not dismiss the analogy; in fact, he developed it a little further. "It can certainly look that way empirically," he replied. Then he said: "The historical hour isn't turning around, nor is this star becoming compact again, as it were, or returning to its accustomed size and luminosity. It would undoubtedly be false to expect that a sort of historical shift could take place, that the faith will again become a large-scale mass phenomenon that dominates history." Buried in the image, which borrows both from cosmology and Thomas Kuhn's "paradigm shifts" in the history of science, is another favorite Ratzinger metaphor—the Church as faithful remnant. The remnant collapses back into itself, separating itself from the heresies and dilutions of the age, becoming a *"gens lucifuga,"* the "true" Church as a people fleeing from the light of day to preserve themselves intact for better times.

The idea of the austere remnant also has ancient lineage harking back to the third-century father of the Church, Cyprian, Bishop of Carthage, who saw the pure and continent body as an image of the determined survival instincts of an embattled Church, surrounded by self-indulgence, betrayal, and apostasy. Cyprian admonished the Christians of Carthage and Rome to resist even a hint of "effeminate weakening of the hard resolve of the Christian," which would prove disastrous to the Church.

They must resist lust, anger, jealousy, and ecclesiastical pride, and be prepared even for martyrdom.

The remnant strategy has been most recently advocated in actual practice by Cardinal Schönborn, the leader of the Catholic Church in Austria, following his disavowal of progressive reforms in the Church. He has announced that the Church will in future have a smaller and more committed membership. In expressing such an outcome, Schönborn is in conflict with his predecessor as president of the Austrian bishops conference, Bishop Johann Weber of Graz-Seckau, who rejects the idea of a Church confined to "a small flock" of committed believers. Weber commented in March 1999 that the Church would remain a body for all baptized people, who "in some form or other," belonged to it. "Everyone can have a hand changing and renewing the Church."

The inclusivist images of the whole body, and the exclusivist images of the decaying star establish the contrasting metaphors that power the tensions in the Church today. The tensions have been a factor in Christianity from the very beginning, and they have formed the religious life stories of countless Catholics over the past five or six decades. Will the polarities they describe be maintained in tension in a conversation between control and freedom? Or will the forces become mutually destructive?

CHAPTER 5

A CATHOLIC PERSONAL HISTORY

> Some autobiographers continue to see themselves in adult life primarily as products of their interrelationship with a powerful parent.
> —Brian Finney, *The Inner I*

MY PERSONAL CATHOLIC HISTORY spanning 1940 to 2000 is relevant in this narrative insofar as it represents the experience of a large proportion of a generation that has seen a paradigm shift in Catholic practice and belief, remarkable changes in the complex fragmenting community we call the Catholic Church. A great many Catholics in North America, Ireland, Britain and its Commonwealth, as well as the countries of West and East Europe, have traveled journeys through faith during this period, enjoying similar consolations, doubts, and challenges. They will have experienced personally, or observed, the same altered principles, dilution of belief, disillusionment, and defections, in the lives of their friends and their children, their own generation and the next. The main features may differ in some essentials from the experience of the hundreds of millions of Catholics in the Third World, but there are analogies and connections which draw them into the same narrative.

The Dilemma

Catholics believe that they are created to seek the face of God. In the long history of the Catholic Church there have been periods when that radical, transcendent quest expressed itself in a self-denying, penitential, Good Friday spirituality. As a boy seminarian, then a senior seminarian, I made an honest trial of that hard, exhilarating, often self-wounding spiritual journey. When I later attenuated my radical Catholic aspirations with experiments in toned-down secular humanism, I felt more content, more calm, but I experienced a sense of mediocrity and loss. As the philosopher Charles Taylor puts it: "Do we have to choose between various kinds of spiritual lobotomy and self-inflicted wounds? Perhaps. Certainly most of the outlooks which promise us that we will be spared these choices are based on selective blindness." Karl Rahner, the Catholic theologian so influential at Vatican II, offers a similar reflection, but with a bias. Writing of the mystery that leads all without exception to God, if only they will listen, he declares: "It forces upon us the dilemma of either throwing ourselves into the uncharted, unending adventure where we commit ourselves to the infinite, or despairing at the thought and so embittered—of taking shelter in the suffocating den of our own finite perspicacity." Many Catholics of my generation have experienced and witnessed the dilemma of those contrasting choices, personally and historically: between a Roman Catholic penitential, radical transcendence, and a Christian secular humanism. Vatican II seemed set to restore our Church by reconciling those apparent irreconcilables, by encouraging the faithful to engage the world while offering the means to transcend it. Forty years on that reconciliation remains elusive for much of the Church. Unless Catholics can restore the spirit of Vatican II, they are due for a shock that will be as great if not greater than the division of Western Christendom five hundred years ago.

Mother Church

I owe my birth to the influence of the Catholic Church. My mother had been severely depressed on discovering she was pregnant for a third time in three years. My father was unemployed. They lived in two rented rooms close to the docks in East London.

I had been conceived just before Britain declared war on Germany in September 1939. The parish priest, Father John Heenan, persuaded her to trust in God and see it through. And so she did. I was baptized by Father Heenan, who, like us, was of East End Irish stock, and I was named after him.

My mother was second-generation Irish. Her people came from Kerry to the East End of London with nothing but their family and their faith. My mother left school at fourteen to work in a grocer's store. When she was just sixteen, her parents died within a year of each other, leaving her, their only daughter, to care for six brothers and to put food on the table. My maternal grandmother was buried in the habit of the Third Order of St. Francis, a lay section of the Franciscans.

My father received instruction to become a Catholic and was baptized in order to satisfy the virtual ban on mixed marriages, but he never went to church. We grew up thinking him a lost soul. His mother—my paternal grandmother—was a secular Jew called Lillian Freeman; she was deemed, doubly, a lost soul. The Irish Catholic contempt for Jews in London's East End was matched only by their fear and hatred of Protestants.

I was educated like my siblings, missionary style, by Irish nuns and Irish laywomen. Most of my school companions were the children of working-class parents; there were no non-Catholics in the school, and its existence in the suburban communities of East London was like a stockade surrounded by hostile natives. When I was approaching my fifth birthday, one of Hitler's V2 rockets destroyed a nearby Anglican church, killing several members of the congregation. Our saintly teacher, Miss Doonan, who taught us so piously to make the sign of the cross, said that these worshipers had been punished by God because they were Protestants.

Our parish priest was now Canon Cooney (Father Heenan had gone on to higher things, eventually to be Archbishop of Westminster). Canon Cooney had iced holy water in his veins. He was a great builder of churches. He lived on cabbage and wore cheap canvas shoes painted black. He fulminated from the pulpit about the wickedness of the world, and the expense of the interest on the church building loan. I grew up with Our Lady and Saint Patrick constantly on my lips, a sense of awe for the Eucharist, and a terror of Purgatory (which a teacher told me was like live burial). Aged seven, I had by heart the entire penny catechism, which contained all the essential truths of the Catholic religion.

"How do I know that Purgatory is true?"

"I know that Purgatory is true through the constant teaching of the Catholic Church."

My elder brother, Terry, recently told me that the Irish ambience was so fierce in our infant years that he thought we were actually living in Erin's Green Isle. To this day I can cross myself in Gaelic. The experience seemed designed to isolate us from the secular influence and temptations of England, in fact to re-create the immersion of monopoly Catholic Ireland. There were processions in the open air, crownings of the statue of the Virgin Mary, exposition of the Blessed Sacrament before forests of candles and flowers, High Mass with cloth of gold vestments and incense. I believed that when we went to Communion we received Jesus into our mouths. Protestants wickedly denied the truth of this, and they hated the Pope. They were destined to burn in Hell for all eternity for their "culpable ignorance"; savages on the dark continents would at least make it to Limbo since their failure to recognize God was due to their "invincible ignorance." We did much praying for the missions in Africa and for the Souls of the Faithful Departed. There was much repetitive prayer in church, litanies, novenas, and the rhythm of the rosary. The parish missions, annual visits by preaching religious, usually Passionists, made a deep impression on all of us, old and young. Even the most obdurate men of the parish, the small minority who rarely came to Mass, would queue for three hours to go to confession during the mission.

Confession was central to our lives, as it had been in my mother's generation, and the generation before that. My mother told me that when she first went to work in the grocer's shop my grandmother would collect her at nine o'clock at closing time each Saturday night to take her to confession. My mother, now in her late eighties, to this day fails to see that this was extraordinary.

When you went before Canon Cooney in the confessional it felt like going on trial for your life. My sister, aged seven, was made to stand up in the darkened confessional box and repeat over and over again that she was sorry for her sins. The priest had evidently judged her confession a trifle perfunctory. Memories such as these have turned my generation against individual confession: we did not want it for our children, and we want it even less for our grandchildren.

Confessions were heard on Thursday evenings after devotions to Our Lady, and for long, long sessions on Saturday morning, afternoon, and evening. It was not unusual to wait two hours to enter the confessional. Sometimes one heard women sobbing inside the box; sometimes a penitent would be heard muttering and sighing within the confessional for as long as an hour. In retrospect I realize that Catholics of my parents' generation were constantly in and out of that confessional, attempting to stay within the ambit of the sacraments and sanctifying grace. There was great fear in those days of being caught by death while not in a state of grace. The priests and nuns, who seemed immune to mortal sin as far as we children were concerned, constantly fueled our dread. In confession the priests demanded a "firm purpose of amendment," which was placed on one's own conscience, of course, as well as avoidance of "occasions of sin." The immense power of the confession-sin cycle was its self-policing mechanism. In a sense the whole of England with its materialist, Protestant temptations was a provocation to sin, but much more so was the marriage bed.

Confession is one of the great Catholic sacraments that has fallen almost entirely into abeyance. The Pope, in his Maunday Thursday address in the year 2001, took heart from reports that the young were returning to the sacrament of reconciliation as it is now called. It could be that a new generation, distanced from the horrors of entering a dark box with a man in a black robe, may return to the sacrament; but I fear that the Pope's gladness on this occasion was more wishful thinking than real evidence of restoration. The official Vatican statistics do not extend to figures for attendance at confession, but my own inquiries in the past year through a wide sample of parishes indicates that the sacrament has fallen out of use except at special occasions like Catholic youth rallies. A typical tale: I asked an old priest friend whether anybody comes to confession anymore in his parish, and he said, "I am available in the confessional every Saturday afternoon like clockwork. For the past ten years at least I have sat there for a whole hour every week and not a single person has come." On the other hand, a pastor in New York tells me that increasingly, in recent years, penitents are coming to him with "real confessions," authentic reconciliations to the faith, rather than the routine laundry list of peccadillos of yesteryear.

The contraceptive pill, even contraceptive devices, were not, before the 1960s, the big sin for working-class Catholics. I learned only when I reached the senior seminary, and received "technical" instruction in these matters, that coitus interruptus and a practice referred to by many Irishmen in the confession box as "whoring my wife," anal intercourse, were the favored methods of enjoying sex (at least as far as the husband was concerned) while avoiding the appropriate consequences—another baby. These inexpensive forms of birth control, however, did not evade mortal sin.

Meanwhile, as a child, something happened to me which defied articulation at the time, and for which confession was wholly inadequate, although the experience imbued me with guilt. I was a victim of abuse. It seems necessary to say, in the current climate, that the perpetrator was neither a priest nor a nun. When it happened—I was aged about nine—I realized for the first time the meaning of fear beyond all words, and evil. One day, in the future perhaps, the sacrament of reconciliation, or confession, may be widened and deepened to enable the young, especially, to voice such encounters with darkness. As it was, had it not been for the sacred rituals, the warmth and light of the Eucharistic sacrament, my soul might have died permanently—soul murder! Still a child, I developed a sense of the healing power of the sacraments: above all, of the Eucharist, of devotion to the Virgin Mary, and of holy water, the rosary, crucifixes, scapulars. I became a daily Mass server.

After Mass one day Canon Cooney asked me what I wanted to be. I said: "To be a priest." So I was interviewed by the diocesan Bishop in a grand house in the suburbs and that autumn, just thirteen years of age, I was dispatched to a junior seminary.

St. Wilfred's, Cotton, the junior seminary for the Archdiocese of Birmingham, was set in the high moors of North Staffordshire, 150 miles from London. One hundred and eighty boys and twelve priests lived in a monastic building of Gothic cloisters, cold class-rooms, and garret dormitories under the eaves. Our existence was more rigorous and austere than that of Trappist monks today. Had I stayed at home, like my siblings, I should have gone to an inner-city Catholic secondary school: one of my younger brothers earned a scholarship to a Jesuit school in North London, a journey of about ten miles each way every day; my sister won a scholar-ship to a local Ursuline convent. Two other brothers were not so lucky; they went to what then was called Secondary Moderns where the leaving age was fifteen.

Catholic education, whatever one's background, was a neces-sity rather than a privilege. In time, improved and free Catholic secondary education made available through Britain's 1944 Act, no less than the dedication of thousands of nuns, brothers, and priests, prompted the breakup of the ethnic working-class Catholic enclaves. The diaspora to the suburbs and beyond con-tributed to mass lapses and defections as the cousins of my own generation (I had six Catholic uncles, all with large families, and four siblings) moved out of the East End to the leafy Home

Counties. Similar patterns were repeated in North America and Australia. In Ireland and many parts of Europe the trend went in reverse: with education and new prosperity, Catholic families fragmented as subsequent generations moved from the country-side to the city.

Our lives in the junior seminary were dominated by the liturgy, almost entirely in Latin, with Mass at its center. I was a member of the choir, which was directed by an expert priest musician who trained us in Gregorian chant and the rich heritage of Palestrina, Vittoria, Carissimi, Mozart. The day was marked out with frugal meals, silent prayer, spiritual reading, cross-country runs, football, cold showers, manual labor in the bracing moorland air. The seminary teachers, all priests and most of them graduates of Cambridge University, gave us a good grounding in Latin and Greek, and encouraged us to read widely within the ambit of Catholic literature: Hilaire Belloc, G. K. Chesterton, Ronald Knox—eloquent apologists all. In contrast, the inculcation of Catholic doctrine was not a matter for discussion. We were educated in the liberal arts but received unquestioningly the content of faith. Our Catholic spirituality focused on the mediation and special virtues of the Virgin Mary—acquiescence and obedience to the will of God. Despite the many hours we spent in prayer and religious duties, many of us were enthusiastic to do more. I have a memory of myself, aged fourteen, coming into the empty church from an afternoon's manual labor on the Feast of the Immaculate Conception, December 8. As I knelt before the tabernacle lit only by the flickering sanctuary lamp I felt a sense of peace and indescribable happiness.

A popular manual of spirituality among students for the priesthood and priests in those pre–Vatican II days was the *Imitation of Christ*, by Thomas à Kempis. "Avoid the concourse of men as much as you can," wrote the Dutch medieval monk, "for the discussion of worldly affairs is very bad for the soul, even though they be discussed with a good intention." It was a spirituality that was funneled straight up to God with no acknowledgment of our social being.

All of us entered the junior seminary more or less at the point of puberty. Masturbation was the single unspoken moral preoccupation that from time to time made our lives sheer psychological torture. Failure for a boy to go to Communion could only mean one thing—that he had "abused" himself the night before. But matters were more complicated than that. A single "impure thought" or even a stray act of touching one's private parts constituted, equally, a mortal sin unless it were unbidden. But how could one be sure that the thought or act was unbidden? "Scruples," overpreoccupation with the fine degrees of intention, were an endemic spiritual and mental disease of the enclosed seminary hothouse. After I had confessed an act of impurity during one confession, the young priest confessor said to me: "How can God's grace be visited upon this house when you have done such a terrible thing?" It took me many years to comprehend the insidious, if well-intentioned, abuse implicit in that comment. Who knows that he had not received similar "counseling" at St. Wilfred's in his own boyhood?

It became a habit of mind to think of our Catholicism proudly and defensively. We were inside a citadel, the portcullis down. There were no women in our lives, save for an order of enclosed nuns who did our cooking, cleaning, and laundry. Somehow that only seemed natural: we called them "the witches." They did not even receive the Eucharist with us; they had a cramped and dismal chapel behind the coal store. We had no links with local communities, nor did we do anything for locals in need except for an annual carol concert for elderly Catholics in a distant village. We had no thought of suffering and deprivation in underdeveloped countries, except for a single visit from a missionary priest who had been tortured in Communist China: he showed us a drawing of a "brainwashing" cell.

We were aware, in theory at least, that one day, as curates and parish priests, we would be involved in care for the bereaved, the sick, and the dying. Some of us would even volunteer for work overseas on the missions. But first and foremost our vocation was to save Catholic souls, administer the sacraments, convert non-Catholics to the one true faith. On my visits home from the junior seminary I came to see more of the organized activities of parish laity. Apart from the Society of St. Vincent de Paul, which gave assistance to the Catholic poor and provided holidays for the children of poor Catholic families, lay groups were mostly concerned with devotional and spiritual matters: the Children of Mary, the Legion of Mary, the Knights and Squires of Columbus, Our Lady of Ransom, the Pioneers of the Sacred Heart who took the pledge not to drink alcohol, the Catholic Women's League, and various third orders and sodalities. These groups were totally in the control of Canon Cooney and the Bishop. In the immediate postwar era, when travel abroad became possible, the most important joint parish effort was the annual pilgrimage to Lourdes, which combined spirituality with work for the Catholic sick.

I arrived in the senior seminary, a neo-Gothic college in the West Midlands, in the autumn of 1958, just as Pius XII died. We were all astonished by the election of a Pope with a paunch, the jolly John XXIII. The contrast with the lean, ascetic Pius XII was almost ludicrous; we had yet to learn of Pope John's explosive decision to call an ecumenical council.

There was no shortage of vocations in those days. The senior seminary, like all the others in England and on the continent of Europe, was packed to overflowing with eager ordinands, most of them from the junior seminaries of England. St. Mary's Seminary, Oscott, was a enormous, gloomy building; one could have driven three buses abreast down the cloisters. Unlike St. Wilfred's and its rural setting, the senior seminary had commanding views over a polluted, industrialized landscape of chimneys, concrete cooling towers, factories, and housing developments. The routine of the day was much as it had been at junior seminary, although we were now trussed up in black cassocks and Roman collars.

The emblematic romanticism, the liturgy, the monastic routine continued. The intellectual regimen was narrow and austere. Our studies, in philosophy, theology, Scripture, and Church history, came packaged in published theses and aging manuals, mostly in Latin. We were not encouraged to read original texts. The tone of most of what we were taught was dogmatic, which lent a similarly didactic ring to our own utterances. These were the final days of an academic regimen that went back almost a hundred years to the reign of Leo XIII, when seminaries were instructed to treat packaged versions of the philosophy and theology of Saint Thomas Aquinas as if they were Holy Writ. I could not warm to the works of the Angelic Doctor, as taught in the seminary; it seemed to me a precarious palace of the mind, with grand, soaring pillars and buttresses; so much interlacing, so much analogous patterning, but pull away one pillar and the whole edifice would collapse.

From Rome there were gathering clouds and distant rumblings: would they bring damaging storms? Or rain for famished lands? In the meantime, things were getting a whole lot worse before they got better. John XXIII, as few people realize, was an archconservative when it came to seminary training. He called for the restoration of Latin lectures in our classrooms and a tightening of discipline. A new rector, replacing the retired octogenarian who had held sway for forty years, went on a tour of Spanish seminaries to learn how it should be done. Rules proliferated, the vigilance of the staff knew no bounds, sanctimoniousness was encouraged, honest intellectual debate was quashed. Young priests coming through from Rome spoke of better days to come. Some of us could not wait, and I was one of them.

I left the seminary and abandoned my vocation to the priesthood after completing the course in philosophy. I left without bitterness and with some happy memories of companionship in community and fleeting periods of spiritual contentment. I had attended early morning Mass every day of those seven years. I left at the very time when the Vatican Council was in preparation.

I went to see Canon Cooney back in my home parish, to explain. His last words to me were: "Keep the faith."

I threw myself into a new life. I was accepted at Oxford University to study English literature. For the first time in my life I felt intellectually free, and stretched. I was in love, for a time, with a girl who was not a Catholic, and religion began to recede from my conscious everyday life. I turned to literature and found a new spiritual sustenance, especially in the Romantic poets. Wordsworth's "spots of time" in "Tintern Abbey" and *The Prelude* described a sense of transcendent mystery that was far more impressive and true, I felt, than any of the sterile propositions about God propounded in our versions of the works of the Angelic Doctor, Thomas Aquinas:

> And I have felt
> A presence that disturbs me with the joy
> Of elevated thoughts; a sense sublime
> Of something far more deeply interfused,
> Whose dwelling is the light of setting suns,
> And the round ocean and the living air,
> And the blue sky, and in the mind of man:
> A motion and a spirit, that impels
> All thinking things, all objects of all thought,
> And rolls through all things.

I knew all about the heresy of pantheism, but this I could feel and understand: it was an acceptable prayer, and it connected with the sense of happiness I had experienced as boy in the moors and woods and lonely hills around St. Wilfred's. I see now that my discovery of the transcendental in the English Romantic poets was a form of extended adolescent immaturity, but the religion I had rejected was no less the inchoate and childish product of a disturbed, infantile imagination.

After Oxford I went on to Cambridge as a postgraduate student. As far as the Church was concerned I was living in sin, and I resented the persistent voices of conscience. I had stopped going to Mass because it only made me feel more guilty; I was not receiving the sacrament. I knew that I would soon have to come to a decision about Christianity itself. Walking one afternoon across Parker's Piece, an expanse of open ground close to the center of the city, I was transfixed by the Gothic tower of the Catholic church in the distance and the very sight of it provoked in me feelings of unbearable tension. I understood for the first time that I had been striving for several years to live my life with two entirely irreconcilable cosmologies in my head. One involved a supernatural realm, just beyond the veil of appearances, in which resided my depictions of Purgatory, Hell, and Heaven—all of which depended on pictorial, literary, and scriptural odds and ends as in a poorly imagined Gothic fairy tale. The other—and it was, admittedly, a vision of juvenile optimism—centered on the wonders of the universe: the stupendous fertility of life on the planet, the dignity, the genius, the resourcefulness of humankind, all of which could be ascertained by means of direct knowledge and understood by the light of unaided reason.

How was it possible to hold two such utterly opposed pictures of reality together? And yet, despite its purely speculative, shadowy nature, the "supernatural" realm, as interpreted by the doctrines of the Church as I understood them at the time, made obtrusive demands on my attention and conscience; it challenged and disturbed all the plans I was laying for myself—plans, so my informed Catholic conscience told me, that were selfish and vainglorious. That day I decided to cease believing as a Catholic and as a Christian. It was a simple decision that brought immediate relief. There were no pangs of conscience, no heart-searching; I was determined that I would not look back. The transition to agnosticism was painless, guiltless, and immediately rewarding. I could get on with my life unhampered by scruples of conscience and intellect. It would take another twenty years for me to return to the faith of my fathers, and keep the promise I had made to Canon Cooney.

Vatican II

While I was a student, the Second Vatican Council (1962–1965) was in progress. I followed it from a distance, and I was aware that there were discontents and tensions between the "progressives" (as Paul VI later called them, without disapproval) and conservatives, although it was not until the late 1960s that the overall shape could be discerned, and the emergent and restored models of the Church could be appreciated in the great conciliar documents.

There was much talk of the Holy Spirit arising within the Church, much talk of love and renewal, of bringing the laity forward to greater participation. After centuries of resistance, the Church was about to move out into the modern world. There were rumors and counter-rumors of liturgical reforms—a great relief and joy to some, but disturbing for others. Individualistic piety at Mass was to be discouraged, communitarian worship was to be encouraged. The reading of Scripture and the Eucharistic rite would be conducted in the local language. Social action, so much missing in my own upbringing, was now to be promoted: everyday Christian life was to be found in the world rather than in cloisters and churches. Christianity was to be exercised in society, politics, citizenship, a sense of responsibility for the environment and the developing world. The Council confirmed that the Church moves with the times, that it can change. It encouraged dialogue with other faiths and our separated Christian brethren.

The Council affirmed the importance of the collegial authority of the bishops together with the Pope; it spoke of the participation of the laity in the ministry and the whole Church. There was talk of reform of the Curia, the Vatican bureaucracy, and even of the papacy itself. There were hopes that authority would be returned to the local and national conferences of bishops in partnership with the clergy and the laity. In the event, despite many far-reaching changes, the papacy remained unreformed. After

John XXIII's death it became apparent that the old guard had challenged the bishops and worn down the aspirations of the Council's hopes for a reformed Church hierarchy.

In the meantime, what had happened to the old confession-sin cycle that had dominated the Catholicism of my childhood and youth and that of my parents' and grandparents' generations? Although there were constant rumors that the Church would lift its ban on contraception, nothing in fact happened; both clergy and laity seemed to languish in a no-man's-land. A number of my priest friends found the pressure of the ambiguities too great: the mid- to late 1960s was a bad time for them. Then, in 1968, came Paul VI's encyclical *Humanae Vitae*, reiterating the ban on contraception. The defections of the laity and their priests, at first a trickle, became a great river. For my own part, Paul VI's encyclical did nothing to encourage me to reconsider my agnostic convictions.

CHAPTER 6

CONVERSION OF LIFE

Do not reject me from among your children.

—Wisdom 9:4

IN MIDDLE AGE, after more than twenty years of confident agnosticism, unexpectedly, and against all my convictions and habits
of mind at the time, I had a religious dream which prompted me
on a journey back to faith. Such was my routine skepticism and
complacent empiricism that nothing could have been more out of
character, emotionally or intellectually, than to be influenced by a
dream, and especially a "religious" one.

It began in New York City, where I had arrived on a business
trip. I was forty-six years of age and an executive on a national
newspaper in London. My wife had her own business, my children were in their teens and doing well at school. I had published
two respectfully received novels by the age of thirty-one, and
a work of literary criticism by the age of thirty-three. But by
the age of thirty-five I had made a mark in the more profitable
ambit of journalism, a profession I now pursued after abandoning
an academic career in philosophy and literature. In time, drawn
by financial rewards, after years of penny-pinching, I was seduced
to the corporate management side of the newspaper business.
Plans to write were routinely postponed. Although I had once
been passionate about literature—I lived and slept literature
through my youth and young manhood—I was now reading little
apart from balance sheets and an obligatory torrent of foreign affairs news and analysis. I had abandoned not only the exercise of

religious imagination, but the poetic imagination, too. As for serious thinking beyond business, my thoughts were with sociopolitical "realities": areas of conflict, threats to the environment, the
arms race, the expanding domination of information technology,
the forces of market economics. Just occasionally, though, I would
find myself brooding on that elegaic reflection: "How with such
rage shall beauty hold a plea / Whose action is no stronger than a
flower?" Poetry had been my first and abiding love as a young
man, but when I considered the contrast between the power of literature and the power of modern technology, which admittedly
was seldom, I found myself echoing with ironic sadness Saul
Bellow's reflection: "to be a poet is a school thing, a skirt thing,
a church thing." Orpheus moved stones and trees, but a poet
can't perform a hysterectomy, send a vehicle out of the solar
system, pick up four hundred people in London and deposit them
seven hours later in New York. "Miracle and power," opines
Charlie Citrine in Bellow's *Humboldt's Gift*, "no longer belongs
to the poet."

After a transatlantic flight I had fallen asleep fully dressed on
my bed in the Dorset Hotel in midtown Manhattan when I had
this dream. I was walking in the garden of what looked like a college campus. The place was unfamiliar, but there was a sense of
sacred presence, of nostalgia and melancholy. Young men dressed
in black robes were approaching in twos and threes along a pathway. They seemed to be the contemporaries of my seminary days.
Their faces glowed with youth and innocence, but I was aware
that I had aged by comparison. I felt ashamed, stained, sinful. To
my relief, though, the first two figures acknowledged me cheer-
fully, and I felt a sense of grief for lost happiness. When I woke I
had the impression that the dream had recurred a number of
times. The pillow was wet.

I had that dream night after night as I traveled down through
Baltimore, Washington, D.C., and Atlanta. It was chiefly remarkable for its overtones of remorse, and yet I felt a sense of satisfaction and peace at being accepted by the holy young men. Each

time I woke I realized that I had been weeping. The dreams only stopped the night after a frightening incident when I was pursued by three muggers in the parking lot of the Hyatt Regency New Orleans. I forgot about the dream, but a few days later I had reason to remember it.

I had rented a car for the weekend in St. Louis, Missouri, and I was taking a drive from my motel on a crisp October Sunday morning. The road was empty, sparkling with ground frost and sunlight. Eventually a white circular church came into view and I had an urge to go inside. There had been a service and the interior of the austere building was filled with incense. I left by a different door and found myself on a campus bordered by low redbrick buildings. With a shock of recognition, I realized that I had walked into my dream. As I stood on a pathway that connected the church with the campus buildings, a bell rang and a group of black-robed men began to spill out of the nearest building. They came in order of age, the youngest first. They were monks. As they passed none spoke, but they all gave a brief nod of friendship.

I had arrived at the Benedictine Priory of St. Louis. The community had been founded by the monks of Ampleforth Abbey in North Yorkshire, England, and I had known some of its members when I was a student. I spent a day and a night with the monks, eating as a guest in the monastic refectory and enjoying their company in the common room. The serenity and healing quality of Benedictine hospitality stayed with me for the rest of my journey.

I now understand that religious dreams are associated in many cultures with an individual's rediscovery of an inner self, a conversion of life—one of the vows all Benedictines take. But how was one to account for the predictive quality of the dream? After returning to England I began ransacking libraries for books on dream psychology. I was also reading a jumble of books about mysticism, the claims of the religious paranormal mystical writings: Julian of Norwich, Meister Eckhart, John of the Cross, Teresa of Avila, Margery Kempe; commentaries on mysticism by authors such as Baron von Hügel, William James, and Evelyn Underhill. I found myself reading, once again, poets whom I had long neglected: Richard Crashaw, George Herbert, Gerard Manley Hopkins. At length I read an intriguing book entitled *The Physical Phenomena of Mysticism* by Herbert Thurston, an English Jesuit who spent fifty years studying tangible evidence for the operation of the Christian supernatural: miracles, levitation, flying Eucharistic Hosts, stigmata. His book, published in 1952, convinced me that the traditions of Christian mysticism, as opposed to the realms of the nonreligious paranormal or the occult, contained the best-documented, the most fascinating, and the most accessible range of popular mysticism available for scrutiny in the Western world.

My colleagues and friends were beginning to wonder about my sanity. I remember an editor saying: "I'm not interested in mumbo jumbo even to the extent of debunking it." I did not doubt my sanity, but I was surprised at how easily I was slipping back into a Catholic perspective: an openness to God's presence in the world through the tangible, a continuity between the symbolic and the real. But I had a professional interest, too. We had spent many hours in editorial conference during this period, talking about the influence of religious fanaticism in areas of conflict. I was fascinated by the influence of individuals and groups who believe they have special access to divine knowledge and power. The Germans refer to the consequences of this power as *Schwärmerei*, or "swarming effect." Interesting as all this seemed, however, and relevant as I considered it to be, I was neglecting my proper duties.

Shortly after Christmas of that year I decided that I could not in good conscience both pursue my obsession and keep on top of my job. I applied for a year's leave of absence without pay. So it was that for the first time in many years I became a free agent, ready to embark on a quest that on the face of it was strikingly simple, even vulgar and, to most of my colleagues, irrational. I would search for the "supernatural made visible" in the world, seeking evidence, wherever I could find it, for claims that God intervenes in the affairs of human beings. The story of that quest is told in my book *Powers of Darkness, Powers of Light* (in the United States, *Hiding Places of God*), and I now know that I started out asking all the wrong questions—providence, I suspect, often works that way—but I depict it here briefly in broad strokes.

I embarked on a pilgrimage, a journey more strange and dangerous, at least to the spirit, than any I had undertaken as a journalist in the world's trouble spots through the 1970s and 1980s. Given the fame at that time of Marian prodigies—bleeding, weeping, moving statues of the Virgin, from Japan to the Republic of Ireland—I chose first to visit Medjugorje in Yugoslavia, the site of a series of apparitions experienced by a group of Catholic children.

At Medjugorje, although I do not think that I understood it at the time, I received the first blessing of my journey. Outside the house where the visions were supposed to take place I felt part of the people who were kneeling there, expectant in the pouring rain. At the appointed time, an eerie silence descended over the entire village. Some gazed toward the window of the house, saying their prayers. Others bent down until their foreheads touched the ground. Those closest to the house itself pressed their faces against the walls.

Pilgrimage is sometimes referred to as "therapy of distance," symbolizing needs and yearnings, satisfied by departure, discomfort, and the rigors of travel. I was conscious of the enormous distances these pilgrims had traveled; they had made sacrifices, many journeying despite sickness and handicaps. But pilgrimage is also arrival, and I felt the goal of every pilgrim's journey: a sense of real presence.

The next day I was invited by the late Father Slavko Barbaric into the room in which the visions took place. On that day Jakov, Marija, and Vicka, three of the leading seers, were present. At the appointed time, as on the previous day, the world went quiet and I was conscious of the crowd on its knees outside. I was a few feet from the visionaries. They stood before a blank wall and began to pray out loud. Suddenly, in perfect coordination, they went down on their knees and continued to pray; then, together, their heads rose and they were now speaking silently, their lips and throats moving quite rapidly, gazing intently as if at a real object. They had entered their ecstasy. The extraordinary thing was that when one of them stopped "speaking," the other, in that same split second, would begin. All three—there was no other word for it—were transfigured.

As I watched the visionaries in the deep peace of those few minutes I had an unusual experience. I saw in my mind's eye, with great clarity and in sequence, each and every one of the images of Mary before which I had prayed throughout my childhood and youth, from the statue of Mary in my mother's bedroom in my infancy to the carved stone Mary Queen of Heaven that adorned the Lady Chapel of the seminary at St. Mary's, Oscott. In a mysterious expansion of a single moment I was somehow aware of each and every prayer I had prayed, every hymn that I had sung to Mary from my earliest Hail Marys to the poignant Salve Reginas at the end of Compline in later years. As the experience faded, I found myself thinking that these memories gave new meaning to the phrase "full of grace," and for a moment I had the impression of something unblocking inside myself. Somehow, unawares, I found my heart inclining.

I was not, however, entirely happy with Medjugorje. When I had entered my dream at the St. Louis Priory that Sunday morning, I had not abandoned my journalistic instincts. The mood of attentiveness in which I found myself was not without questions and scruples. In Yugoslavia, talking with pilgrims, and priests, and pilgrim tour promotors, I detected the exploitation of the pilgrim experience as a form of designer pop religion. The by-products at Medjugorje seemed rooted in a preoccupation with a type of phony do-it-yourself mysticism: visions of spinning suns and holy "sky pictures" (recorded in chance photographs), talismanic weapons against the powers of darkness, holy alchemies that turned rosaries to gold, and supra-scientific "beam-me-up-Scotty" evidence of the supernatural, of which a series of "scientific" encephalogram printouts of the seers' brain waves were an example. Money was not the only objective. The agenda of at least some of the cult promoters was to deal a blow against the perceived enemies of traditionalist Catholicism: the specter of Catholic liberalism.

And yet I was convinced that despite the exploitation on the periphery, Medjugorje was a focus of spirituality that outweighed the sum of its drawbacks. The old peasant people who knelt hour after hour in the silent church were a reminder that the shrine was a place of amnesty from the world's doubts, miseries, and helplessness. It would not be long before this part of Yugoslavia became embroiled in torture, war, ethnic cleansing. Through the worst of the war in Bosnia, Medjugorje was to stay open, a small haven of prayer and peace in a time of injustice, violence, war, and ethnic hatred. For me, it marked the rekindling of a long-dormant faculty. For a rationalist and a skeptic, which I was, it was a humbling admission. It had taken an encounter with popular religion, of a kind that in the past I had vociferously despised, to awaken the religious imagination that had lain suspended for so long in my soul.

Pilgrim people move from one holy site to another, often revisiting shrines where they have felt a sense of presence. Over the next six months I was often following in their footsteps, taking many side trips and losing myself down religious cul-de-sacs. I visited a Marian shrine at the mountain village of Garabandal, Spain, where the winds were so strong that the bells rang of their own accord at night. I interviewed a colonel in the Guardia Civil there who told me that he had witnessed a young seer levitating before his eyes. I viewed a "Eucharistic Miracle" at Lanciano, Italy, where bread and wine had "transubstantiated" into a piece of meat and a globlet of blood, so it was alleged, to assist the faith of a Basilian monk in the Middle Ages. I saw another "Eucharistic

Miracle," a piece of rust-red Communion bread, guarded over by five Carmelite nuns living in a walk-up apartment in the Bronx: the prodigy, they believed, was in reparation for the activities of a neighboring abortionist. I talked with Professor A. J. Ayer, who had been somersaulted by a vivid "mystical" after-death experience when he died for six minutes in a West London hospital: he had seen, with his own eyes, he said, "the spirits of time and space." I met a depressed Marian visionary in Queens, New York, who was awaiting a second coming of the Virgin, and I viewed the wounds of a stigmatic woman in Montreal, a former concert pianist who, lacking a piano, played a paper keyboard. I peered at the tears of Our Lady of Siracusa in Sicily, and scrutinized the liquefaction of the blood of San Gennaro in the Naples cathedral. I investigated the claimed prodigies of the Shroud of Turin, and the extraordinary screaming flights of Saint Joseph of Cupertino. I met Archbishop Milingo and witnessed him "slaying" his congregation "in the spirit"; I listened to holy women speaking in tongues. I brooded over accounts of satanic possession and exorcism and met a terror-stricken young man who had been undermined by a Black Mass. I went to see the Holy House of Loreto, transported by angels, so it was said, from the Holy Land to the Adriatic coast.

In time, and predictably, I became bored by these alleged prodigies. A token of my disgust was my disinclination to even walk a few yards to witness the incorrupt body of Saint Bernadette when I traveled through Nevers one month. I had begun to discern more clearly the difference between the apprehension of a mystery on the one hand, and crude "magic" masquerading as supernatural "evidence" on the other. And this growth in discernment had much to do with the conviction that I was no longer interested in "evidence" as a manifestation of explanation and control. Power was in the imagination—the metaphor, the symbolism, the sacrament. The significance of the Virgin's tears in Siracusa was not about evidence of literalist supernatural intervention, but the meaning of a mother's sorrow. I found myself returning to the Gospel miracles as stories that exemplified redemption.

Toward the end of my journey I went to Dublin to meet Sister Briege McKenna, a nun credited with a charism of healing. She ran a renewal ministry for priests at All Hallows College in Drumcondra and she invited me to spend time on retreat there. She was a remarkable woman. In her presence I felt a sense of purity of heart and great courage. She had dedicated her life to helping troubled priests. She told me horrifying stories of priests who had been involved in diabolism. She related the case of a priest, half mad with despair, who had taken part in a Black Mass ritual in which he pushed the Sacred Host into a woman's vagina. Priests came to Sister Briege from all over the world for healing and reassurance.

Late in the afternoon Sister Briege prayed over me in private and recommended that I read the Book of Wisdom, chapter 9. "I feel that the Lord has a special word for you there," she said.

Instead I went out to a pub called the Cat and Fiddle on the Drumcondra Road with a priest who had been an army chaplain in Beirut: this was more to my taste, I thought, than nuns and the religiosity of the retreat house. We drank a lot and laughed a lot. We got back late, somewhat unsteady on our feet. I felt restless. Before retiring I thought of Sister Briege's counsel and went down to the retreat chapel. I sat for a long time alone in the sight of the Blessed Sacrament tabernacle wondering whether it was possible to pray without faith. Did it make sense for an agnostic to seek guidance and help from a God who might be no more than a figment? Was it not akin to someone adrift at night on the ocean who sends a signal that may never be seen? Then I noticed a Bible on the chair next to me. I picked it up and turned to Wisdom, chapter 9. It began with the lines: "O God of my fathers and Lord of Mercy, Who has made all things by your word . . . do not reject me from among your children. . . . We can hardly guess at what is on earth, and what is at hand we find with labor."

The words seemed to open my heart, and the phrase "do not

reject me from among your children" echoed the yearnings I had felt in my dream in America when I seemed to encounter, face-to-face, the religious ambience of my childhood and youth. I wanted to believe this, and I was moved to tears by the apt sentiments expressed in the passage. I felt that I had found an acceptable prayer to pray. In the silence and stillness I was prepared to believe it possible that my tears were a token of the "loving-kindness of the heart of our God," who gives "light to those in darkness."

On leaving Dublin I was conscious of no great spiritual conversion. I felt a sense of dryness, of cynicism even, at the exercise I had put myself through: the journalist in search of God and of one or two good stories on the way! And yet regardless of my explicit (and my hidden) motives, I realized that I had been disturbed. I had further to go before I could begin another journey toward home.

After returning to England I had an urge to drive up to the Peak District to visit my old junior seminary in its remote and secluded glen. As I drove down the country lane where the college stood in the lee of a hill, the place looked much the same. But as I parked my car, the extent of the calamity that had occurred brought tears to my eyes. The refectory, the classrooms, the libraries, and the cloisters were in ruins. An item of graffiti across the wall of a dormitory proclaimed: "This is a shit hole!" The gardens, once beautifully tended, were overrun by weeds. The college that had survived two hundred years educating countless generations of priests was an abandoned shell.

As I stood in the ruins of St. Wilfred's I seemed to grasp a truth that I had been trying to articulate with difficulty for many months. As a boy I had once walked in these cloisters and gardens thinking how happy I should be to live the life of a contemplative monk. How I had longed for the courage to love God so much. All these years later I was only beginning to understand that the desert wilderness of spirituality is not to be found exclusively in those convents and houses of prayer where men and women dedicate themselves to the service of God. The desert may lie at the very heart of a person's life, in the depths of one's being. Many people who appear to have turned from religion, sometimes with a sense of hatred, to embrace skepticism, agnosticism, even atheism, are as much in the desert, the "dark night of the soul," as any contemplative. What we are fleeing, perhaps, is not God at all, but the false or inadequate representations of him which hinder any possibility of ever making progress in coming to recognize him or reach out for him.

As I walked through the devastated, deserted gardens and cloisters of St. Wilfred's, my young self seemed to come to meet me: without reproach or condemnation on his part, and without remorse or self-recrimination on mine.

My Catholic identity—which I intend to keep, come what may—is not like the renewal of a club membership, agreeing, once again, to abide by a set of rules. It is, for me, a daily creative action and interaction with the world, like a language. First and foremost I am a Christian, but my Catholic expression of Christianity, which I consider a special privilege of grace as well as accident of birth, parenthood, and education, is a way of using my imagination in prayer, in the liturgy, and in the work and encounters of everyday life, in reaching out to God, and being reached by God. Some theologians call this "sacramental" language. For me it is best understood in a striking passage of Scripture.

I saw one like a Son of man, dressed in a long robe tied at the waist with a belt of gold [writes John in the Book of Revelation]. His head and his hair were white with a whiteness of wool, like snow, his eyes like a burning flame, and his voice like the sound of the ocean. In his right hand he was holding seven stars, out of his mouth came a sharp sword, double edged, and his face was like the sun shining with all its force.

The polarities of snow and fire, rushing waters and roaring furnace, the majesty of the sun and stars contrasting with the tactile tensions of brass and wool, combined in the single image of a being both youthful and ancient, human and divine are the language of poetry. In drawing together Scripture and poetry like this I am suggesting that a crucial key to understanding religious experience can be reached through artistic imagination. The poet Samuel Taylor Coleridge describes imagination as a shaping power that "dissolves, diffuses, dissipates in order to re-create," extending our consciousness by providing a new unity to our perceptions; it is an "echo," he once wrote, of the imagination of God himself in his "eternal creation." He is saying that we can perceive God's action in the world through language, images, nature, and human relationships. He is suggesting that God is to be apprehended not as an object competing for our attention with other objects in, or outside, the world, but in whatever form the imagination expresses itself as it opens up the human heart. In this way, writes Coleridge, it is possible to discover "transcendence" in "the incidents and situations of common life."

During my sabbatical I'd returned again and again to the writings of Coleridge, especially his notebooks. His favorite image of transcendence in nature ("counterfeit infinity" he called it) was the waterfall or the fountain. Observing a waterfall in the Lake District, he commented: "What a sight it is . . . the wheels, that circumvolve in it—the leaping up and plunging foward of that infinity of pearls and glass bulbs—the continual change of the matter, the perpetual sameness of the form—it is an awful image and shadow of God and the world."

The idea of the meeting of finite and infinite in a single image prepares us for the idea of symbol as something that, in Coleridge's words, "partakes of the reality which it renders intelligible," as something that shares in the power, the mystery, the presence of what it represents.

As I moved away from the temporary allure of the paranormal, and from "voluntarism"—the temptation to place power and control at the center of religious experience—it seemed to me that imagination, in Coleridge's sense, lay at the heart of religious practice and experience: in the reading of Scripture, in prayer and acts of faith, in worship, and in the highest mystical states, as widely endorsed by contemplatives such as John of the Cross, and Teresa of Avila. As I renewed my faith it became clear to me that I needed to understand it as I would understand a poem or a piece of music rather than to seek explanations for power and control.

In time I began to write in this vein, and my views had a hostile reception in some quarters. The principle opposition came not from theologians but from Catholic fundamentalists who were in the habit of subjecting "supernatural" encounters to management, exclusive ownership, and manipulation—voluntarism. For the fundamentalist, the religious imagination is too inclusive, too open to religious pluralism, too available to rival denominations and religions, and even to agnostics and atheists.

The religious imagination comes in various guises and in various degrees; through love; through poetry, music, art; through nature; through compassion for those who suffer or who are in need; through Scripture, prayer, and ritual. For some it may take the prodigies of folk mysticism to kindle, or rekindle, the jaded religious imagination.

The awakening of religious imagination does indeed open the transcendental to all, for it is surely central to what it means to be fully human.

CHAPTER 7

THE GREAT ADULTERATION

These acclamations of the people, these cries of the Christian soul, have come down to us through the ages as a heritage from the early Christians, and still form a link between the Churches of the East and the West. Even to this day the sun never rises without hearing the same words uttered in the midst of the same mysteries.

—Fernand Cabrol OSB, *Liturgical Prayer*

WHEN I BEGAN to go to church again after breaking faith twenty years earlier, I felt personally and belatedly the full force of a despondency shared by many at the deterioration and adulteration of traditional Catholic worship. The first service I attended at a Catholic church in Northamptonshire was Mass on Christmas morning. At the moment of the Consecration the choir broke into a schmaltzy "Happy Birthday to You . . . Happy Birthday, dear Jesus." I had to go outside to catch my breath. I had the feeling that I wasn't going to make it. It wasn't just a feeling of nostalgia for the sense of mystery, the rhythm and repetitions that hallowed the rest of the day; it was the sheer ugliness, the uncouth jauntiness, the dumbed-down populism of what had become of Catholic worship. I now realize that I was making an overhasty generalization, and that there were parishes where the reformed liturgy—in efforts for greater participation—was performed with dignity and prayerfulness; but, also in time, I came to understand that there was loss, destruction, and deterioration which went some way to explaining the unhappiness, and the defections of many Catholics.

In subsequent weeks I looked around for alternative liturgies which resembled something closer to what I had been used to. I sought at first the Latin Tridentine Mass, which had been in constant and universal use for three hundred years before the Second Vatican Council. The rite had been banned after the Council, but eventually it was allowed a restricted catacomb existence. I found a church in London where it was celebrated once a week. There was a "supply" priest from somewhere in South America. He was too young to have known the rite and had to manage on poor Latin and an old pocket missal. It was a mess. But observing at least the ghost of the old Mass, I felt I was watching a museum piece. The congregation looked elderly, dispirited, and alienated from what was occurring faraway on the altar, with the priest's back to them. I never went to another Latin Mass until I attended a private Mass of the Pope in his chapel in the Vatican: it was in the new rite, and the fact that it was said in Latin seemed irrelevant.

Not long after this I went with my wife to a Trappist monastery in the East Midlands, Mount Saint Bernard Abbey. The liturgy was austere and meticulous, according to the new rite, and in English, but we were upset by the way in which the monks sang and mumbled to themselves: the congregation was denied music sheets, and there was no attempt to encourage us to sing the responses or even join in the hymns. Afterward my wife wrote to the prior complaining about the lack of participation. She received a letter of rebuke, roundly telling her that Mount Saint Bernard was an enclosed religious community and that she should go to her own parish if she wanted participation.

In the first two or three years after my return I became something of a wanderer. While I went to many churches where the congregations seemed happy and involved, I did not feel drawn in. While I liked in principle the idea of participatory worship and seeing women at the altar (formerly they had been denied access even to the sanctuary), I felt that I had parachuted down into a religious and aesthetic wasteland. In the inner-city church where an old seminary friend was pastor, I was shocked to discover that he had installed elaborate hi-fi equipment which he could regulate from the high altar or the pulpit with a touch of a button. He told me that when he didn't like his own choir he would drown them out with a tape of the Sicilian Vespers sung by the Sistine Chapel Choir.

Many of the churches I went to had retained the old high altar and its plaster reredos and simply inserted a table facing the people (some of these objects looked as if they were shop counters); the temporary had become permanent. The Blessed Sacrament had in many cases been relegated to a wooden cabinet somewhere to the side of the altar, and invariably lacked a sanctuary lamp. Out had gone the prominent statues of the Virgin Mary, for whom I had renewed my devotion; in had come execrable abstract murals, or badly executed scenes of caring and sharing. In many of the churches I visited, the sign of peace had become a free-for-all; in some churches a "charismatic" priest would bound down the aisle with an evangelical grin, grabbing members of the congregation at random. In others, old-fashioned priests would leave it out altogether. My old friend the late Father Philip Caraman SJ, then in a parish in Devon, told me ruefully after Mass one day: "I don't want homosexualists French-kissing in my church before Communion."

Songs of Praise

The *Constitution on the Sacred Liturgy* (*Sacrosanctum Concilium*, 1963) was the very first document issued at the Second Vatican Council. It was a crucial piece of writing because it influenced the direction of the whole Council project. It pictured the Church as a diversified people of faith gathered around its Bishop and regarded the liturgy as the summit toward which all the varied activities of the faithful are directed, the fount from which the power of the Church flows. "In the earthly liturgy," goes the text, "we take part in a foretaste of that heavenly liturgy which is celebrated in the Holy City of Jerusalem toward which we journey as pilgrims." The document set enormous store by the study of liturgy through history, the recovery and restoration of what is best and authentic; at the same time, it called for liturgical creativity and outreach. Liturgy should adapt to the needs of the time; it should promote greater unity among all Christians, and draw in all cultures and peoples. "Even in the liturgy the Church does not wish to impose a rigid uniformity in matters which do not involve the faith or the good of the whole community," counsels the document. "Rather does she respect and foster the qualities and talents of the various races and nations. Anything in these people's way of life which is not indissolubly bound up with superstition and error she studies with sympathy, and, if possible, preserves intact. She sometimes even admits such things into the liturgy itself, provided they harmonize with its true and authentic spirit."

But where lies the dividing line between anything goes and the restoration of what is most authentic? Was it "cafeteria Catholicism" or healthy pluralism that led a priest in New York City to advocate the à la carte options in his church? At St. Ignatius Church on Park Avenue a celebrant remarked to me after Mass that "smart" pastors were offering a range of worship. He listed: "masses with singing, masses without singing, masses with guitars, masses with Mozart, masses for children, masses for women, masses in Spanish, masses in Polish, masses in Latin, masses partly in Latin . . ."

Occasionally I found a church where, because of the mix of the congregation or an unusually gifted celebrant, or celebrants, it turned out to be an uplifting occasion. I am thinking of a packed and rousing Sunday evening Mass at the campus church at Stanford University in California; a Mass at the shrine of the Virgin Mary at Medjugorje in Yugoslavia at which the late Father Slavko Barbarbic sang in Latin, according to a traditional Gregorian chant; a Sunday morning Mass conducted by St. Lucians in the West Indies; a Mass at the Benedictine Priory of St. Louis, in

Creve Coeur, Missouri; Mass at the Benedictine Abbey of St. Wandrille near Rouen in France. But these were exceptions rather than the rule.

Mostly I was appalled at what I encountered. Something was badly wrong with the singing, the translations of the Latin rite, the manner of participation. In my own part of the world, the Northern Hemisphere, it seemed that the invitation to participate had broken down, leaving congregations stranded in a profane and banal milieu: almost everywhere I went I sat among people who did not even attempt to sing the dreary and tricky renderings of the Creed and the Gloria on offer, not to mention the hymn choices—"Kumbaya," "Michael, Row the Boat Ashore," "Amazing Grace," "Happy Birthday to You"—or if they did, it was hesitant, feeble, and uncoordinated. I felt I was witnessing a spiritual and cultural disintegration of flabbergasting proportions.

My Catholic friends told me that I was lucky. I had been spared, it seems, many of the excesses of the early period of outright anarchy: masses on coffee tables, masses with dancing girls, masses in which it was difficult to detect where the recognized Catholic rubric started and finished. But I was quickly made aware of the existence of continuing anarchy: masses (and I am referring to experiences in Dublin and just outside Rome) where ministers engaged in "slaying of the spirit," deliberately encouraging hysteria; children's masses where the celebrant dresses up as Mr. Magic and clowns around on the altar; masses where, according to the musicologist Tom Daly, middle-aged nuns swayed their bare breasts to the incantations of goddess worship, or where basketball teams dribbled balls up and down the aisle. I encountered ecumenical hybrid celebrations which indicated something more ominous. One priest friend told me how he had suffered a heart attack in a scuffle that had occurred in the university ecumenical chapel where he worked as a chaplain. His Anglican co-chaplain had decided, without consultation, to bring together the two separate Communion tables—Catholic and Anglican—as an ecumenical gesture. My Catholic priest friend had tried to separate the tables and had collapsed with a myocardial infarction in the process. To cap it all, my own son, at the time studying in a Catholic college in Britain, told me of Catholic priests "concelebrating" with a Lutheran woman minister during a "lunchtime" Mass.

Meanwhile, the choice of hymns involved a disturbing narcissism—the focus on self, "I" and "me"—owing more to the cult of "self-help" therapy than to the traditions of Catholic spirituality and liturgy. Tom Daly cites Psalm 90–91, which speaks of God's abiding protection. "Analyse the same text as found in the song 'Eagle's Wings' by Michael Joncas," he writes. "Note the enormous difference. The Joncas work, an example of the reformed-folk style at its most gushing, does not proclaim the psalm publicly; it embraces the text—lovingly, warmly, and even romantically. That moaning and self-caressing quality of the music, so common in the reformed-folk style, indicates that the real topic of the words is not the comforting Lord but 'me' and the comforts of my personal faith." Daly demonstrates how many religious songs with first lines such as "Come to me," "Be not afraid," "If you belong to me," "I" and "me" do not refer to the individual worshiper, but God himself. But through the "miracle" of contemporary folk music the congregation becomes the Voice of God. Daly believes that the Catholic Church has entered a power struggle in which the egotistical providers of music and liturgy are taking over the true center of real presence, which should be the Eucharist.

Revisions

Gomar De Pauw, a former dean of a seminary, and a combative traditionalist, has spoken for a broad constituency of Catholics in his condemnation of the liturgical reforms as "schismatic, sacrilegious, heretical, and possibly invalid," warning that it could in

time destroy "the whole basis of the Roman Catholic religion."
But one does not need to be a conservative in De Pauw's sense to
be disturbed by the new rites. One of the most contentious areas
of the new liturgy has occurred over revised liturgy and texts.
Vatican II recommended that revisions be preceded by careful investigation of theological, historical, and pastoral aspects. But the
anthropological dimension of ritual was entirely neglected. The
Council document advocated, for example, that "the rites should
be distinguished by a noble simplicity. They should be short, clear,
and free from useless repetitions. They should be within the people's power of comprehension, and normally should not require
much explanation."

It has taken an Anglican theologian, Catherine Pickstock of
Cambridge University, to demonstrate the theological enfeeble-
ment and loss in the new translations of the Roman missal
through the elimination of "needless" repetitions. As Pickstock
shows in her influential book *After Writing*, this involved the
failure to understand the "liturgical stammer" of the ancient rites
of the Roman missal. These "stammering" repetitions and dox-
ologies are invariably exemplifications of the Trinity, references
to the Father, Son, and Holy Spirit, enacting liturgically the central mystery of Christianity—the three persons in one God. She
argues that fallen humanity requires the "constant rebeginnings"
contained in the old rite. Each Eucharistic act must embody both
the possibility and the impossibility of approaching God, the par-
adoxical tension between the finite and the infinite, matter and
spirit. Commenting on Pickstock's thesis, the Catholic historian
Eamon Duffy writes: "In eliminating or muffling these tensions,
the new rites crassly rush in where, quite literally, angels fear to
tread." Here the reduction of music to dumbed-down ego-cen-
tered populism combines with accusations of the spread of a neo-
Pelagianism (the denial of our fallenness). Duffy, again, writes:
"The calamity of the new Mass in its English guise is that it constantly occludes the provisionality of the present world order,

constantly nudges us towards a smugly pelagian sense that we possess the mysteries we celebrate with longing." At a conference on the Eucharist at Duke University in 1998 an American participant told Duffy: "The nun who had prepared my children for First Communion had taught them to say not '*Domine, non sum dignus* [Lord, I am not worthy]' before reception, but 'Lord, I *am* worthy to receive you.' " More worrying are recent reports of lack of respect for the Sacred Host among children. A recent correspondent to *The Tablet* writes: "I was shocked to see the irreverence and lack of respect amongst the children for the Host. I believe the same is true in parts of the Americas." A local Catholic catechist told me that she saw a young boy taking the Host and putting it into his pocket. When she remonstrated with him, the boy's mother abused her loudly in the church. The family never returned.

Syncretism

In the developed Northern Hemisphere with its deep European roots, the conservative unhappiness with adulterated Catholic worship is understandable and its protests laudable. But in a Church that has emerged from a process of European outreach, parallel to colonial imperialism, and into a state of globalization, the internal tensions over ritual expression are complex and ominous. One of the most bitter conflicts between the Roman center and the south (outside of Europe and North America), where some 70 percent of the world's Catholics live, is between the application of centralized discipline, especially of worship or liturgy, and the tendency for local Catholics to mix native non-Christian beliefs and practices with orthodox Catholicism.

The tensions go back a long a way, and there are many strong arguments on both sides, but it is evident that Rome believes that it could be losing a crucial battle for the future integrity of Catholic ritual, and hence for the Church itself. The tension be-

tween liturgical conformity and anarchy involves problems that
lie beyond familiar arguments about a male-dominated priesthood or the participation of the laity.

The heated quarrels between Rome on the one hand, and bishops, pastors, and missionaries in countless far-flung enclaves on
the other, have their origins in the Church's modern, post-
Counter-Reformation missionary past. Films like *The Mission*
and *Black Robe* have been influential in creating a largely mythi-
cal and sentimental portrait of Catholic evangelizing in the sixteenth and seventeenth centuries. The process was never without
difficulty and tragedy. An example is the remarkable mission of
French Jesuits to the northern woodlands of America, traveling
months by canoe beyond present-day Montreal. The Jesuits
aimed to purchase souls for Heaven and many are the tales of
their saintly heroism and martyrdom. But they were also attempting to reclaim the northern New World from the Protestant
Dutch and English. Their scheme was to evangelize the native
Americans of the northeast so as to create an indigenous Catholic
empire. The entire continent of North America would then be
evangelized by a domino effect: ultimately the Protestants would
be thrown out to reclaim the new Eden of America for the
Catholic Church. They first targeted the Hurons, a relatively advanced indigenous people numbering about twenty thousand, living close to Lake Ontario. After some twenty years of supreme
effort, living among the people in their longhouses, the Jesuits realized that they were making little headway: the Hurons found
Christianity obnoxious, and were cooperating for material rather
than spiritual gain. Food was often traded for baptism. Instead of
working patiently with Huron culture and traditions, the Jesuits
hardened their line and attempted to destroy the native web of
beliefs and impose Catholic dogma by fear. The story of this tragic
mission is to be found in the many volumes of *Jesuit Relations*.
"To prevent backsliding and to encourage conversion," writes the
anthropologist and historian of the Huron people Bruce Trigger

in *The Children of Aataentsic,* "the Jesuits continued to emphasize the torments that they believed would be inflicted on a
non–Roman Catholic or an apostate after death." The consequences were not merely psychological and cultural dislocation
but the physical destruction of an entire people. Their social and
familial structure fatally weakened, the Hurons were rendered
vulnerable to their traditional enemies the Algonquins who in-
habit present-day upstate New York. In the end, devastated by
disease, famine, and violence, the Hurons numbered a mere six
hundred when they started their diaspora to the safer haven of
Quebec. Such disasters of missionary activity, through to the
twentieth century, were repeated in many parts of the world.

The bad old days of destructive, heavy-handed, first-contact
missionary zeal have long gone, and the Catholic Church now approaches with a deeper understanding complex situations involving local socioeconomic predicaments and mixes of postcolonial
and local native influences. Anthropological awareness is second
nature to Catholic missionaries today, but efforts to spread the
Gospel while respecting and even working within local culture are
often in conflict with centralized Catholic authority.

The view of Vatican II, in its *Pastoral Constitution on the
Church in the Modern World,* was this: "The Church is faithful to
its tradition and is at the same time conscious of its universal mission; it can then enter into communion with different forms of
culture, thereby enriching both itself and the cultures themselves." The concept of such cross-fertilization had a further boost
following a special Synod on Evangelization (1974), which explored the need for recognizing cultural pluralism. At about this
time theologians started to use the term "inculturation," meaning
the mystery of incarnation in which the Word of God "becomes"
flesh in a particular human society and culture. The notion is revealed in combinations of local and orthodox Catholic ritual and
belief, widely referred to as "popular Catholicism." Michael
Amaladoss SJ writes: "The people who have the gospel pro-

claimed to them have already their culture, animated by a religion. What happens then is an intercultural and interreligious encounter. This can only be a process of dialogue." But popular
Catholicism has come in for much harsh criticism in conservative
quarters, giving rise to accusations of syncretism. Syncretism
means the creation of hybrids of different religions, as in blend-
ing local demons or spirits with the theology of angels, or mixing
pagan creation myths with the Genesis account.

While the guardians of orthodoxy are rightly alarmed by syncretism, missionary work informed by anthropological sensitivities is shedding light on the continuing, perhaps expanding,
problem of projecting a "European" Church on a global Church.
In their book *Popular Catholicism in a World Church*, editors
Thomas Bamat and Jean-Paul Wiest bring together seven case
studies of "popular Catholicism" in Third World settings to
demonstrate the scope of inculturation in the Church today.

Being a Catholic, they point out, can have very different meanings and consequences in different places. Sometimes local cultural
traditions blossom under Catholicism, sometimes Catholicism undermines local cultural tradition. Writing in *America* on May 29,
1999, Thomas Bamat commented:

> Aymaras in Peru say that being Catholic—rather than Evan-
> gelical or Adventist—provides the liberty to be faithful to
> their traditions. But Dagomba Catholics in Ghana and
> Catholic parishioners in Hong Kong struggle with troubling
> accusations by compatriots that, as Christians, they are no
> longer truly Dagomba or truly Chinese. In Ghana, Christian-
> ity is often called a "white man's religion," and in Hong Kong
> there is a saying, "one more Christian, one less Chinese."

Bamat and Wiest report that popular religion shows remarkable resilience to "modernity's cult of the market, its individualism and the process of secularization." But to what extent can
orthodox Catholicism accept admixtures before it becomes some-

thing other than Catholicism? Bamat gives some examples of what he considers benign inculturation:

> I found myself praying with young Dagomba Catholics amid the huts of a Muslim-dominated village in Ghana, witnessing the expulsion of vociferous demons during an all-night prayer vigil in Tanzania, participating in the community blessing of an Aymara home that had been struck by lightning in Peru's high plains, watching rehearsals for a Holy Saturday ceremony that retraces the slave history of banana farmers on the Caribbean island of St. Lucia.

Rome's concern about syncretism in the far-flung regions of the world (as well as places closer to home) is clearly justified: Rome is also right be concerned about the importation of syncretism into Europe and North America. I once attended a terrifying syncretic service in the Eternal City itself, conducted by Archbishop Emmanuel Milingo. Milingo, now married outside the Church, was a charismatic Zambian prelate who was ordered to Rome to account for his tendency to mix local spirit worship with Christian teaching. He remained obdurate in his practices and beliefs, so he was given a job in a department within the Holy See and lodged in a Vatican apartment. He began to conduct illicit services, which immediately became popular among Italian Catholics. During Mass, which he celebrated in the Ergiffe Palace Hotel on Rome's beltway, he incorporated a "healing" ceremony. I watched as Milingo whipped up hysteria in the congregation at the most sacred point of the Mass—the Eucharistic rite. As he moved among the people, sprinkling them with "holy water," people were screaming, groaning, and gripped with fear. I saw a middle-aged woman go down on the floor, writhing and shaking in an obscene fashion as if she were having an orgasm. Then a young man went down in front of me and began to paw and scrape the floor, barking and whining like a dog.

Mixtures of Catholic ritual, witchcraft, and pagan attachment to demonology are to be found in many parts of Africa, Brazil, and the Caribbean. One of the best-known forms of Catholic-pagan syncretism is Santeria, developed in Cuba and combining elements of local Yoruba superstition with Catholicism. Santeria developed out of the adaptation of the ancestral religion of African slaves to the Catholic influences of their new communities in the New World. The Yoruba pantheon of gods, or *orishas*, were equated with Catholic saints: for example, the thunder god Shango is equated with Saint Barbara, who is invoked during thunder and lightning. It is not difficult to see why the Vatican authorities and local hierarchies are suspicious of Bamat's approval of rituals connected with houses struck by lightning, or that they are alarmed by the link between the Easter Vigil and the slave histories of banana farmers. Would this not be a short step to the superstitions of Santeria initiates who believe that through special rituals they can be "possessed" by the *orishas*? With immigration, Santeria has spread to parts of the United States, where the practitioners have clashed with the civil law over animal sacrifice.

It is difficult to estimate the extent to which Catholicism has become adulterated with admixtures from non-Christian religion and New Age beliefs and practices. Where should the line be drawn? Should Cardinal Ratzinger allow the use of goat's flesh and milk at the Eucharist in parts of the world where bread and wine are unobtainable? Should priests in New Mexico be allowed to celebrate youth masses using Pepsi-Cola and Big Macs? And while the majority of experimenting pastors would stop short of sorcery, many are open to what anthropologist Father Michael Amaladoss terms the "cosmovision of popular religiosity." "I think that the new age movements," he writes, "are efforts to explore this world-in-between of human powers beyond the reach of ordinary science through techniques which Asian, Hindu, and Buddhist masters have developed and perfected over the centuries." They do "not deserve rejection," he goes on, "but deeper study." Catholic figures like the late Father Bede Griffiths (a

Benedictine monk who formed an ashram in India), or former
Catholic Father Matthew Fox, who combined mysticism (favoring
Hildegard of Bingen) with a theology close to panentheism (the
indwelling of God in the earth), have attracted enthusiastic followers among Catholics and non-Catholics alike. When Fox got
into a dispute with Cardinal Ratzinger, he published a full-page
letter in a newspaper inviting the prelate to engage with him in a
dance with a white witch called Starhawk. Father Fox has since
joined the Episcopalians.

Catholic conservatives point to these "flexible" approaches to
Catholicism and indeed Christianity as a whole as evidence of
prevalent syncretism even within the developed north. Commenting on the sociologists' self-congratulatory description of America
as "incorrigibly Christian," Father Richard John Neuhaus spoke
for many conservative Catholics when he pointed out the danger
of "flexibility" which "reaches a level of promiscuity."

> We are inclined to view Santeria and similar religious expres-
> sions as impossibly "primitive," but it may be that Christian-
> ity in this most advanced society of ours is, at least to a
> significant extent, a kind of American Santeria. Some sociolo-
> gists of religion have also referred to American Shinto, mean-
> ing a culturally pervasive but doctrinally indeterminate
> religiosity similar to Shintoism in Japan.

Father Neuhaus evidently believes that Catholicism should
and can be preserved from this kind of taint through stricter centralized control—conformity to Rome's orthodoxy. But is it that
simple to foster an authentic, unpromiscuous, popular Catholicism by control from the top downward? From the center outward?

While liturgical reform has been evidently successful in certain
places and applied to certain rites, such as baptism, liturgists
complain bitterly of the return and expansion of clerical patriarchalism. "Perhaps more serious," writes liturgy scholar Aiden

Kavanagh, "is the increasing speed with which parish liturgy may become a celebration of middle-class values, creating a narrow new elitism which tends to exclude the lower classes and alien ethnic groups." This tendency, according to Kavanagh, is "splintering the Church," and "the organic sacramentality of the Church as redeemed humanity standing worshipfully and in unity before God in Christ by the Holy Spirit falls away." Idiosyncratic individualism is flourishing, according to this view, and worship becomes the plaything of its celebrants. The participation intended by the fathers of Vatican II fails, and the consequence is empty churches.

CHAPTER 8

DILUTION OF BELIEF

I like the idea of preserving something even for one's grandchildren.
—Cardinal Ratzinger

ABOUT TWELVE YEARS AGO, the daughter of a friend sat next to me during a family baptism. She had been brought up Catholic and was now in her mid-twenties. "Are you still practicing?" I asked. "No," she said. "I'm trying Buddhism. But I suppose I'll go back to Catholicism in the end. We all do, don't we!"

Born in the 1960s, she was a member of perhaps the last generation of Catholics who had received a distinctive grounding in the faith—clear practice, allegiance to authority, well-defined beliefs familiar as "Catholic identity" to my generation and that of my parents and grandparents. The following roll call contains a necessary if not complete set of those beliefs and practices familiar to that generation: devotion to Mary as Mother of God; the indissolubility of marriage, and the inadvisability of mixed marriage; the real presence in the Eucharist; venial sin and (deserving Hell for all eternity) mortal sin; the necessity of confessing mortal sin; the immortal soul, the resurrection of the body; Purgatory and the scope for praying for the souls therein; infallibility and the primacy of the Pope as successor of Saint Peter, the role of bishops as successors of the Apostles; the intercession of the saints; the reality of Satan, and of demons and angels; a hostile antagonism toward atheistic communism; the inadmissibility of contraception, abortion, premarital sex, adultery, homosexuality, and remarriage; the inadmissibility of worshiping with non-

Catholics; weekly attendance at Mass, holy days of "obligation";
and the imperative to avoid meat on Fridays. There were other
Christian beliefs, which we Catholics shared with other Christian
denominations, but those cited above were, in retrospect, as distinctively Catholic as the burning of a sanctuary lamp before the
Blessed Sacrament and the papal coat of arms somewhere in the
church porch.

Confidence that one can return home to a Catholic space and
set of everyday beliefs and worship assumes that the prodigal has
a clear sense of what and where home is, which gives point to the
protestations of conservatives who argue that the content of the
Catholic faith has become so relativized as to be indistinguishable
from other Christian denominations or even the quasi-spiritual
sentiments of those with no particular religion. That is not how
religions survive.

In contrast to the pre–Vatican II definition of core Catholicity,
a new list of Catholic priorities, according to many surveys, has
emerged. They are as follows: belief that it is possible to have a
personal and loving relationship with God; belief that God took
human form as Jesus Christ to redeem the world and bring us to
God; and commitment to a relationship with God through public
and private prayer, worship, and reading of Scripture, principally
within the faith community and sacramentals of the Catholic
Church. Unlike the pre–Vatican II list of priorities, these post–
Vatican II Catholic convictions are shared with other Christian
denominations. Commitment to a relationship with God within
Catholic sacramentals—Marian devotion, belief in the real presence in the Eucharist—makes all the difference. But this add-on
qualification seems desirable rather than imperative, and has to be
balanced against a decline in confidence in the Catholic Church as
an institution.

Recent international studies led by British sociologist of religion Professor John Fulton in six Western countries have shown
that a group characterized as "core young adult Catholics" (meaning regular churchgoing young Catholics), aged currently between

eighteen and thirty, continue to subscribe to the "more open" definition of Catholicity while confirming that allegiance to moral teaching based on external authority has virtually disappeared. Research indicates that profound cultural and social changes have influenced the majority of young Catholics (even those who practice their faith regularly) to the point where values and moral choices tend to be individual and personal. As we shall see later, these findings link with the thesis of the Jesuit moral theologian Professor John Mahoney, who argues that nowadays the faithful see moral questions in terms of a totality of consequences. For example, young Catholics tend to view contraception in the light of overpopulation and stricken families as well as in terms of moral "absolutes" focusing on the "purpose" of the sex act.

At the same time, recent surveys show that the location of the sacred and the good has shifted from traditional Catholic sacramentals to reverence for the environment and attention to the dignity of human beings prompted by their suffering: in other words, a more secular set of concerns in this world rather than in a sacralized, symbolic, or cloistered world, or reality beyond the "veil of appearances." I shall return to these crucial studies, but first it is important to emphasize that questionnaire-based statistics also show a dilution of traditional Catholicity right across the generations. The difference between the old and young Catholics is that my generation knows what has been lost or diluted, whereas today's young have not received that detailed, distinctive Catholic grounding to make the distinction. Will the children of my friend at the church baptism have the confidence to say: "We all go back to being Catholic in the end, don't we?"

Catechizing Young Catholics

The consensus of sociologists of religion is that Catholics, old and young, are making up their own minds about the content of their belief. But catechesis—the teaching of the faith—has also played an important role in the way young Catholics understand their faith. Catholic catachesis of the past twenty years has contained little that is recognizable from the days of the pre–Vatican II catechism.

I have before me the "level two" textbook (ages eleven to thirteen) entitled *Community-Story-People,* which is part of a series of books titled Weaving the Web. It was developed by Catholic religious education experts for use throughout Catholic schools in the dioceses of England and Wales, and published in 1988 with frequent reprintings up to the end of the 1990s. It has its counterparts throughout the English-speaking world and in other languages, and it has formed an essential ingredient of the religious education of many hundreds of thousands of Catholic children in the early years of secondary school. The material is more in keeping with a course in secular civic responsibility than religion: reading through, one can sympathize with conservative complaints that "liberal" Catholicism is actively imparting a relativistic attitude to the faith.

On the first spread, which is a busy format of pictures and "tasks," there is a single segment describing "Plural Community": "In this country there live followers of all the main world religions: name some of these religions which are present in your community (plural means more than one)." No attempt, here or later, to provide a religious underpinning of pluralism, the imperative of respecting the dignity of all people, whatever their differences, including belief and value systems; no attempt to acknowledge that there are people of no particular religion who also have dignity and value systems derived outside religion. The principal thrust from the outset then is certainly relativistic, but it also curiously reactionary.

As the text develops, there is much about helping others and being nice to people, until finally, on page 14 of eighty pages, there is a single page entitled "Religion in the Local Community" which sees Catholicism as one option among many, and includes this task or question: "What do you think about the idea of women being priests?" The sop to the women's ordination lobby, however, is undermined by the absence of a sensible treatment of the place of women in society, including their battles for equality through the twentieth century.

On the opposite page, under the heading "Exploring a Diocese," an exact equivalence is given to the Anglican and Catholic dioceses, and bishops are equated with "superintendents" or "mayors" or "the head of the town council." No word about the successors of the Apostles. Meanwhile, Jesus does not put in an appearance until page 21, when we come upon a headline "Jesus the Servant of Others." The leading paragraph runs: "For Christians, Jesus is the person who is to be followed. . . . Christians try to live the way Jesus lived, not by dressing the way he dressed, but by following his way of living for others. This is sometimes called Service." On the following page we have another headline: "Jesus the One Who Was Concerned About Others." Jesus, then, is seen as a kind of social worker, one among a number of caring prophets, but there is still no hint that Catholics are supposed to believe that Jesus is the Son of God. And so it goes, through the suggested "Christian" virtues of helping, caring, serving others, with not the remotest hint of the Christian virtue of loving others as oneself, or the underpinning of that love in the destiny of each individual to God.

Page after page the young reader is informed about the importance of friendship, making promises, failed relationships, the police, the injustice of apartheid, falling in love, growing up in a Jewish community, and various emotions, until on page 72 we have a picture of Jesus with his arm around a man. The caption reads: "Jesus the Pilgrim: in the gospels, Jesus spends much of his time travelling from one place to another preaching the good news about the kingdom of God." Below, the pupil is asked to "act out the human journey from childhood to old age." Then on page 76 buried in a box at the bottom of the page, for the first and only time we have a description of Jesus Christ:

> Jesus of Nazareth
> born in Bethlehem about 2000
> years ago.
> Killed on Friday during the
> Jewish Passover Feast.
> Innocent, but proved guilty
> at "fixed trial."
> Occupation: Son of God.
> Also prophet, teacher
> and friend of the poor

But is Weaving the Web and its counterparts in many Western countries a symptom of an era in which doctrinal relativism is dominant? Or is it a contributor to the process? As a measure of the dilution that it represents, a new secondary program called Icons has been in the making in Britain for eight years. Canon Peter Humphrey of the Catholic Education Service has declared that the course focuses "rightly" on the Trinity, which "infuses every unit." He goes on: "Original sin, life after death, and Mary all receive full treatment in particular sections of their own," and the program is based "firmly on the catechism." All this in contrast to the vagaries of Weaving the Web.

Sections of the Church in Britain evidently realize that several generations of Catholic youth have gone through school missing out on a distinctively Catholic education. But the Weaving the Web generation of teachers are still in the schools and are likely to react defensively to the new orthodoxy. At the same time, Weaving the Web pupils are today's and tomorrow's parents; it is unlikely that they will welcome a new and belated doctrinal traditionalism in their children's classrooms. In the meantime the society and culture of Catholic youth appears to have undergone a deep structural transformation.

Core Young Catholic Adults

Professor John Fulton's study—*Young Catholics at the New Millennium*—which includes monopoly Catholic countries such as Ireland, Italy, Malta, and Poland, as well Britain and the United States, indicates that young Catholics have been profoundly influenced by changes in culture and society as well as by changes within their Catholic communities. The authors of the study, a group of sociologists, employed interviewing techniques that elicited life stories rather than mass questionnaires. They were looking at three types of young Catholics in the eighteen to thirty age group: core, intermediate, or distant. In other words they were studying regular participants in Catholic life, occasional participants, and what were once called the "lapsed."

Researchers found that young core Catholics' faith is not weaker than that of previous generations. But their experience of the faith is decidedly different: there is no trace of the sin cycle–guilt syndromes of my generation and that of my parents and grandparents. Nor is their allegiance to Catholicism merely a matter of superficial consumer choice. They are not a generation of flaneurs. Amidst the large intermediate group, however, there are clear signs of superficiality, especially in monopoly Catholic countries where the tendency is to induce religion from without rather than from within.

According to the report, "The young sense of the sacred lies in new places and new subjects." The sacred is still engaged in the spheres of institutionalized religion in music, liturgy, sacramentals (such as devotion to the Virgin Mary, lighting candles, honoring the saints). But at the interface between moral consciousness and moral agency and the world, the Catholic young commit themselves in terms of environmental protection, the abolition of poverty, homelessness, support for justice and peace in the Third World, the disadvantaged, the wrongly imprisoned, the tortured. Most of the young Catholics interviewed put strong value on human life in the womb, the prisoner on death row, the patient suffering pain. Yet opposition to euthanasia and abortion is qualified by respect for the individuals who are involved in making such choices. Most are enthusiastic about supporting Third World countries and doing something about poverty and homelessness in their own countries.

There are widespread indications that the coincidence of religious consciousness and social conscience have been encouraged by Catholic bishops and parish priests. There is strong evidence, however, of a gap between the institutional Church's position on personal morality and the views and practices of most young believers. This is most apparent in the gulf between young Catholics' sense of personal responsibility for moral judgments and the Vatican's determination to impose its top-down teaching on sexual morals. The report puts it this way:

> For young modern Catholics, morality has become internal first and external only second. There is no doubt that the present generation of young adult Catholics and former Catholics varies significantly from their forebears. They are significantly more "Protestant" in their outlook and much less distinct from their secular counterparts than previous generations and will do what they feel right and proper rather than what has been announced by the Pope.

The most drastic decline, in pluralist countries like the United States, Britain, Canada, and Australia, is reflected in a Catholicism based on folk, national, or ethnic associations. But despite their dwindling numbers in church on Sundays, there are still appreciable numbers of young people who are keen to pass on their Catholicism to their children. "But," says the report:

> whether their children will experience the same depth of conviction as their parents is debatable. There is no longer the massive support provided by external forces of ethnic identity, the sin cycle of yesteryear, the high sacrality of Latin liturgy. . . . If and when religion is passed on [it] seems to be

an issue decided only partly in the family, sometimes reinforced in school, and sometimes only decided upon in early
adulthood. From then on it is sustained by individual commitment, but with some community extensions that reinforce belief and galvanize moral and social action.

While these findings apply internationally across a spectrum
of Western countries there are likely to be objections from individual countries, for example, the United States, which enjoys, or
suffers, a glut of statistics and surveys on Catholic youth. Surveys
in *America*, the Catholic weekly, broadly agree with the above
findings. But the generally downbeat tenor of the findings has
been challenged by one of America's leading commentators on
the sociology of religion, Father Andrew Greeley.

Greeley accepts that Catholics in their twenties "are Catholic
on their own terms," but so, he goes on, is everyone else. He con-
firms, however, the point made above, that in the United States
"the four most important aspects of the Catholic identity of those
under 30 is the need to help the poor, the real presence in the Eucharist, God's presence in all the sacraments, and Mary the mother
of Jesus." And you can't, of course, get more Catholic than that!

Father Greeley's endorsement of this research commands our
respect, but while he suggests that core Catholic young adults are
enthusiastic about traditional sacramental values, the findings are
not necessarily at variance with those of Professor Fulton's team.
Finding God in the sacraments may be an admission made by
many who nonetheless take no advantage of those benefits: confession, for example, or the breaking of Catholic marriage vows
(Catholics divorce at the same rate as non-Catholics in most
northern countries; in the United States Catholics divorce at a
higher rate than Protestants, or so Father Greeley tells us). But
Greeley's commentary also puts an important gloss on the attitudes of all "good" Catholics, both young and old, and it deserves
quoting in full despite the fact that it is an "impression" rather
than a researched set of findings:

Many Catholics are weary. They are tired of ideological has-
sles, of decisions about Jews and indulgences that embarrass
them, of parish conflicts, of people who tell them what they
must do to be "good" Catholics, of excommunications and
heresy trials, of autocratic priests, of insensitivity to women,
of incompetent Catholic school principals, of uneducated and
domineering parish staff members, of nasty parish controver-
sies, of true believers on the right and the left and, above all,
of poor liturgy and bad homilies. While in overwhelming
numbers they support the reforms of the Second Vatican
Council, they wonder if the sour aftermath of the council will
ever end and if the church will ever get around to treating
them like adults.

How this is to be remedied is a question that sets Catholics at
each other's throats (and I shall give space to Greeley's recommendations for reviving the Church along with others in the final
chapter). But more important is the question as to how this sorry
state of affairs is to be understood. The central items in the cata-
logue of woe involve a weariness with authoritarian pressures.
The language says it all: "people who tell them what they must
do," "autocratic," "domineering," all of which supports the trend
Fulton found in the Catholic young toward personal moral
choices and away from external authority.

The polarization of the center and the periphery, including old
and young, has created an unbearable tension between the ad-
monishing papacy and the "erring" laity. Throughout the 1990s
John Paul and successive Catholic leaders have denounced the
spread of "secularism" as the fount and origin of the ills that are
afflicting the Church: from empty pews to divorce to contraception to plummeting vocations.

The Vatican has focused its attention on German Catholics
since, like the United States, Germany enjoys a large, wealthy,
and sophisticated Catholic population within a prosperous, highly
pluralistic society in transition, with a large young Catholic population. If there is to be a sudden and influential change of direc-

tion prompted by a local European church it is likely to happen in Germany. As a token of the Vatican's anxiety Cardinal Ratzinger told a press interviewer in 1999 that Germany's Catholic population no longer has a common point of view on moral and religious issues. He accused German Catholics of treating issues with political correctness rather than moral perspective. "This creates the possibility that God will be considered a remote hypothesis in Germany, and that everything concerning religion will be pushed into the realm of the subjective." He went on to say that the reunification of Germany had increased the influence of agnosticism and atheism in the country.

In fact, there is no common point of view on the progressive-traditional divide on the part of the hierarchy of the Church in Germany. Germany's bishops share many features of the antagonism that prevails between progressives and conservatives. Archbishop Meissner of Cologne, for example, along with like-minded bishops, urges exclusiveness rather than compromise; he believes that it is imperative for the Church in Germany to define and differentiate what it means to be a Catholic. He tends to pour scorn on those who disagree with him. On the other hand, Archbishop Lehmann, head of the German bishops conference, and Bishop Camphaus of Limburg see signs of hope and are intent on finding common ground between the hierarchy and the laity.

Conservative groups meanwhile live and work in hope of reviving the distinctive Catholic identity, especially the practice of regular confession. Groups of the young, including Opus Dei, Communion and Liberation, Focolare, and Neocatechumenates, represent a range of expressions from moderate to extreme, and a range of agendas from liturgy to sexual morality. Catholic groups, operating like sects within the Church, have vigorously targeted the young, organizing youth rallies with an emphasis on chanting, flag-waving, and the adoption of uniform dress. Youth rallies have been a regular feature of papal visits and celebrations, and the Pope has shown his satisfaction. But while turnouts have occasionally reached a million, they hardly reflect the inexorable trend of the majority of young Catholics in their flight from papal authority.

In the United States one of the leading conservative lay organizations is Catholics United for the Faith. Founded by H. Lyman Stebbins in 1968, the group is devoted to bearing "corporate and public witness to the Faith, and to pledge fidelity to the Roman Catholic Church." It sees itself as a "rallying point for the multitude of Catholics who are bewildered by the surprising confusion of thought and clamor of voices within the Church itself." Its principal target in the year of its formation was the denunciation by Father Charles Curran of Paul VI's encyclical *Humanae Vitae*, which Stebbins saw as a declaration of war on the Church.

CHAPTER 9

CATHOLIC "SEXOLOGY"

Nowhere is the discrepancy between the official teaching of the Catholic Church and the actual convictions of many believers so great as in the domain of sexuality and marriage. Yet nowhere do faith and life touch each other so closely as in this domain.

—Edward Schillebeeckx

NOT SO LONG AGO a young journalist colleague, who is a Catholic, asked me a question over lunch. "Why is it," she said, "that there are two kinds of Catholic?" Margaret (that is not her real name) has been married for two years, to a man with whom she lived for the previous three years. They are saving to buy a home in London, where property is expensive, but currently they are renting an apartment where it would be difficult to raise a child. She is on the contraceptive pill.

"My husband," she explained, "is Irish, brought up a Catholic from childhood; but it never worried him that we were sleeping together before we married, and it doesn't worry him that I'm on the pill. But it worries me."

Margaret is also a born Catholic and it is obvious that she takes things to heart. She is a serious person.

"Ideally we shouldn't have been living together before marriage; but I don't think our relationship could have survived. The problem was that when I went to church I felt terrible, because I know what the Church's teaching is. And it's the same now. I don't want to go to church to feel bad. Then I see everybody going up to Communion, including my husband, and I just can't do it.

The Pope teaches that I am in mortal sin; and perhaps I am. So I've stopped going to church altogether. Most of the girls I knew at school are in the same boat. We've all stopped going for more or less the same reason."

Margaret was voicing a dilemma that millions of Catholics have faced since the availability of the contraceptive pill in the early 1960s. The teaching of the Catholic Church on sex and on marriage, what Pope John Paul calls "sexology," is clear and uncompromising. According to the *Catechism of the Catholic Church* (1994), all baptized faithful are called to chastity "whether they are married or single." Sexual activity is only chaste when it is performed within the state of marriage and while "open" to fertility, or at least in principle (couples that are sterile or impotent are not deliberately frustrating the sex act, even though they cannot have children). Homosexual acts, premarital or single sex, extramarital sex or fornication, adultery, masturbation, coitus interruptus, oral and anal sex, and deliberate pleasure derived from pornography are all regarded as "gravely disordered" according to the teachings of the Catholic Church—in other words "mortal sins" and deserving of everlasting damnation. In a speech on March 13, 1999, Pope John Paul underlined the Church's teaching that sacramental confession was required for the remission of mortal sins, and that those who received general absolution—that is, collective forgiveness bestowed by a priest on a congregation—must either have confessed their mortal sins or intend to do so at the first opportunity, and that confession must precede Communion. Since confession has all but ceased in the Church (and, according to the Pope's directive, general confession—absolution bestowed on an entire congregation—does not count for mortal sin), it appears from the figures of those Catholics who practice contraception, who are divorced and remarried, who sleep with partners before marriage and out of marriage, and who practice homosexuality, that the majority of practicing Catholics, in the view of Rome, are cut off from the Eucharist. And yet—quite obviously—they are not. So how long can this situation persist before the Pope's authority is eroded to the point of extinction?

Marriage

Marriage in the Church was traditionally seen down the centuries as a contract. Marriage was not recognized officially as a sacrament of the Catholic Church until twelve hundred years after the death of Christ. The absolute requirement of its enactment in public before a pastor did not emerge until the Council of Trent in the sixteenth century. Since Vatican II matrimony has been considered a covenant, which echoes the covenant between God and his people and between Christ and and his people—the Church.

The sacrament is contracted by the consent of the partners. "Authentic married love," states the *Catechism*, "is caught up in divine love." Until the sixteenth century, Catholics in Latin Christendom married by exchanging consent: the individual spouses being the "ministers" of the sacrament, invariably without a priest or witness present. Desertion of spouses, and the habit of subsequent denial of marriages conducted in privacy, led to the obligation (laid down in the Council of Trent, 1545–1563) for couples to marry before an authorized priest and two witnesses. Conjugal love, according to Catholic teaching, is "undivided and exclusive," requiring "inviolable fidelity of the spouses." It is "indissoluble."

Contraception and abortion are grave sins. During the so-called safe period sex is permitted, although this period should be used with discretion so as to preclude a "contraceptive mentality." The safe period is characterized by the *Catechism* not as contraception, as such, but as "periodic continence: that is, the methods of birth regulation based on self-observation and the use of infertile periods."

The Pope and the Vatican are in deadly earnest about the inadmissibility of contraception in all its forms and in every circumstance without exception. Despite the drives throughout the world for safer sex, in successive pronouncements the Vatican has declared that it is gravely disordered for a partner suffering from AIDS to use a condom. In July 2000 Archbishop Christophe Pierre, apostolic nuncio in Uganda, where some 10 percent of the population suffer from AIDS, urged the country's youth to ignore calls to use condoms to prevent the spread of the disease. The nuncio was addressing young people on the issue in contradiction to the Uganda vice president, Speciosa Wandir Kazibwe, a medical doctor, who had criticized religious leaders who opposed the use of condoms. The same month, a priest in Brazil who had been distributing condoms as part of a one-man campaign to halt the spread of AIDS received a "letter of condemnation" from his Bishop, Claudio Hummes of São Paulo. Hummes said there would be further punitive actions "to correct this regrettable situation" if the missionary, who has spent twenty-two years in Brazil, does not comply with official Church teaching. The priest, Father Valeriano Paitoni, an Italian, said: "If the condom protects life, there is no reason not to view it as a lesser evil. . . . It deals with a greater good."

Since Catholic moral teaching does not admit to a moral hierarchy in the realm of mortal sin, questions as to the comparative evil—of infecting a partner with AIDS, as against using a contraceptive device to avoid passing on a fatal illness—do not arise. The Church expects heterosexual couples which include a partner suffering from AIDS to practice continence.

To enjoy the pleasure of the sexual act without concomitant openness to fertility, according to the Church, is "disordered," a mortal sin. Abortion, moreover, constitutes the taking of a human life which potentially begins at the moment of conception. Morning-after pills, or contraceptive pills that work by destroying embryos, are regarded as abortifacients, and hence are equivalent to abortion.

The Church does not require that couples live together when it has become impossible for whatever reason, including the departure and remarriage of one of the partners. "In this case," continues the *Catechism*, "the Church permits the physical separation of the couple and their living apart." But the former spouses continue to be married in the eyes of the Church. Each is expected to live a continent life, and neither is free to contract licitly a new union.

In some cases the Church grants an annulment to a couple whose marriage has broken down. This means that in the view of canon lawyers no marriage has taken place: it is not a divorce, it is a statement that the marriage, as a sacrament, was null and void in the first place. Very few annulments were granted before Vatican II, but in the past thirty years the grounds for an annulment have expanded to include new standards of extenuating circumstances, including immaturity in one of the partners, or lack of "discretion."

After an annulment the Catholic is free to marry another partner in the Church and receive Communion. If a Catholic marries a divorced partner, or divorces and remarries without an annulment, he or she is deemed to be severed from the sacraments of the Church. In July 2000 the Vatican publicly reaffirmed that Catholics who divorce and remarry cannot receive Communion unless they agree to abstinence from sexual relations in their married lives.

Catholic moral teaching on sex and marriage is founded in Scripture, the Christian tradition of the centuries, natural law, and papal teaching. The Church's understanding of the sexual act and the state of matrimony owe little to contemporary biology and psychology. The sex act is still largely understood from the point of view of the ancient Greek philosophy of Aristotle and the medieval philosophy and theology of Thomas Aquinas. Modern biologists see sexual reproduction in terms of complex statistical (or stochastic) processes with a large element of wastage (for example, half of all embryos are lost before implantation), rather than the end goal of all-or-nothing purposive acts. Contraception is sinful, according to the Church, because it frustrates the prime purpose of the sexual act—procreation. The Church's view does not admit the separability of the reproductive "purpose" of the sex act from the biological, social, and psychological functions of bonding.

Our understanding of the nature and complexity of sexual bonding has been immeasurably broadened in the twentieth century by advances in anthropology, gender studies, psychology, psychoanalysis, sociology, genetics, reproductive biology, and cognitive science. Catholic theologians have not failed to keep abreast of these developments and have raised many questions as a result. Karl Rahner, one of the most influential theologians of the century, once commented on the natural wastage of human reproduction: "Will [theologians] be able to accept that fifty percent of all 'human beings'—real human beings with 'immortal' souls and an eternal destiny—will never get beyond this first stage of human existence?" At the same time, biologists argue that the beginnings of potential human life are more accurately linked with the implantation rather than fertilization. But the official teaching sources of the Catholic Church continue to draw largely on premodern philosophy of religion. While John Paul II has employed modern philosophical methods (phenomenology) to explore sexuality, his conclusions—aimed at combating what he characterizes a "Culture of Death"—tend toward absolutes and immutable "purposes." He is intransigent on the intrinsically evil status of certain acts, such as contraception.

As we have seen, there was widespread hope in the mid-1960s that Vatican II would pronounce favorably on a less rigid interpretation of the ban on contraception. In the end, after much agonizing, Paul VI reserved the verdict to himself, setting aside the views of many of his bishops and various lay consultants. The fact that a modern predecessor, Pius XI, had pronounced on the issue in the encyclical *Casti Connubii* (1930) is said to have influenced his thinking. Paul VI reiterated Pius XI's ban on contraception, prompting a crisis within the Church between Pope and hierarchies, hierarchies and priests, hierarchies and people.

Catholic Heterosexuals

The split between teaching and practice in matters of heterosexuality, marriage, and divorce in the Catholic Church has settled into a set of chronic divisions, giving rise to the appearance of institutionalized hypocrisy. The faithful, en masse, have rejected a crucial set of Church teachings. Such a predicament cannot continue without affecting respect for Church authority in other matters: disregard one set of core moral imperatives and it becomes easy to disregard others. If the Church, in the eyes of the faithful, is out of touch in one sphere, then it is likely to be deemed out of touch in others.

Throughout the world, contraception is practiced by the majority of married Catholics, typically by 90 percent in Western countries, and the same proportion do not think contraception is wrong, any more than do Catholic partners outside of marriage. Contraception is seldom confessed, and in many countries priests are under instruction not to inquire about their penitents' contraceptive practices.

In the United States 80 percent of Catholics, according to one poll conducted in 1999, believed that they should make up their own minds on issues such as contraception and abortion. Only 17 percent of Catholics believed that the Pope should always be obeyed on such issues, while 3 percent were unsure. A similar poll conducted in April 2000 in Germany revealed that 90 percent of Catholics did not consider contraception a sin.

Three-quarters of Catholic Americans, according to one poll, think that *extramarital* sex is always wrong. And while three in every four Catholics thought *premarital* sex was always wrong in 1963 (regardless of how many were nevertheless participating), by 1994 only one in six American Catholics believed that premarital sex was always wrong. What is more, when unmarried Catholics engage in sex they do so more frequently than their average non-Catholic fellow Americans; those who actually practice sex as single persons naturally tend to be even less likely to think that it is always wrong. In Germany (according to a reputable public opinion survey), 82 percent of Catholics are against the prohibition of premarital sex, while only 6 percent of Catholics support the Church's ban on birth control.

According to surveys conducted by the National Opinion Research Center (1989 to 1991), only a little more than a third of single American Catholics were chaste in the previous year, and of the group described as "sexually active single Catholics" 38 percent engaged in sexual intercourse every week (as opposed to 31 percent of sexually active other single Americans).

Since official Catholic thinking on premarital sex is partly based on the view that the resulting offspring of a sexual union should enter life under the protection of married parents, the advent of convenient and highly effective contraception in the 1960s robbed the Catholic argument against premarital sex of at least part of its force. According to Andrew Greeley, another feature of the change in Catholic attitudes is a result of altered views of Church authority. "It is evident that Catholic leadership has little credibility with its people on the subject of single sex," Greeley wrote in 1994. "A large proportion of Catholics no longer accept the thesis that sexual pleasure must be limited to married persons who are open in each sexual act to the possibility of procreation."

According to a widespread reading of the gulf between practice and teaching, the timing of Vatican II had sudden and far-reaching consequences for Catholic sexual morality. Just as the Catholic Church was announcing an amnesty from its traditional counter-cultural opposition to the world, so Western societies were going through an unprecedented "sexual revolution." The explosion of "youth culture" lifestyles in music, film, television, clothes, dance, concerts, and drugs, attended by the collapse of norms of sexual behavior, coincided with the apparent relaxation of moral norms in the Church and a new emphasis on individual conscience following the Council. Many, in retrospect, believe that the apparent lifting of old strictures left Catholics particularly vulnerable to the prevailing new culture. The sense of amnesty fueled the brushfires of general sexual permissiveness and promiscuity, consuming overnight the age-old scruples and disciplines of laity, religious, and clergy alike.

Some commentators, moreover, directly blame the split between practice and official Catholic teaching on the new "spirit" within the Church. According to this view, the Council prompted a profound alteration in the way in which bishops, priests, and the laity think, write, and talk about morality in general and sexual morality in particular. Moral theology had traditionally been packaged in manuals which focused on a narrow and legalist view of sexual behavior. Sexual "deviations" had been described as "intrinsically evil," and finely dissected and graded as if exclusively for penitential diagnosis in the confessional. By emphasizing the fundamental freedom of all human beings, the Council implicitly encouraged primacy of conscience in forming moral decisions.

Catholic moral theologians tend to see the gulf between laity and the official Church on sexual matters as a shift in moral perception that is unlikely to revert. According to Professor John Mahoney, author of *The Making of Moral Theology*, the period since Vatican II has seen a "reaction to the excessively analytical approach . . . which had characterized moral theology since the end of the nineteenth century." Mahoney sees the alteration in terms of a preparedness to take sexuality as a "totality," to consider, for example, overpopulation, poverty, and the difficulties experienced by single parents. Moral absolutes, he argues, are no longer seen in "isolation from other factors, whether of the whole of human nature with its variables as well as its constants from which they claim to be derived, or of the whole complex of circumstances in which such human nature finds itself immersed when it comes to act."

The gap between contemporary approaches on many nonsexual issues and sexual morality as expounded by the Vatican, and mostly accepted if not preached by the hierarchies of the world, is increasingly noticeable. In the United States, for example, the bishops have explored and expounded on the morality of two major issues—the just war, and the U.S. economy—not by appealing to abstract absolutes alone but by embarking on extensive consultations, the gathering of evidence, the examination of consequences and situations, allowing consideration to time and circumstance.

Rome may yield to the shift that has taken place among theologians and bishops on a range of issues; in the meantime, the Pope appears increasingly, on sexual issues, a lone voice in the wilderness. The tragedy is that the world at large is less likely to listen to the Church's central teaching authority on a range of other crucial areas of morality while it appears eccentric and out of touch on the one issue with which the entire Church has disagreed with him, and defied him.

Catholic Homosexuals

In the first week of July 2000, some 200,000 gays and their supporters collected in Rome from many parts of the world to conduct what they described as a World Gay Pride fest which ended with an extravagant parade featuring the flaunting of exhibitionistic transvestite costumes in temperatures over ninety degrees. Barred from areas close to the Vatican City and St. Peter's, after a row lasting many weeks between the city's political leaders and the Vatican, the demonstrators paraded around the pagan environs of the Colosseum and the Circus Maximus. There were a number of figures from Italian public life present, including the Italian minster for equal opportunities Katia Elillo. One of the marchers wore a paper mitre which declared: "God also loves me." A Catholic priest from Avellino gave a speech in which he "outed" certain high-ranking prelates.

After it was all over the Pope expressed his "bitterness" at the demonstration. He said it was "an affront to the great Jubilee." It was "an offense to the Christian values of a city so dear to the hearts of Catholics worldwide." The Pope went on to quote from the *Catechism of the Catholic Church* which describes homosexual acts as contrary to the natural law, but acknowledges that the "number of men and women who have homosexual tendencies is not negligible. They do not choose their homosexual condition: for most of them it is a trial." He emphasized that, according to the *Catechism*, homosexuals "must be accepted with respect, compassion and sensitivity" and that "every sign of unjust discrimination in their regard should be avoided." They were called to "fulfill God's will in their lives" and, if they were Christians, "to unite to the sacrifice of the Lord's Cross the difficulties they may encounter from their condition." The crowd in St. Peter's Square cheered him on, but throughout Italy and many parts of the world, his words prompted criticism and controversy among Catholics, gay and straight alike.

Attitudes toward homosexuality, including the self-identity of homosexuals, have gone through a rapid series of transformations since the Second World War. In many Western countries homosexuality was still regarded as a criminal act, or a treatable form of "deviancy" or mental illness, until the 1960s, when the orientation became widely accepted as a legitimate choice of lifestyle and hence open to aspirations for social and political liberation. A significant event was the police raid on the Stonewall Inn, a venue for gays and lesbians in New York City. The arrests by the New York Police Department culminated in a full-scale riot and a series of clashes between law enforcement officers and gays occurred across the United States. From this point on gays and lesbians began to reject the appellation "homosexual" and to promote a new, open, and self-confident identity. By the mid-1970s, researchers in the expanding scientific disciplines of neuroscience and genetics were claiming hard evidence for homosexuality as biologically determined, enabling the gay communities to find parallels between homophobia, racism, and sexism. A key book in the campaign for acceptance of genetically predisposed homosexuality was Simon LeVay's *The Sexual Brain*. LeVay, a British neuroscientist based at the Salk Institute in La Jolla, California, claimed that neurons of gay individuals were a different size from those of straight individuals. The findings are still subject to heated debate.

The Catholic Church has been only partially affected by these social and scientific developments. But there has been much heart-searching in Rome, possibly a result of the large and growing gay priesthood (of whom a significant proportion are evidently sexually active), but almost certainly in response to campaigning by Catholic homosexuals themselves. There are a growing number of highly organized Catholic and ecumenical homosexual networks in the world today. They have their own chaplains, websites, newsletters, and liturgies. They are telling Rome and their bishops that whatever the Church's teaching, they want to belong. The leading groups include: in the United States, Dignity, Conference for Catholic Lesbians, Courage, New Ways Ministry (the network established by the silenced religious Father Robert Nugent and Sister Jeannine Gramick); in the U.K., Quest (taken out of the Catholic Directory because of its refusal to make clear its dissociation from active gay sexuality); in Germany, Homosexuelle und Kirche (HuK); in France, David et Jonathan (some twenty-five local groups); in Spain, Coordinadora Gai-Lesbiana; in Italy, an extraordinary proliferation of independent groups based in different parts of the country, Davide e Gionata (Turin), Il Guado (Milan), La Parola (Vicenza), L'Incontro (Padua), Chiara e Francesco (Udine), L'Arcipelago (Reggio Emilia), Il Gruppo (Florence), Nuova Proposta (Rome), and Fratelli dell' Elpis (Catania); in the Netherlands, Stichting Dignity Nederland; in Mexico, Otras Ovejas; in South Africa, Pilgrims. Many of the participants organize prayer meetings and retreats, and make common cause in their desire to keep the faith without hiding their sexuality. They are calling for official recognition of permanent partnerships, arguing that this is the surest way to curb the practice of homosexual promiscuity.

The official Church condemns homosexual acts and has done so since the early Christian period. Vatican documents appeal principally to natural law, which, according to the giants of moral theology, Augustine of Hippo and Thomas Aquinas, was placed in us by God at the creation and is immutable. In other words there are certain acts which are inherently evil and for which there can be no exceptions: homosexual acts are of that nature. Aquinas states that certain sins are "contrary to heterosexual intercourse . . . [namely] male homosexual union, which has received the special name of unnatural vice."

In the immediate post–Vatican II era, Paul VI reiterated the ban on homosexuality by linking it in his encyclical *Humanae Vitae* (1968) to the principle that "each and every marriage act must remain open to the transmission of life." The Church's views on gays and lesbians were further expanded in a declaration published in December 1975 by the Congregation for the Doctrine of the Faith (CDF), stressing the immutable and universal nature of the ban and rejecting the notion that subjectivity or intention can enter into the question. The document nevertheless called for sympathy and understanding of those who were homosexual by "constitution" as opposed to "transitory circumstance," such as bad example or false education. Nevertheless, all such acts are "disordered," states the declaration, and under no condition can they be condoned.

A few months after the declaration, in August 1976, an American Jesuit priest, John McNeill, as if in direct contradiction to the Vatican ruling, published his book *The Church and the Homosexual*, which had been given a local okay by the diocese. In the preface to the fourth edition, McNeill states, "I naively assumed that by granting me an *Imprimi Potest* [a local stamp of theological approval], the Church, in the liberating spirit that followed Vatican II, was ready and willing to reexamine its teaching on homosexuality." He goes on to comment that the theologians who reviewed the manuscript believed, as he did, "that the new evidence coming from the fields of scriptural studies, history, psychology, sociology, and moral theology seriously challenged every premise on which the traditional teaching was based." The following year, in June 1977, the venerable Catholic Theological Society of America (CTSA) published a book on sexuality edited by many hands, contradicting Vatican teaching even more fundamentally than had McNeill. The society dismissed the Thomistic approach as "oversimplified" and advocated an approach that focused on the psychological, emotional, social, and moral aspects of the whole person. "Homosexuals," the society declared, "enjoy the same rights and incur the same obligations as the heterosexual majority." The theologians went on to argue the importance of "wholesome and moral sexual conduct," which properly involved such standards as regard for "the other," honesty, loyalty, personal responsibility, service to life, and joy.

McNeill was the following year forbidden by the Vatican to even discuss the issue of homosexuality and morality in the public arena; in obedience, he maintained silence. Ten years after the publication of McNeill's book and the CTSA collection, the Vatican was again moved to pronounce on the issue in a document entitled *Letter on Homosexuality*. The document concentrated on the blamelessness of homosexuality as a "constitutional" circumstance, but reiterated in even stronger terms the sinful nature of homosexual acts. "Homosexual activity is not a complementary union able to transmit life. . . . [Homosexuals] confirm within themselves a disordered sexual inclination which is essentially self-indulgent."

The document had harsh words, besides, for what it characterized as the "pro-homosexual movement in the Church," and its "deceitful propaganda," claiming that these tendencies were the work of "homosexual persons who have no intention of abandoning their homosexual behavior." The Vatican statement condemned active homosexuals as people who "either ignore the teaching of the Church, or seek somehow to undermine it."

Even AIDS, characterized in the document as a "gay disease," did not dissuade homosexual advocates from considering the "magnitude of the risks involved." Actively homosexual persons, announced the document, "should not have the support of bishops in any way."

In 1994 in a revised edition of the *Catechism of the Catholic Church*, the official line was again reiterated: "Homosexual persons," states the *Catechism*, "are called to chastity. By the virtues of self-mastery that teach them inner freedom, at times by the support of disinterested friendship, by prayer and sacramental grace, they can and should gradually and resolutely approach Christian perfection."

In subsequent years, the bishops toed the line. After the fall 1997 conference of the U.S. Catholic bishops, a directive was issued to the heterosexual faithful to accept with "respect, compassion, and sensitivity" all homosexuals. At the same time it was stated that "homogenital behavior is objectively immoral."

In February 1999 the trustees of Notre Dame University came in conflict with faculty and students when they threw out a proposal to ban discrimination against homosexuals on campus. The students reacted by calling hunger strikes and demonstrations. The trustees explained that their decision was taken in the context of increasing tensions over the gap in moral values between secular society in the United States and official Church teachings. "Whereas in a secular environment this is seen as a simple matter of civil rights," declared the trustees in a public statement, "that's not the way it's viewed through the Catholic prism."

But the Catholic prism is a fragmented instrument when it comes to attitudes toward homosexuality. The following story reveals how gay Catholics would be treated following a further lurch to the right in the Church. Father Ralph McInerny, a Catholic commentator, writing in the conservative periodical *Crisis* under the headline "The Bleat of the Wolf," reports the story of a parent who in the spring of 2000 brought his son to Notre Dame, entered the chapel of the residence hall, and found a prayer card entitled "Toward a Spirit of Inclusivity at Notre Dame." The card, according to the magazine, had been distributed at all the masses in the residence halls of the university. It read: "Because we welcome and value lesbian and gay members of our Notre Dame community, help us to be an inclusive people." McInerny commented:

> This is the heart of a truly corrupt effort to cloak the homo-sexual agenda in Christian terms, indeed to make it a Christian obligation in charity and justice to regard the Church's negative judgment on homosexual activity as a lapse in charity and, consequently, something to be overcome. Let's stop thinking of homosexuality as a sin. Rather, let us make the negative moral judgment on it sinful. No one animated by the truth of Christianity could have composed this bogus "prayer" and foisted it on an unsuspecting student body. If ever there was a wolf in sheep's clothing this "prayer" is it.

McInerny concludes: "This was done under the auspices of campus ministry. It marks one more instance in the continuing effort to put campus ministry at the service of those who seek to corrupt the morals of young men and women."

Divorce and Annulment

In the United States, when the Catholic population was just over 60 million in the year 1995, some 302,919 new Catholic marriages were registered: in other words, 5.0 per 1,000 Catholics. But back in 1950 when the Catholic population was only 28.6 million, there were 327,317 Catholic marriages: that is, 11.4 per 1,000 Catholics. Had the percentages remained constant, some 687,000 Catholics would have married in the Church instead of 302,919. J. C. Harris, pondering these figures in the Catholic weekly *America* in 1999, assumed that large numbers of Catholics were choosing increasingly not to be married in the Church in the United States. But Pierre Hegy and Joseph Martos point out in their book *Catholic Divorce* that since some 45 percent of all marriages in the United

States are accounted for by second marriages, and since between 80 and 90 percent of divorced Catholics do not get annulments, it is more or less certain that many of the 384,000 marriages "missing" in 1995 were absent from the Church registries because of the Catholic ban on remarriage. "If this situation continues," declare the authors, "the U.S. Catholic Church will be losing perhaps half of its newlyweds every year. And since rejected divorced Catholics are less likely to foster the Catholic faith in their children, the Church is likely to lose the children of these marriages as well." According to the Center for Applied Research in the Apostolate (CARA), Catholics are divorced at about the same rate as the U.S. population as a whole.

The decline in Catholic marriage is not restricted to the United States. In Britain, one in every two marriages fails; and many Catholic couples are choosing to cohabit, but the latest statistics show that cohabiting couples with children have even less chance of staying together than the marrieds: more than half will split up by the time their child is five compared with 8 percent of married couples (http: www.divorcereform.org). Recent figures show a steep decline in Catholic marriages in pluralist Christian Western countries over a period of fifteen years, despite fairly stable Catholic populations in Europe: in Britain and in the Netherlands over the same period marriages have halved.

In the United States, however, the rate of annulments since Vatican II reveals the extraordinary phenomenon of a form of ecclesiastical divorce previously unknown in the Church's history. In 1968, the year of Paul VI's *Humanae Vitae*, a mere 368 annulments were granted by diocesan tribunals in the United States. That figure has risen to a current average of more than 50,000 a year (having dropped from an all-time high of 63,900 in 1991 after an attempt by the Vatican to clamp down). But when one compares even the slightly reduced U.S. figures with other countries, indeed whole continents, the full extent of the local American annulment bonanza can be seen for the extraordinary phenomenon that it is. In 1998 in Germany, a mere thousand marriages were annulled in a Catholic population of 28 million; in Brazil, 741 in a Catholic population of 139 million; in Africa as whole, 429 in a Catholic population of 116 million.

Taking all the figures between 1989 and 1996, the annulments in the United States indicated that 6 percent of the world's Catholics received 75 percent of the world's annulments. The American situation has been boosted by the Church's greater financial resources, and the Vatican's decision to streamline the annulment process since 1970. For example, tribunals can now deal with cases from within the diocese in which the petitioner is currently living, rather than in the diocese of the parish in which they married. But the true significance of the U.S. annulment phenomenon is the extent to which it undermines the meaning of Catholic marriage, indicating that the Church, in the United States, is moving inexorably toward ecclesiastical divorce by default.

The petitioners themselves, however, are not deceived. Many testimonies reveal the extent to which appellants are disgusted by a charade whereby they acknowledge that their marriages somehow never took place. According to a recent *Continuum* study on divorce and annulment, a petitioner found herself encouraged to make false statements to support the notional invalidity of her first marriage: "The monsignor who was conducting the hearing repeatedly tried to get me to say that I thought from the very beginning that the marriage wasn't going to last forever or that I wasn't committed from the very beginning. I never agreed to that because it wasn't true." Writing of her sister's attempt to get an annulment, an informant told *Continuum* authors that the tribunal had attempted to extract a statement that she had not had a sacramental marriage the first time. "In conscience [she] could not agree with this. She felt to do so would be hypocritical and a violation of her conscience, as she knew in her heart she had received the sacrament of marriage."

For the most part, Catholics seeking annulment are attempting to marry for a second time within the Church in order to remain communicating members of the faithful. While it is clear that the marriage tribunals of the United States are doling out annulments in blatant contravention of the traditional spirit of such procedures, it indicates that in America, at least, a significant proportion of the Catholic faithful are prepared to go to considerable lengths to mark their new marriages with a sacramental beginning.

Abortion

The widespread practice of divorced and "illicitly" remarried Catholics receiving Communion reveals a process of powerful change within the Church. Lay people, with the acquiescence of pastors, appear determined to seek the empowerment of Catholic sacramental life while repudiating crucial Catholic teaching.

There are indications that groups of Catholics are similarly rejecting self-exclusion over the abortion issue, which, in the latter half of the twentieth century, replaced divorce as the litmus test of authentic Catholicism.

The Catholic crusade against abortion exerts its influence not only within the Church but beyond, manifesting itself in vigorous campaigns which at times erupt into violence. Active Catholic pro-life campaigners use shock tactics to ram home their message, not infrequently invoking parallels with the Holocaust and King Herod's slaughter of the innocents. When Austria introduced its morning-after pill, called Myfegine, which resembles RU-486, the Archbishop of Cologne, Cardinal Meissner, compared it to Zyklon B, the gas used in the Second World War to exterminate concentration camp inmates.

While official Catholic opposition centers on the belief that abortion is tantamount to mass murder, the Vatican has for many years linked abortion with wider, and in its view, sinister anti-Catholic aims in the Third World. As long ago as the summer of 1970, I had an interview in the Vatican with the late Cardinal John Wright, originally from New England, which started with a question about Vatican investments and led immediately to the question of abortion. At that time, Wright was a member of the Curia with responsibility for the "discipline of the clergy" and a keen interest in Church finances (his friend Bishop Paul Casimir Marcinkus had recently been made secretary of the Vatican Bank). Wright became extremely angry when I asked him about the Church's views on environmental issues. Was the Church concerned, for example, when companies in which it invested proved to be guilty of pollution? There had been a scandal near Genoa that year when a company in which the Vatican reputedly had shares—ERG—was accused of causing damaging floods through polluted culverts on a river above the city. Wright deflected the discussion by pointing to a link between environmental groups and abortion. He said that on a recent visit to the United States he had seen stickers in many cars proclaiming "The pollution bomb is your baby!" He also saw links between what he termed "Anglo-American Protestant foundations," Jewish foundations, and contraception and abortion in Latin America and Brazil. He said: "The aim of these foundations is to promote contraception and abortion in order to create smaller families which will in turn create ideal markets in the Third World for American products. The Church needs adequate finances to counter these influences—sufficient funds to finance publishing, broadcasting, higher education." In the period following Vatican II, it appeared, the Curia viewed abortion not simply as a painful choice to be made by individual women, but as part of a Protestant strategy aimed at furthering the ends of American capitalism.

Wright was certainly correct in believing that the incidence of abortion was about to multiply, in both the First and the Third Worlds. But in the view of some Catholic lay groups, the prevalence of abortion in North America and elsewhere is less a result of a Protestant foundational plot than the result of a lack of education and preparedness to use contraception.

An estimated 50 million abortions are performed worldwide every year. Of these, 20 million are obtained illegally. This indicates that a quarter of the 200 million pregnancies known to occur each year are resolved by abortion. Approximately 1.5 million abortions are performed in the United States annually, a figure that has remained constant for the past two decades. American Catholic women, according to a Gallup survey, have abortions at the same rate as non-Catholic Americans. According to the Alan Guttmacher Institute, however, 29 percent of Catholic women are more likely than Protestants to have an abortion. A CNN survey published in 1999 (www.cnn.com/HEALTH) claims that according to researchers the highest rates of abortion are a result of inadequate availability and use of contraception. Women using a method of contraception are only 15 percent as likely as women using no method to have an abortion.

Meanwhile, eastern Europe has the highest rate of unplanned pregnancies and the highest abortion rate of any area of the world: 90 abortions per 1,000 women of childbearing age. Western Europe has the lowest abortion rate, 11 per 1,000 women, athough its abortion laws are similar to those in East Europe. In the United States, according to Guttmacher (1999) the rate of abortions per thousand women is 22.9. In France, where 85 percent of the population is nominally Catholic, there are currently 220,000 abortions a year (AP Online, October 4, 2000) or 12.4 per 1,000 women. France was the first country to allow the sale of the "abortion pill" RU-486, which claims a 96 percent success rate if taken with a prostaglandin. The drug now accounts for about 30 percent of all abortions. Nearly 40 percent of all births in France are out of wedlock (eurodata newsletter, www.lmzes.uni-mannheim country profile). In Italy the number of abortions is 11.4 per 1,000 women. In Germany, it is 7.6 per 1,000 women.

Most Catholics endorse the Church's teachings on abortion as expressed, for example, in John Paul II's encyclical *Evangelium Vitae* (1995), on the principle that while it may be difficult to say precisely when human life begins, a moral perspective on the sanctity of human life and the rights of the unborn child demands that the line is drawn somewhere. Younger Catholics, however, are increasingly prepared to take a less condemnatory view in the light of individual circumstances, especially in the case of rape and incest. Catholic laypeople, moreover, find themselves at odds with their Church over issues relating to the complexities of pluralist societies where abortion is legalized. Their views on abortion, in other words, do not necessarily translate into political action, an important consideration in the United States where a quarter of the electorate are Catholics. In 1984 when Governor Mario Cuomo of New York spoke at the University of Notre Dame on the issue he explained how he saw the dilemma: "I have a salvic mission as a Catholic. Does that mean I am in conscience required to do everything I can as governor to translate all my religious values into the laws and regulations of the state of New York or the United States or be branded a hypocrite if I don't?" The Catholic public official, he said, accepts "the truth that to assure our freedom we must allow others the same freedom even if occasionally it produces conduct by them we would hold to be sinful." When Cuomo repeated his views in Tucson, Arizona, in 1989, Bishop Austin Vaughan of the New York archdiocese said the governor was running a "serious risk of going to hell."

In Germany and elsewhere Catholics are increasingly in conflict with their hierarchies and the Vatican over the issue of abortion counseling. The official teaching on abortion is thus challenged from inside the Church by Catholics who appeal to principles not only in the domain of public health, biology, and political science, but who also appeal to arguments from within Catholic moral theology itself.

The Catholic view on abortion stems from two considerations: the starting point of human life, and the sanctity of human life. The *Catechism* is clear that "human life must be respected and protected absolutely from the moment of conception. From the first moment of his [her] existence, a human being must be recognized as having the rights of a person—among which is the inviolable right of every innocent being to life."

Saint Augustine, in the early Church, and Saint Thomas

Aquinas, in the Middle Ages, however, condemned abortion on the grounds that it frustrated procreation, the purpose of the sex act. For Augustine and Thomas there was no clear verdict on the starting point of human life any more than there was a biological understanding of the nature of sperm, egg, and embryo in the modern sense. The notion prevailed, in fact, that "ensoulment"— the endowment of the fetus with a human soul by an act of God—coincided with hominization: that is, when the fetus achieved a physical human body. That moment, it was variously argued, was different in male fetuses than in female fetuses, where ensoulment was delayed by a considerable period of days. Only in more recent times, starting with Pius IX in 1869, has the Church insisted on the universal adoption of the "ontological" view that human personhood begins at the moment of conception. In his 1930 encyclical on sexual morality, *Casti Connubii*, Pius XI endorsed that doctrine, but allowed that surgical intervention might take place, even late-term, when the life of the mother was in danger—for example, because of uterine cancer or an ectopic pregnancy—and where the principle of double effect could be invoked: in other words, if the death of the fetus would be an inevitable result of surgery, but not its purpose.

Throughout the twentieth century, papal teaching reinforced Church teaching against abortion on the basis of the right to life implicit in the potential for human existence which begins at the moment of conception. Vatican II asserted that "life must be protected with the utmost care from the moment of conception; abortion and infanticide are abominable crimes." Paul VI reiterated that same view in his controversial encyclical *Humanae Vitae* (1968).

Five years after *Humanae Vitae*, in the United States the courts appeared to throw down the gauntlet to the Catholic Church. In January 1973 the Supreme Court of the United States reached its *Roe v. Wade* majority opinion (7 to 2) declaring that laws prohibiting abortion during the first twenty-four weeks of pregnancy were unconstitutional. The thinking that went into that precise number of weeks was based on the "viability" of the fetus and the average development of the central nervous system and hence its ability to feel pain. In response, the Vatican published a special declaration on abortion in 1974, emphasizing that "freedom of opinion" cannot be invoked when it comes to "most especially the right to life."

In 1987 John Paul II declared that "the inalienable rights of the person must be recognized and respected by civil society and the political authority.... Among such fundamental rights one should mention in this regard every human being's right to life and physical integrity from the moment of conception until death." Linking abortion with capital punishment and euthanasia, John Paul also extended the principle to the exploitation of human embryos "as disposable biological material." The ruling can now be applied to research that exploits human embryos as a source for stem cells, the special "mother" cells that can form replacement tissue using cloning techniques.

In the United States the hierarchy has led the Catholic Church, clergy and laity, in urging the inadmissibility of abortion in society as a whole. In other words, Catholic bishops do not accept the moral relativist stand that the Church should not dictate in this instance to the consciences of those who disagree with it. Unlike other issues, such as divorce and birth control, the bishops have emphasized the heinous nature of abortion by declaring that it cannot be permitted in a society ruled by law. Some bishops have even insisted that Catholic public figures who defend or support a public policy of choice on abortion may not receive Holy Communion. It is evident that there is disagreement on this tough stand among bishops, theologians, and certainly among the laity. Professor John Fulton's survey, as we have seen, found that core young Catholic adults tend to be against abortion but insist on a measure of understanding for those women involved in the predicament of an unwanted pregnancy.

Meanwhile, there has been a long-running battle between lay Catholic "free choice" activism and the American hierarchy over the issue. A key group ever since the *Roe v. Wade* ruling in 1973 has been Catholics for Free Choice (CFFC). With headquarters in Washington, D.C., the organization depends on volunteer activists around the country. The group claims to work to "reduce abortion" while increasing women's "choices in childbearing and child rearing through advocacy of social and economic programs for women, families, and children." The hierarchy has a particular animus toward CFFC precisely because it claims to speak in the name of Catholicism. The potential for splits within the Church over the issue were evident in the clash between the bishops and CFFC over the Democratic vice presidential candidate in the 1984 presidential campaign, Geraldine Ferraro. CFFC paid for a full-page ad in the *New York Times* highlighting the diversity of views on abortion among committed Catholics and arguing that "even direct abortion, though tragic, can sometimes be a moral choice." The statement was signed by about one hundred prominent Catholics, including some nuns. The Vatican responded by making an example of those who were vulnerable to ecclesiastical sanctions. Disciplinary action was taken against several of the religious signatories, sparking a row between Catholics throughout America. Consistently critiquing the hierarchy's stance with a "Catholic" perspective of its own, the CFFC has countered the bishops' pro-life campaigns with calls for "mutual understanding," "reflection on the meaning of respect," and a plea for "listening sessions." CFFC's campaign for moral pluralism was profoundly challenged, however, by Pope John Paul's encyclicals *Veritatis Splendor* (1993) and *Evangelium Vitae* (1995), the first of which stressed the intrinsically evil nature of abortion, with no exceptions, and the second of which eloquently warned that "a new cultural climate is developing and taking hold, which gives crimes against life a new and—if possible—even more sinister character . . . broad sectors of public opinion justify certain crimes against life in the name of rights of individual freedom."

Meanwhile, in Germany, despite the Pope's rallying cries, abortion was fast becoming an issue that has divided large sections of the laity from the bishops and the Pope. The focus of the dispute was not a controversy over attitudes and beliefs but a practical issue concerned with abortion counseling and the role of Catholic social workers.

Abortion in Germany

The issue of abortion counseling in Germany has raised crucial moral questions for Catholics who seek to accept social responsibility within a pluralist society while at the same time attempting to heed a Pope and hierarchy who condemn them for failure to adhere to moral absolutes. The German predicament reveals an historic outcome in the clash between lay Catholics, their bishops, and Rome in a developed, pluralist, multicultural society which has recently absorbed a mainly atheistic population separated by war and ideology.

Under a German law passed in June 1993, a woman is allowed to have an abortion within the first twelve weeks of pregnancy on condition that she has received counseling from a state-approved organization. Abortion advisory services exist to inform women about alternatives and available support should they decide to proceed to term. The woman must be able to produce a *Schein*, a certificate, confirming that she received counseling at least three days before an abortion. In September 1993 Archbishop Johannes Dyba of Fulda refused to collaborate with the state consultation scheme, standing out against his brother bishops, who supported it.

Two years later, in September 1995, the Pope criticized the German abortion law and noted his unhappiness at the apparent ambiguity of the Church's involvement—the certificate, he pointed out, could be taken as a permit for abortion. The letter sparked a series of debates among bishops and the faithful in Germany, but the majority of the hierarchy wished to stay within the state system, believing that it enabled the Church to persuade thousands of women every year not to end their pregnancies. But the Pope con-

between absolutism in Rome and the pressures on lay Catholics to handle complex moral and legislative issues in the local church.

These tensions are set to become more frequent and intense in the next generation of Catholics, who see the need to strike a balance between absolute principles and individual moral choices.

CHAPTER 10

PRIESTS

Fr. Andrew Greeley, in a 1993 article, estimated that 100,000 men and women had been abused by 2,500 priests—6 percent of priests in the United States. Financial losses have reached $1 billion, according to Fr. Thomas Doyle, who in the mid-1980s was the canon lawyer for the Vatican Embassy in Washington [and] entreated bishops to form a response policy.

—Jason Berry, *National Catholic Reporter*

There is little doubt in the minds of priests that the Church stands at a precarious point at the turn of the millennium.

—Donald B. Cozzens

MOST OF US CATHOLICS love and respect the Catholic priesthood, even if we sometimes have occasion to deplore individual priests. Priests are a living paradox: in the world but not of the world. In the words of George Herbert's poem to prayer: they are the "engine against the almighty," "the soul in paraphrase." Most of us treasure these men who hallow our marriages, usher our children into the life of grace, console us in bereavement. Priests seldom become close friends to the laity, but they are the embodiment of Christ's intimacy in our lives. The special place of priesthood in Catholic consciousness only serves to make their current tribulations all the more tragic.

Not long before he died, one of my close priest friends who had a position of responsibility as chaplain in a Catholic residential college told me on his sixty-ninth birthday that he was currently attempting to seduce an eighteen-year-old male student into a sexual liaison. Wise and evidently good in countless ways, he was a stirring preacher and a man who loved his priesthood, but I came to see that his life was profoundly dislocated. I realized that although I had been acquainted with him for twenty-five years, I hardly knew him at all. He said, "I'm convinced that I cannot become fully human until I've had sexual relations with this young man." At one point he said, "Oh, the body is just a playground; it's the soul that matters."

I did my best to dissuade him, not so much for his sake as for the young man's and for the community of his college. He never spoke of it again, and he died suddenly soon afterward. My friend, sadly to say, now takes his place in a distressing set of statistics.

The trust that the faithful once placed in the Catholic priesthood has suffered a reverse. Rumors of abuse, actual abuse, and false allegations of abuse have affected the identity of the Catholic priesthood, damaging the collective reputation of many of the finest men in the world. The percentage of pedophile priests is said to be 7 percent in the United States and the numbers are probably typical for Europe as a whole. Some one thousand cases have been examined in the United States to 1998 and a billion dollars paid out in compensation and damages. To put the figure in context, that is equal to the annual budget for ten years of the Knights of Columbus in the United States—a foundation with a five-billion-dollar endowment.

In recent years the shocks have come with sickening regularity. Just when the crisis seemed to have peaked, there were new and unexpected ramifications. In the first week of September 1995, when the pedophile priest scandal appeared to have reached its zenith in Britain, Cardinal Basil Hume of Westminster addressed an international conference at Salford University on the priesthood; Cardinal Danneels of Belgium was present and bishops had traveled to attend from all over Europe. Cardinal Hume complained of the way in which priests had been unfairly stigmatized by the pedophile behavior of a minority: "It is wrong when the impression is given that all celibates are in some way failing to live up to their promises if any of us fails to do so." But a horrible irony was in store for the delegates. The keynote talk was given by Father Michael Hollings, a British priest with a reputation for personal holiness and pastoral success. Hollings talked about the imperative for priests to follow in the footsteps of Christ, while being available to others as was Christ. He emphasized that they should try to love themselves, as otherwise they could not love anyone else.

Two months later Father Hollings, then aged seventy-four, was suspended by Cardinal Hume from his parish duties in London after he was accused of having sexually abused a youth of seventeen whom he had taken into his house twenty-five years earlier. A newspaper had persuaded the alleged victim to trap Hollings into an admission of his misdeeds with the use of a concealed tape recorder. Hollings's ambiguous acknowledgment of inappropriate behavior was published in Britain's largest circulation Sunday newspaper, *News of the World*. He was reported as saying to the individual: "Please forgive me for what I did. Accept I wanted to help, not harm you." No charges were brought by the police, and although Hollings was officially cleared by his diocese of improper behavior, a cloud hung over him until his death in 1998. Many of Hollings's friends, and I number myself as one of them, find it difficult to believe that he was guilty of abuse. But his plea for forgiveness—"for what I did"—was at least a qualified admission of guilt and, in that light, his glowing reputation was seen by the media as hypocrisy. If a man of holy reputation is infected, what hope for the priesthood at large?

The ordained ministry is of central importance for the spiritual welfare of the Catholic Church. The Catholic Church cannot function without its ordained priests; but by the end of this decade, unless a turnaround currently reported by the Vatican bears fruit, the supply of priests throughout the world will be half the number recorded in the mid-twentieth century but with twice the numbers of faithful in their care.

In the generations since the Second Vatican Council the Catholic priesthood has undergone a dramatic self-reassessment, an alteration in identity that has renewed and strengthened the commitment of countless priests but left many others confused and demoralized. There have been mass defections (some 100,000 since the late 1960s) and a calamitous drop in recruitments. The Vatican is currently taking heart from a recent improvement in the numbers entering seminaries, and a return of up to 20 percent of those who have defected from their ministries. But the trends have been so bad over the long term that local and recent improvements may prove insignificant except to provide a much-needed boost for the fainthearted. The Cardinal Archbishop of Chicago claimed early in 2001 that entrants to his seminary had quadrupled; in the English College in Rome for the year 2000–2001, however, there was only one new entrant, and for the first time in four hundred years there has not been a single novice for the British Jesuit province. Enrollment figures, in any case, do not translate into ordinations at the end of the six-year course for diocesan priesthood; in countries like Britain, the average perseverance of ordained priests in the ministry is only seven years.

In the United States, according to CARA online information, there were 8,325 seminarians enrolled in 1965, compared to 3,474 in 2000. Some 60 percent of seminarians are over thirty, compared to the pre-Council pattern of seminarians enrolling straight from junior seminary at eighteen. This means that the active careers of priests of the future will be drastically foreshortened. According to projections to the year 2015, made by sociologists Richard A. Schoenherr and Lawrence A. Young, unless there is a dramatic revival the total decline in the current clergy population will be in the region of 46 percent.

Catholic priests are a dying breed in Western Europe and North America. In most Western countries priests are predomi-

nantly in their mid-fifties. In Europe, according to Professor Jan
Kerkhofs, the number of active priests declined almost everywhere except Poland and the trend continues downward.

It is also an aging population. The average age of diocesan
priests in the active ministry in the United States in the year
2000 was fifty-nine, and the average age of members of religious
orders was sixty-three. Some 44 percent of active priests are older
than fifty-five in the United States, whereas those under thirty-
four make up less than 5 percent. From 1995 through 1999 there
were 1,247 diocesan ordinations in the United States, but there
were also 2,654 deaths and resignations from the priesthood.

Members of religious orders, themselves a graying population,
are working in parishes rather than pursuing their traditional
roles in other areas, such as education, in order to fill the gap in
the provision of diocesan priests. When the current generation of
older stalwarts—diocesan and religious—retires or dies off in the
West, the true extent of the calamity will become apparent. Positive figures, such as reported in Holy Week of 2001 by the Vatican, are undermined by a negative balance between ordinations
on the one hand and the number of deaths and retirements on the
other.

The most immediate impact of the decline in numbers is upon
priests themselves. Pastors who once shared their workload in a
single parish with the assistance of one or more curates now
struggle alone to run more than one parish. In 1992 around 33
percent of what had hitherto been regarded as parishes in Europe
in the mid-century had no resident pastor and the number of
priestless parishes continues to expand. In France, parishes with a
resident pastor numbered 15,597 in 1976, as opposed to 12,184 in
1992, indicating that 3,413 parishes became priestless in the space
of sixteen years. It is now common in many rural areas of France
for parishioners to listen to a tape recording of a homily recited
by a pastor who lives many miles distant while a lay Eucharistic
minister distributes Communion. In the United States parishes

without a resident priest have risen from 549 in 1965 to 2,843 in 2000.

Since 1965, according to official Vatican figures, ordinations in the United States have declined by more than two-thirds (from 1,575 in 1965 to 460 in 1998). And Professor Jan Kerkhofs believes that the falling numbers of priests in Europe represents the most serious problem for the future of the Church. On the continent as a whole, many dioceses have parishes—between 30 percent and 50 percent—with no resident priests, and in the provinces religious orders are reporting a reversed age pyramid. In Ireland, once the provider of priests for the world, ordinations (both diocesan and religious) dropped, according to St. Patrick's College, Maynooth, from 259 in 1970 to 43 in 1999. In Poland, ordinations rose by a third between the mid-1970s and mid-1980s, but according Kerkhofs, all kinds of vocations have been decreasing there since the fall of communism. In Germany ordinands declined from 744 in 1979 to 181 in 1999. But if things are bad in the Northern Hemisphere, the ratio of priests to faithful in developing countries is already disastrous. In Africa, the proportion of members of the faithful to priests rose from 3,251 to each priest in 1978 to 4,483 in 1998. In Latin America as a whole, during the same period, the proportion rose from 6,000 to each priest to 7,000.

As the workload of a largely aging priesthood expands, the problem is not simply that of providing Mass and a homily to congregations in more than one location. The priest is still in demand for baptisms, marriages, and funerals, as well as visitations to the sick, the aged, and the dying, whose numbers and needs do not diminish. At the same time, the increase in bureaucratic stress adds to the workload. Priests are obliged to continue working long beyond the retirement age of most other professions: in many dioceses in the West priests are not expected to retire until at least the age of seventy-five. Many continue to work, despite ill health, until they die.

The progressive-conservative divide promotes opposing solutions: the call for married and women priests on the one hand,
and for greater discipline and asceticism on the other. Generalizations about the status and fate of priestly celibacy are deeply
problematic, and there is no clear consensus, even among Catholic
specialists who study the issue. When Richard W. Sipe, a psychiatrist and former priest, stated that many priests are not mature
celibates, Father Greeley retorted: "Sipe's study . . . is garbage,
and would not be taken seriously if it were on some other subject." On the conservative side, however, there is a tendency to
criticize the Catholic married laity. As an old-fashioned priest of
my acquaintance puts it: "The lack of priests is a token of all those
unborn children who might have had a priestly vocation had they
not been deprived of life through the epidemic of contraception."

The world of the Catholic faithful, it is true, has undergone a
transformation since the 1960s, and families are not nurturing
priestly vocations as they did in the past. But considering the difficulties in which priests find themselves, considering the nonstop
scandals that are afflicting the image of the priesthood throughout the developed world, it is small wonder that Catholic families
are not encouraging their sons to enter seminaries. But there are
other considerations which involve the changing face of the
priesthood in a culture that is inimical to their ideals and purpose.

The Changing Face of the Priesthood

When I was a boy, a young man of the parish who had been in the
seminary returned to be ordained. The Mass of ordination was
one of the most moving and impressive religious experiences of
my childhood. The choir sang: "Thou art a priest forever according to the order of Melchisedech." There was an enthralling moment when the young ordinand lay prostrate, facedown, before
the altar; his hands were anointed with oils and bound; his
priestly robe, known as the chasuble, was unfurled. After Mass
the parishioners lined up to receive the young priest's first bless-

ails. He handed out holy picture cards
r our prayers. In the parish hall a group
is and a dozen or so priests sang a rous-
nultos annos! Ad multos annos . . . [For
r many years to come . . .]." When I
of a priest recently I found that little
vening years: the beauty of the cere-
joy and of noble commitment. But the
d, and the circumstances of the minis-
try, have altered dramatically in the interval of more than forty
years.

When I became a seminarian before the Second Vatican Council our teachers used to remind us that our calling was greater
than that of Mary herself. In the still-popular *Imitation of Christ*,
which many of us read every day, the section on the priestly vocation declared: "High is the ministry and great the dignity of
Priests, to whom is given that which is not granted to the
Angels. . . . You have not lightened your burden; you are now
bound by a stricter bond of discipline, and are obliged to a greater
perfection of sanctity." A priest was a priest for all eternity; ordination bestowed an indelible character on the soul. A priest was a
man who had died to this world and had risen to a new life. Defections from the priesthood were so rare as to be virtually unknown. In those days it was widely accepted that the celibate and
chaste life was attainable and laudable; there were, besides, many
domestic, institutional, and disciplinary frameworks in place, not
least the companionship of fellow curates in the priests' house.

But the priesthood, for all its high spiritual aspirations, was imbued with patriarchal privilege. The pastor in those days was
chairman of the school governors, unquestioned ruler in his
parish, ultimate arbiter of finances and building programs, confessor of sins, marriage counselor, a preacher who brooked no contradiction. Revered by women, adored by children, fussed over by
nuns, respected by men, Father was the parish, and Father knew
best.

In the lifetime of the generation of priests aged sixty and above, the role and nature of priesthood altered, undermining the patriarchal privilege and inviting the pastor to draw closer to his people. The calling has become especially demanding for priests lacking maturity and people skills. In his recent book *The Changing Face of the Priesthood*, Father Donald Cozzens, a seminary rector in the United States, quotes a series of contrasts summarizing the emergence of a new priestly identity in the post–Vatican II era: "from pedestal to participation; from classical preacher to contemporary mystagogue; from the lone ranger style to collaborative ministry; from monastic spirituality to a secular spirituality; from saving souls to liberating people." The patrician, honored and respected for his office, has become a servant among peers who must earn their respect on a daily basis. At the same time, the nature of the priesthood—that essential transformation with the oils of ordination—is subject to searching questioning. One ex-priest summed up for me the new understanding of the priesthood like this: "It was a mistake for people to think that ordination left an indelible mark on our souls. Being a priest is just a job; and people routinely throw in their jobs." Once upon a time it was a help and a consolation for priests to believe that they were not like the rest of us: nowadays they often find themselves working among lay Catholics who resent the idea of privileged ministry and charism. In a Church in which the laity aspires to ministry it is not surprising that priests feel that they have all the drawbacks of the religious life and none of its consolations.

While many priests have grown in maturity and effectiveness as a result of the altered identities following Vatican II, others have been destabilized. The priests who stayed were obliged in the early years, following *Humanae Vitae*, to cope in confession with an expanding gap between practice and Church teaching. Some priests took this in their stride and found joy in liberating their congregations from the burdens of the sin cycle. Others found the split impossible to handle and left. A few took the dilemma heavily upon their own consciences. "In the days when they still came to confession," a priest friend told me, "I would tell them God loved them, that contraception was not something to confess. But I would lie at night wondering whether I would roast in Hell."

There can be no doubt that Vatican II lifted many of the checks and disciplines that made a celibate and chaste life feasible. Nor can one ignore the sudden impact of sexual permissiveness, under which priests came to live their lives and through which a new generation of priests was emerging. The Vatican had made it relatively easy (at least under Paul VI, if not John Paul II) for diocesan and religious priests to be released from their celibacy; about 70,000 have been officially released since the mid-1960s. The effect on those who remained has been incalculable. A Jesuit friend, now in his early seventies, told me recently: "As we saw our fellow members of the society leaving in their dozens, their scores, and eventually in their hundreds and thousands, we were left speechless. All we could do was weep and hug each other." Many who remained found themselves leading ambiguous, unhappy, and stress-laden lives, robbed of esteem and status, their morale constantly under pressure, their worth minimized.

Priestly Sexuality

According to Cozzens, "At the core of a priest's crisis of soul . . . is the search for his unfolding identity as an ordained servant of Jesus Christ." Priestly identity—what it means to be a priest in the world today—raises questions about personal integrity, personal relationships, and one's capacity for human intimacy. In recent years I have talked with many priests involved with priestly formation and priestly renewal in Britain, Ireland, and the United States. One, a priest psychologist, insisted that no one should remain within the priesthood who is not capable of conducting an intimate but "non-genital," as he put it, relationship with a woman or a man. A former seminary rector told me that it was nowadays difficult to advise student priests about depth of intimacy in their relationships, "how far should they go," whether with men or with women. "Priests," he said, "are not hermits; a vow of celibacy is not a vow to live without loving relationships." But where does this place the individual priest, with his uncertain identity and collapsing framework of disciplines, living in a culture that believes chastity to be warped and, in fact, unfeasible? Within the confessional box many priests have been routinely releasing their parishioners from strict observance of the Church's sexual teachings. How does this affect their own celibacy and chastity?

Since the 1960s about a third of the priestly caste of the Catholic world abandoned their calling. This made for a generation of "survivors," some embittered, some nostalgic for the past, some immeasurably transformed and strengthened, and many who are grateful just to have clung on. "The important thing," one priest in his early seventies told me recently, "is to enjoy life and to see it through." The climate has not been conducive, evidently, for the recruitment of new priests; it has not prevented the steady growth of relationships between priests and women, nor has it challenged the entry into the priesthood of actively gay men who in more rigorous times would have been rejected.

Diocesan priests, in particular, live in virtual solitude many miles from brother priests. Educated in seminaries, which are still modeled on cloistral monasteries, their priestly formation has taken place in the exclusive male companionship of an enclosed institution. Candidates for the priesthood are not encouraged in their seminary training to socialize within the communities in which they live. Student priests are to this day encouraged to develop a spirituality more suited to what the social anthropologist Erving Goffman characterized a "total institution"; the hope is that they will continue the routines of prayer and disciplined living adopted in the seminary. But there is a stark contrast between peer-group student interaction, backed up with constant supervision by seminary staff, and the solitude of celibate pastoral life.

Most priests fend domestically for themselves. For many their solitude is gregarious. They are alone and yet they rarely have time and space to call their own. Having supper with a priest friend of mine in the East End of London not long ago, I recorded that he rose from the table sixteen times to answer the door during our first course. He had cooked the meal, as usual, by microwaving deep-frozen pre-prepared dishes from the supermarket. Past midnight, as we sat having a nightcap, he was called to the door by a parishioner who asked him to sign a passport application form. He had suffered two heart attacks by the age of forty-five.

At the opposite extreme, a significant number of priests cut themselves off, refusing to answer the phone: the TV, Guinness six-pack, and the whisky bottle have become the friends of all too many priests. Many survive by predictable means of escape. At a renewal weekend for priests in Dublin several years ago a priest charged with counseling large numbers of priests declared to more than a hundred of his clerical brothers: "Well, we all get by, Fathers, don't we, on the three excesses: excessive whisky, excessive golf, and excessive masturbation!"

More scientifically, a survey based on 1,500 personal biographies of priests conducted in Germany and the United States produced the following statistics on the sexual activity of priests: occasional sexual activity, 40 percent; sexual relations with women, 28 percent; homosexual relations, 10 percent; complete chastity, 10 percent.

In many parts of the Third World priests routinely take mistresses and are expected to do so. As a correspondent in South America in the early 1970s I came across such liaisons among members of religious orders in Peru, for example. In many parts of Africa celibacy is seen as a form of deviancy; according to reports, priests and even bishops commonly live with women and the faithful do not object. The Vatican acknowledged in March 2001 the sexual abuse of women religious by priests. Earlier, in a March 16, 2001, article in the *National Catholic Reporter*, aid agencies and women's religious congregations had alleged that in Africa particularly, a continent ravaged by HIV and AIDS, young nuns were sometimes seen by the clergy as safe targets of sexual activity. In some instances, according to the documentation, priests had impregnated nuns and then encouraged them to have abortions. There is widespread belief in Africa that having sex with virgins is a cure for AIDS. One agency alleged that there were cases of nuns who had contracted AIDS from the priests, and that they had been thrown out of their community houses to live, and die, on the streets.

Equally disturbing is the claim, originally published in the *Kansas City Star*, on November 4, 2000, that priests in the United States are suffering AIDS at a higher level than in the general population. Documents in fourteen states where death certificates are available indicate that the AIDS death rate among priests is more than double that of all adult males in those states, and more than six times that of the general population. The available data, according to Richard Selik, an AIDS specialist at the Centers for Disease Control and Prevention in Atlanta, "shows that the HIV death rate is higher among priests than it is in the general population of men twenty-five and older." Among the estimated 500 priest victims of AIDS, according to an investigation conducted by the *Star* in 2000, were a priest who had served as an AIDS consultant to the Vatican, a rector of a seminary in the Midwest, two seminary directors, three college chaplains, the spiritual director of a seminary, a Catholic prep school principal, and a former employee of the National Conference of Catholic Bishops. Bishop Thomas Gumbleton of the Archdiocese of Detroit told the *Kansas City Star* that the death statistics did not even take into account the numbers of priests now living with AIDS or those who had left the priesthood. Many of the informants of the *Star*'s investigation commented that there is remarkable silence and denial of the AIDS incidence among priests. All informants, especially those connected with priestly formation, concurred that the predicament within a group vowed to chastity and celibacy indicates a profound psychological and spiritual dislocation.

In 1995 Bishop Emerson Moore, an auxiliary in the New York archdiocese, became the first Catholic bishop known to have died of AIDS. In the 1980s he had become addicted to alcohol, cocaine, and crack. John Cardinal O'Connor of New York stood by him. Cardinal O'Connor told the press: "If a bishop of mine were to die of AIDS, it would be nothing to be ashamed of."

There is no indication that priestly AIDS victims and priestly pedophiles are one and the same group. But in Britain a potentially explosive link was made after an Oratorian priest, who had served as a school chaplain, was discovered to have died of the disease in 1998. Father David Martin, who was forty-four when he died, was in 1997 appointed chaplain and governor at the Roman Catholic Oratory School in London (where the sons of Prime Minister Tony Blair were enrolled). When he was ordained in 1994 by Cardinal Hume of Westminster, Martin's superior knew that he was a homosexual and that he had AIDS. Father Martin had been expelled from another order, the Rosminians, when his homosexual activities were discovered in the late 1980s. The superior of the London Oratorians, Father Michael Scott Napier, did not see Martin's predicament as a barrier to his appointment as chaplain to young boys in the junior department of the Oratory School. According to allegations made by pupils to a child protection agency, Martin lured boys to his room at the house of the Oratorian order in London and sexually assaulted them. The case came under scrutiny by police and child protection agencies after two pupils asked to be tested for HIV. A police investigation was conducted after the priest's death, and has proved inconclusive at this time of writing, but every such story is a setback for the charism and freedom of the priest-hood.

Abusing Priests

The principal devastation caused by priestly abusers is, of course, to their victims and their families who must pay for a lifetime in psychological suffering. But the damage done to the image of the priesthood and future recruitment—and hence the Catholic Church and its ministry—is incalculable. The trust of the faithful has been badly shaken; self-doubt and a poor self-image affect even the many priests who have been faithful to their calling. One priest told me: "I feel as if the work of my vocation over twenty-five years has been entirely destroyed." Another said: "When children approach me in the schoolyard, like they do, clinging on to you, my only thought is whether I am going to be accused of something. Priests can no longer afford to be alone with children for one moment and they certainly cannot come into bodily contact with them."

In the seminary we were told that our spiritual fatherhood toward children would make up for the renunciation of children of our own. That consolation now sounds like a cruel joke. Whether the priesthood has become irreparably damaged remains to be seen. The crisis appeared to reach a high point in the mid-1990s. Since then, various strategies have been employed, including immediate suspension and collaboration with the police. But widespread denial is also in evidence, and so is the tendency to make liberal Catholicism the scapegoat.

The crisis has given impetus to those groups within the Church who want to see a return to greater clerical discipline, vigilance, and segregation of the priestly and religious caste. Anecdotally, at least, some seminaries and traditionalist groups, such as Opus Dei and Legionaries of Christ, are enjoying a boost in vocations. In Rome, the practice of wearing soutanes, or cassocks (virtually banned in many seminaries), is again in vogue among the more rigorously disciplined seminaries. Since pedophiliac activity among priests is normally same sex, the circumstance has aided the agenda of those groups who deplore the presence within the priestly ranks of gay student priests, pastors, and bishops.

Some time before I began researching this book, I was assured by a seminary rector that the crisis is over, that the worst has come to light, and that the wounds should now be given time to heal on both sides. But at this time of writing a spate of new cases reveals that Church authorities are still failing to detect and deal with the problem at every level. In the month of October 2000, a priest in Normandy, France, Father René Bissey, was jailed for eighteen years after being found guilty of assaulting eleven young boys over a period of years. He was described by one witness as "truly perverted." The priest's Bishop, Pierre Pican of Bayeux, also faces trial on charges of conspiracy for failing to report the crimes when he was told of them by the parents of the victims. During the same month a priest of the Archdiocese of Cardiff, Wales, Father Joe Jordan, was sentenced to eight years imprisonment for various pedophiliac offenses; two of his victims were nine and ten years of age. Jordan had been ordained as recently as 1998 and committed his most recent offenses between his ordination and the year 2000. His Bishop, who had been warned of Jordan's potential pedophiliac tendencies during his first year in the seminary, refuses to acknowledge that he has a case to answer.

The pedophile crisis reveals that there are defects in the recruitment, formation, and discipline of Catholic clergy. For some experts the situation indicates profound problems inherent in the celibate status itself and the manner in which priests relate to their communities and societies as a whole. The notion that celibacy could be optional for Roman Catholic priests has been thoroughly repudiated by John Paul II in the document *Pastores Dabo Vobis*, where he reiterates that clerical celibacy is "profoundly connected" with Christ's desire that the priest imitate himself in giving his whole life to his Church. On a psychological and cultural level, the idea that celibacy is damaging or immature is also is repudiated by sociologists like Andrew Greeley.

Yet despite the imposition of safeguards, the priesthood, according to some Catholic commentators, remains hospitable to pedophilia and other forms of abuse. Richard Sipe reports that an American Bishop whom he had interviewed on the question of priestly pedophile behavior said: "The thing that pains me about the organization to which I belong is that it is rotten from the top down." As the facts of the Jordan case in Britain demonstrate, even when the pedophile crisis was at its peak there was a lack of competence in screening and an astonishing breakdown of communication and trust among those responsible for ordinands. When forty-three-year-old Father Jordan was sentenced in October 2000, he had left his seminary in Rome only two years earlier. He was found guilty not only of pedophiliac acts but of possessing 500 items of child pornography which the judge described as "totally depraved." To entice his victims he routinely set up boys' football teams, offering them massage treatment after games. A former teacher, Jordan had been before a court on charges for pedophiliac behavior even before he entered the seminary. He had been acquitted then, but the education authority for which he worked nevertheless considered him unsuitable to teach in school. Unsuitable to teach children, Jordan had nevertheless thought himself an ideal candidate for the priesthood; and so did those concerned with recruitment and assessment of ordinands. He applied to Bishop Christopher Budd of the Plymouth diocese in England, who had him enrolled in the premier seminary for England and Wales, the Venerable English College in Rome. Before Jordan's first year was completed, however, Bishop Budd grew suspicious on learning more about Jordan's earlier court case. But with the help of the college rector of the time, Jordan succeeded in changing dioceses and so remained in the same seminary but under a new bishop, Archbishop John Ward of Cardiff.

Ward eventually vetted Jordan personally by inviting him to

stay in the cathedral house for a period of time. But Ward ignored warnings from Bishop Budd, who had advised him that Jordan should be scrutinized by a psychiatrist experienced in dealing with pedophiles. Archbishop Ward arranged for Jordan to be interviewed by a retired psychiatrist with no expertise in pedophilia, and Jordan was allowed to complete the six-year course for the priesthood. Complaints by fellow students that he was evidently unsuited to the priesthood went unheeded by the rector, who appeared to notice nothing unusual about this ordinand. The complaints made by Jordan's fellow students are interesting. While there was no immediate evidence that he was a pedophile while in Rome, they found him "foul-mouthed" and "threatening." Those he suspected of being gay, and there were evidently gay students within the college, he called "shit-stabbers" to their faces in the seminary refectory.

Whatever conclusions can be drawn from the experience of pedophiliac abuse by priests, it certainly calls for humility and a readiness to admit that there is something seriously and structurally wrong with how our priests are chosen and assessed. Defensive reactions to the effect that this is just more "Catholic bashing," or that the ministers of other denominations are equally guilty, are as out of place as to suggest that the crisis is due in some way to the permissiveness of the Second Vatican Council. While commentators talk of the phenomenon as "erupting" in the mid-1980s, and of the scandal "spreading in recent years," it is clear that a range of abuse of minors was perpetrated by a minority of priests and religious well before the mid-1960s. A proliferation of cases involving Christian Brothers in Australia, Sisters of Charity in Scotland, and the nuns in charge of Magdalen workhouses in Ireland reveal that the preconciliar period was no golden age of innocence in respect to abuse of many kinds.

In my junior seminary, where we lived closely with twelve young priests, I had a brief brush with the phenomenon in 1957 when a priest, now long since dead, asked me during confession in his room if he could look at my penis. His excuse was that I might have a deformed sexual organ which was causing "overstimulation"; to inspect my penis would satisfy us both as to whether I suffered this condition. The word was rarely used in that context in those days, but I had the sense to realize that his suggestion was inappropriate and I declined his offer, but I wonder to this day how many other boys fell for this tactic.

The American journalist Paul Hendrickson, a seminarian in the United States during the same period, has a similar story to tell in his book *Seminary: A Search*. Under the direction of his priest spiritual advisor, Hendrickson went through the following ritual once or twice a week for more than five years:

> I would go in, sit in a chair beside his desk, talk for a short while, await his nod, unzipper my trousers, take out my penis, rub it while I allowed impure thoughts to flow through my brain, and, at the point where I felt myself fully large and close to emission, say, "Father, I'm ready now." He would then reach over and hand me a black wooden crucifix . . . and I would then begin reciting the various reasons why I wished to conquer this temptation. . . . The power of the crucified Savior in my left hand as overpowering the evil of impurity and the world in my right.

According to Hendrickson, a number of boys in the seminary were subjected to this spiritual "therapy," and it never occurred to him, or to them, that their spiritual director was a pervert. Nobody thought to report the priest to his superiors. Parents are nowadays more vigilant and victims more knowing and ready to come forward with their stories.

Priestly sexual abuse has been committed in every country in the West and involves every rank from lowly curate to bishops and at least one cardinal. Of the 7 percent estimated by Sipe to be priestly abusers, he claims that 2 percent of the priest population can be classified as true pedophiles, with a three-to-one preference for boys (this gender attraction is reversed in the general population), while two-thirds of priestly abusers, or 4 percent of the priest population, are sexually involved with adolescents with gender preference more evenly distributed.

Donald Cozzens complains that although he sat in on more and more diocesan crisis meetings to discuss how to manage the phenomenon, he recalls "no thoughtful discussion about the causes of the problem, its meaning or implications. Attempts to do so were often met with a certain suspicion that a particular agenda was at work."

In Britain, the Joe Jordan case evoked diametrically opposed reactions from the progressive and conservative Catholic press. The conservative *Catholic Herald* defended the local Bishop, John Ward, while *The Tablet* called for his early retirement. The *Herald* was not, of course, defending the deplorable behavior of Jordan so much as objecting to criticism of a Bishop in the absence of clear evidence against him. Meanwhile, in the United States, some officials have reacted by reminding laity and clergy that the dioceses have a duty to protect their funds from predatory false claims. But while the liberal-conservative divide often uses the crisis to further their separate agendas, the crisis has not gone away. Cozzens is concerned that we are only seeing the tip of the iceberg: "Diocesan officials would be naive to think that there are not numerous incidents of clerical misconduct with minors that have not come to their attention." He echoes the concern of psychiatrist William H. Reid, who has written that "careful studies have indicated . . . that child molesters commit an average of sixty offenses for every incident that comes to public attention." Sipe predicted that there would be fresh cases involving bishops as well as priests. On June 1, 1998, Bishop Joseph Symons of Palm Beach, Florida, resigned after he admitted sexually molesting five teenage boys during his earlier career as a priest. There is also an outstanding accusation involving Cardinal Hans Hermann Gröer, former Cardinal Archbishop of Vienna, once a Benedictine Abbot. In February 1998 four Austrian bishops asked Gröer to respond to charges that he had been guilty of sexual abuse of young

men. In 1995 a former monastic student came forward to claim
that Gröer had abused him some years earlier. The Cardinal has
refused to date to answer the charges despite many calls for him
to do so by brother bishops. By remaining silent, say the bishops,
Gröer has put the Church in an invidious position. If the charges
are false he should attempt to clear his name; if they are true, he
owes a public confession and an apology. A Vatican delegation announced at the time of the charges that it was to initiate an investigation, but at this time of writing it has failed to report.

Gay Priests

"One of the untold stories of the priesthood at the close of the
twentieth century," writes Cozzens, "is the large number of life-
giving, joyful, loving friendships between celibate priests and
their committed friends." There are spiritual directors who argue,
in fact, that the existence of committed friendship is a prerequi-
site for a deepening of the soul and the experience of genuine
love. Cozzens is referring to both gay and straight priests, and acknowledging that while there is often a struggle to maintain a
friendship within celibacy, the benefits outweigh the drawbacks
and the dangers.

It is, of course, difficult if not impossible to gauge accurate es-
timates for the number of gay priests and student priests in the
Church today, and in any case the prevalence of an orientation
does not indicate gay sexual activity. According to an NBC report
on celibacy and the Catholic priesthood, anywhere between 23
percent and 58 percent of the Catholic clergy in the United States
nowadays have a gay orientation. The younger the priests, the
higher the proportion of gays. Elsewhere, reasonably reliable
studies have put the figures as 48.5 percent for priests and 55.1
percent for seminarians. Individual seminaries, according to
Cozzens, have gay populations as high as 75 percent. The phenomenon of gay priesthood spreads throughout the European
Church and, by recent accounts, is prevalent in Italy. The journal-

ist Marco Politi, Vatican correspondent for *La Repubblica*, has firsthand testimonies of gay Italian priests in his book *La Confessione*, published in January 2001. The book discloses a network of gay priests throughout Italy as well as informal "self-help" groups whose members live in fear of their superiors or bishops discovering their orientation. On a weekly news program in Italy, Father Antonio Mazzi, a well-known priest who runs a drug rehabilitation community, said that homosexuality was spreading "above all in seminaries." He said that homosexual clergy lead "tormented lives."

The problem of gay diocesan priests and ordinands also has its counterpart within the religious life. Again, reliable figures are difficult to come by, but a remarkable example of the presence of gays in monastic life was evident in a recent episode involving the famous Benedictine community of Montserrat in northeast Spain. The national Spanish newspaper *El País* revealed in the autumn of 2000 the circumstances surrounding the resignation of two of its previous abbots. The report claimed that the abbots were forced to resign by Vatican-appointed Visitors (outside adjudicators) who had discovered splits within the community because of a sexually active minority of gay monks. Monks were quoted in the paper as saying there was a "pink lobby" within the community which upset the majority. The row led to the decision by the Archbishop of Barcelona, Cardinal Ricardo María Carles Gordó, not to preside at Mass to celebrate the Jubilee Year at the abbey. Cardinal Carles was reportedly angry with a past abbot's comments on Spanish radio pleading for a more liberal approach to homosexuality.

While it seems clear that among diocesan priests and seminarians, at least, the figures for gays could be as high as 50 percent, it is difficult to estimate how this contrasts with figures before the Second Vatican Council. We know that very large numbers of priests left the ministry in order to marry, which has depleted the number of heterosexual priests.

Again, while impressions and anecdote are the only guide, the numbers of gay applicants to the priesthood in the preconciliar days probably reflected the numbers in the population at large for one very good reason. Before Vatican II a large proportion of students came from junior seminaries (which they had entered prepuberty); hence it may be assumed that they were on the law of averages mostly heterosexual: in other words, the notion that the priesthood was an option for adult gay men entering the seminary after the age of thirty was a thing of the future. I was aware in my seminary of perhaps three or four students of homosexual leaning out of 120 (this was long before the "gay" appellation), but this preceded the days of gay self-consciousness and awareness. In any case we took it for granted that, like the rest of us, these men were not sexually active.

But what, then, is the significance if any of the rise of gay men in the Catholic priesthood, when one assumes that they accept, just as do straight priests, that sexual liaisons offend the need to be not only celibate but chaste? For Cozzens and others, the impact of the increase in a gay ministry is already evident in the presence of "a gay subculture," which Cozzens claims is present in most of the larger U.S. dioceses and seminaries. Whereas most laypeople are reasonably tolerant, even sympathetic, to the notion of a pastor with a gay orientation, the knowledge that their pastor is part of a gay subculture—adopting a particular mode of dress, creating a social milieu, frequenting gay bars—would be a different matter. In one North London parish in 2000 the arrival of a new priest, allegedly gay, with his partner at the presbytery was enough for the entire congregation to insist on his removal.

In the seminary, where many young men live together in an enclosed community, the potential for a gay subculture presents problems of a different order. Cozzens quotes the Master of the Order of Preachers, Timothy Radcliffe, on the emergence of a subculture within a seminary or religious order: "It can threaten the unity of the community; it can make it harder for the brethren to think of themselves in a way that is not central to their vocation." According to Annabel Miller of *The Tablet* the existence of many gays in a seminary community can lead to the departure of the straight students:

> One criticism often made of the current seminary intake is that it is largely homosexual, and that the resulting ethos of the seminary causes the heterosexuals to leave. This was recognised in Fr. David Smith's [a seminary rector, now a bishop] paper for the bishops' conference in 1994. "With a higher proportion of homosexually inclined entrants," the document read, "very often the heterosexual can feel in the wrong place. The image of the seminary is compromised."

According to recent reports, the Vatican is preparing to "tackle homosexuality" by revising guidelines for seminary life. In a report in Britain's *Catholic Herald* the director of Italy's National Vocations Center, Monsignor Luca Bonari, said the Holy See viewed the negative effects on the priesthood as "a very serious problem and is determined to take steps to correct it." He said that the guidelines would acknowledge "greater risks" to celibacy among homosexuals and require "careful discernment" as to whether gay candidates could live out their sexuality "with serenity."

The perception that the Catholic priesthood may become a largely gay institution may not spell the doom of Catholicism, but it has led to splits and fragmentation in an already fractured Church. Those sections of the Church—including religious houses, seminaries, and even whole dioceses—which take a strong line against homosexuality and deny the priesthood to gays on principle, whether they are active or not, find themselves increasingly isolated and antagonistic toward gay priests. The likely result could be mutual condemnation leading to the schismatic separation of the "straight" groups. Up to this point in time, the boot has been on the other foot. Bishop Gaillot of Evreux was sacked from his diocese for espousing the cause of gays; and Cardinal O'Connor of New York, for all his support of Bishop Moore, outlawed special masses for gays in his diocese.

If it is true that the numbers of gay seminarians are driving out the straight candidates to the priesthood, the existence of a predominantly gay priesthood after the older generation has died off or retired looks a virtual certainty with far-reaching potential for further divisions.

Married and Women Priests

The face of the priesthood, as Father Cozzens suggests, is in the process of change. The ordination of mature married men seems inevitable; and the precedent already exists not only in East Europe but in England where more than a hundred married Anglican clergy have been ordained as Catholic priests. The precedent might pave the way for some of those priests who left the priesthood to marry to return to ministry. One compromise solution, widely discussed in the Church today, is the possibility of establishing groups or orders of priests who are allowed to be married, while the tradition of celibacy continues in the mainstream of the priesthood. It should be possible under such a system for priests who decide to marry at a later stage to join the caste of married priests.

Few Catholics, least of all priests and religious themselves, would wish to reject the ideal of chastity and celibacy chosen with freedom and love by those who wish to do so. Historically, the lives of celibate and chaste clergy and religious bear splendid testimony to a radical form of spirituality and commitment. History also bears witness to the misery, strife, and despair occasioned by celibacy under coercion and the forces of internal Church politics.

Despite the lip service paid to the state of marriage by John Paul and the Vatican, the notion persists that celibacy is a more perfect spiritual state than marriage. In 1987 I attended a talk given by John Paul in Canada to a group of religious in which he insisted that celibacy endows individuals with a "youthful spirituality." He was laudably encouraging their commitment, but at the expense, it seemed to me, of the value of unitive love through which individuals draw intimately closer to each other. In a key survey conducted among American Catholics by Andrew Greeley and Michael Hout in 1996 some 69 percent of respondents said that they would favor the election of a Pope who would sanction married priests.

The issue of women priests is discussed elsewhere in this book; at this juncture, however, it is an apt point to raise the possibility that the ordination of women could bring an end to the crisis occasioned by dwindling numbers of priests in every part of the world. In the same Greeley-Hout survey some 65 percent of American Catholic respondents hoped for a Pope who would permit women priests. But it is unlikely that Rome will sanction ordination for many years to come, welcome as it might be to the laity. The widespread discussions and arguments that took place through the mid-1990s, after John Paul's declaration that women could never be admitted into the priesthood, have continued with increased rancor into the new century. The issues of doctrine, as well as justice and equality, have not gone away. The campaign continues within the Church rather than outside, guaranteeing that the issue will return again and again to plague future papacies.

The Women's Ordination Conference (WOC) in the United States, with affiliates from around the world, has focused persistently on Christ-related themes in its meetings and publications rather than feminist themes. While the Vatican defines the male exclusivity of the priesthood by citing the single act of Jesus in choosing men as apostles, the advocates within WOC point to the social and anthropological significance of the totality of Christ's life in the Gospel story, illustrating the Christian imperative of inclusiveness. As one WOC respondent put it in response to a survey of opinions on the issue: "If Christianity teaches that all are redeemed in Jesus Christ then it is a contradiction to exclude women in the full ministry. It is a denial of redemption. Either Jesus is savior of all or what we believe is false." Another writes: "The ordination of women will demonstrate the universality of God's call, without distinction or human-ordered restrictions." Another young pastoral counselor comments: "If the most important thing about Christ is maleness, are women saved? The Vatican's Christology is warmed-over misogynistic-androcentric daydreaming."

CHAPTER 11

A DISGRUNTLED LAITY

Pro-change Catholics' sense of Catholicism is grounded in the view that interpretive authority is diffuse in this understanding, interpretive power in the Catholic Church is not located solely in the official hierarchical power structure, but is dispersed, seen in the everyday activities of ordinary Catholics.

—Michele Dillon, *Catholic Identity*

NOT SO LONG AGO I was sitting close to a group of priests who were talking theology over lunch in a retreat house. They were engaged in a fairly learned and heated discussion about papal authority and Catholic hierarchy.

I had not been introduced, and I was unknown to the good fathers. But I listened in and made it obvious that I was interested—to the discomfort of the oldest member of the group, who rebuked me with a look as if to tell me to mind my own business. At a certain point in the discussion I intervened to ask a question, a rudimentary question about the First Vatican Council. Whereupon this priest turned to me without a glimmer of irony and said sharply: "Don't worry your pretty little head."

I do not intend giving the impression that priests today are so discourteous, still less that they routinely discuss such recondite matters when they come together over lunch. But the incident, small in itself, revealed an old-fashioned attitude and personality, that persists between clerics of a certain age and laypeople in the Catholic Church. It was not that the old priest thought I was stupid (for all he knew or cared I might have been a professor of

Church history), but he was giving me to understand that I was a member of the laity and that as such, in a clerical milieu, I should hold my tongue and concentrate on my soup.

While such attitudes, relevant to lunchtime discussions in retreat houses, have largely changed, a profound gulf remains in more significant matters. There is a huge rift between the lay and the clerical Church on the score of the Church's teaching authority, education policies, human and financial resources, and decision making. Clifford Longley, the veteran British Catholic religious correspondent, puts it bluntly:

> As citizens we are required to be critical of authority where necessary, to have regard to our rights, and to stand up for them. How come that in our lives as Catholics—surely the most important part of what we are—we somehow have to contrive to become completely different people: docile, passive, uncritical, with no power or influence, no right to information, no right to be consulted? Is it even possible to switch over like that, from active citizen to passive churchgoer; or do we just pretend we have done so, hiding what we really feel? Does this not lead to a kind of Catholic infantilism, where we have to cease to be adults because the only room for us in the Church is as children?

A token of Longley's indignation is a remark made by Archbishop Karl Lehmann of Mainz, the chairman of the German bishops conference, in response to a "church referendum" on change which started in Germany in 1995. Lehmann said he was "more and more coming to loathe this churchy navel-gazing which is typical of an affluent Church and its spoilt children." Small wonder that in Europe, where dissatisfaction runs even deeper than in the United States, the laity is increasingly angry, vociferous, and divided from the institutional Church. International lay campaigns like We Are Church, nationwide referendum groups balloting for change, and forums such as Dialogue for

Austria are insisting that the voice of the laity should be heard and that they should be drawn into every level of decision making: formation of priests, choice of pastors, choice of bishops, determination of doctrinal questions, and even executive membership of the Vatican congregations.

The laity are excluded from a full role in the Church's life and administration, and the Pope, the Curia, and the hierarchies of the world have no plans for such an eventuality. The situation is sufficiently deplorable as to cast doubt on whether the clerical sector of Catholicism believes that the Holy Spirit dwells within the entire Church.

The full scope of the crisis over lay participation is yet to be recognized for what it is and what it will become. That will only occur when the current graying of the clergy reaches the point where there is a drastic shortage of priests. A Church lacking priests, which is the grave reality of Catholicism's future, is destined to become a Church of the laity, and increasingly the women laity. Beliefs, principles, and moral values will be increasingly shaped by the views and the reception of the people. Sacramental ministry will be shared among lay participants, women, and married ministers living their everyday lives in a secular environment. Such a future, however, calls for a seasoned and mature laity if the Church is not to fragment into warring groups.

A diversity of lay groups, and mixed lay-clerical groups, already exists within the Church, exhibiting a less than healthy pluralism. Opus Dei, Focolare, Neocatechumenates, Communion and Liberation, and the Legionaries of Christ have been encouraged in various ways by John Paul II; but in the view of many middle-of-the-road Catholics, they have a tendency to be secretive and devisive. Parishioners complain, for example, that the Neocatechumenates take over whole parishes, excluding members of the community who are not initiated into their movement. They are tantamount to a parallel Church. The same accusation is leveled at Opus Dei, which is allowed to operate outside of the local Bishop's jurisdiction. Fiercely loyal to the Pope, overrigorous in their regulations, demanding discipline reminiscent of private sects, the groups are favored by the Pope as they appear to challenge the incursions of Protestant evangelicalism. But papal favoritism toward these groups is unlikely to advance the maturity of the laity as a whole.

The word "laity" originates from the Greek word *laos*—people—meaning the new "chosen people" of the whole Church, and the distinction between lay and clerical was not at first hard and fast. Significantly, as Vatican II scholars noted, Jesus chose his disciples from among the nonpriestly caste of Jews. In the early days of Christianity the communities were led by "lay" men and women who preached, taught, and celebrated the rituals of prayer and worship. It took at least two hundred years for the clerical caste to form and distinguish itself from the "laity." But in time the word "laity" came to mean the uneducated dependents of the clerical governing elite. Despite the education of the laity in the post-Enlightenment world, the stigma of being uninitiated—religiously, spiritually, intellectually—passive, unempowered, and unconsulted persisted until the mid-1960s. In the 1870s in Germany the Catholic laity had combined in strength and action to combat the persecution of Bismarck's Kulturkampf, but the twentieth century saw the papacy undermining lay Catholic activity in democratic politics. Catholic political parties in Italy and Germany were disbanded at the insistence of the Pope and Curia. In the meantime, Pius XI, Pope during the 1920s and 1930s, encouraged lay nonpolitical cadres known as "Catholic Action," but these groups and their aims remained firmly directed toward nonpolitical, spiritual, and devotional activities and under the aegis of the clergy and the hierarchy. Pius XI described Catholic Action in crushingly ponderous terms as "the organized participation of the laity in the hierarchical apostolate of the Church, transcending party politics." Catholic organizations in my childhood, as I related earlier, centered mainly on devotional activities and internal Catholic works of self-help and charity, all firmly under the wing of the priests and the bishops.

While the laity took a scandalously small part in Vatican II, it was envisaged that the "whole people of God" would be beneficiaries of the conciliar teaching. New emphases on participation, broader definitions of ministry, and openness to the world were aimed at drawing the lay faithful into a transformed Church. When the fathers of Vatican II referred to the Church in terms of the image of the "People of God" they offered the prospect of a new identity for ordinary Catholics—in other words, the 98 percent of Catholic men and women who are neither priests, bishops, nor members of religious orders. In a key document titled *On the Apostolate of the Laity*, the Council fathers attempted to restore an earlier ideal of universal participation of all baptized Christians with restored scope of responsibility, action, and a share in a wide range of ministries.

Laypeople are collaborating in liturgy, catechetics, education, pastoral work, parish management, and many regional and national Church projects, especially in youth ministry and social services. But since the 1960s, and despite a World Synod on the Laity in 1987, the vision of a Church transformed for and by the laity has fallen drastically short of lay aspirations and potential, not least in the formation of Catholic teaching.

Above all, there has been a failure on the part of the clergy to listen on the crucial question of sexual morality. One of the most remarkable statements of Vatican II was the second chapter of the document *Lumen Gentium* in which the Council declares that "the body of the faithful as a whole, anointed as they are by the Holy One, cannot err in matters of belief." It continues: "Thanks to a supernatural sense of faith, it manifests this unerring quality when 'from the bishops down to the last member of the laity' [a citation of Augustine of Hippo] it shows universal agreement on matters of a faith and morals." This is not a recipe for a democratic style of dogma creation—doctrine by a show of hands or the ballot box—nor is it an extravagant notion best ignored for its uncomfortable implications for centralized authority. It is an essential ingredient of Catholic belief that God's protection from doctrinal error involves the guidance of the whole Church and not simply the Pope in isolation; that central tenet of the faith has been rejected not by the faithful, but by an increasingly centralized Church authority despite the correctives of Vatican II.

It is not too much to say that failure to heed the importance of "reception" of doctrine by the laity has led the "official" teaching authority into the deep crisis of mistrust and division in which the Church finds itself today. Professor Nicholas Lash of Cambridge University, a leading Catholic theologian, sharpens our insight, citing John Henry Newman, who was a crucial witness and contributor to the original debate that preceded the definition of papal infallibility. Lash writes:

> Newman admits [in his *Apologia Pro Vita Sua*] that "the multitude" may "falter in their judgement." But according to him, when the whole Church in due course rests and acquiesces in a deliberate judgement, that is "an infallible prescription" and "a final sentence" against such portions of the Church as may "protest and secede."

Newman believed that the definition of infallibility was unnecessary since it could be used as a weapon by factions in the Church (true enough), and that there were too many precedents of popes who had got things wrong. Elsewhere Newman spoke of the need for "an echo" from the faithful before dogma could be said to have settled into unerring truth. As he saw it, the Pope and the bishops were engaged in the task of "active" infallibility, while the whole faithful endorsed that teaching activity by its eventual assent, or called it in question by nonassent. And yet the gap between teaching and practice, which is living evidence of nonreception, is so often characterized by Catholic conservatives today as apostasy and heresy. The crisis of teaching and nonprac-

tice, however, is occasioned not by the apostasy of the laity, but by
the Vatican's failure to listen to the echoes that come back from
the Church at large.

The single and outstanding issue that has created an historic
crisis of mistrust and division within the Catholic Church and the
marginalization and rejection of vast numbers of believers was
Paul VI's encyclical *Humanae Vitae*, which reiterated the ban on
contraception. As Lash comments:

> There is little doubt that the teaching of that encyclical has
> not been "received"—not, at least, in the exact form that it
> was given. Since then, the Church at large has become less
> trustful of its bishops, and especially of "Rome," and "Rome"
> has become increasingly less trustful of theologians and of the
> Church at large.

There is a view among many conservatives and liberals alike
in the Catholic Church that the birth control question is dead and
buried, that the faithful have made up their own minds and are
simply getting on with it. It is certainly true that the question is
rarely discussed nowadays, and as we see from repeated surveys,
Catholics have largely made up their own minds. Yet it is clear, as
I suggested in chapter 9, that the split between official teaching
and practice is both remarkable and untenable, and that the situation of this great moral standoff affects the authority of the
Church on a great many other moral issues. Why should people
take any notice of the Church when Catholics en masse ignore
one of its central teachings?

But the most crucial issue is the damage inflicted on what Vatican II described as a "sense of the faith," the feeling of the whole
people of God. What we have is a contemptuous rejection of the
faithful's "reception" of doctrine and a scornful conflation of
Newman's "echo" with mere "public opinion." The distance officialdom has come since that conciliar recommendation of reception was evident in the 1990 Vatican instruction titled *Donum*

Veritatis (Gift of Truth) which asserts that "not all the ideas which circulate among the People of God are compatible with the faith." All the more so, goes on the document, "given that people can be swayed by a public opinion influenced by modern communications media." Against this background, the idea of "reception" of doctrine becomes defiance and erroneous dissent, and the Holy Spirit is seen to dwell not in the whole Church, including the lay faithful—but exclusively within the milieu of clerical officialdom in Rome. A token of the extent to which this damaging prejudice has become hardened is the way in which the papal decree on women priests (*Ordinatio Sacerdotalis*, 1994) was handled, backed up by the instruction that the question may not be discussed even among competent theologians (*Responsum ad dubium*, 1995). The conservative reaction to criticism of the Pope's stance is that the teaching on ordination for women had been stated clearly in a Vatican declaration made in 1976 under Paul VI. But the views of the laity had no more been sought under Paul VI than they have been under John Paul II. How can there be "reception" when all discussion has been preempted? How do the Pope and his officials entrusted with Church teaching know that the doctrine concerning women priests has been "received" by the Church at large when it is forbidden to discuss it before soundings have been made?

Laity Against the Vatican

While the lay Church in the United States, for all its stresses and internal divisions, shows signs of qualified health and optimism, the situation of laity vis-à-vis the institutional Church in Europe, and especially within German-speaking countries, looks distinctly perilous. The clashes between people and Pope, people and bishops, are hardening into full-fledged lay rejection of official authority. Adherence or trust in authority appears to be at an all-time low in Germany. A Forsa Institut survey dated April 2000 returned the following indices in the 27 million strong

Catholic Church in Germany: 90 percent do not consider contraception a sin; 81 percent do not accept the Pope's official teaching as the ultimate authority; 85 percent question the infallibility of the Pope; 77.8 percent think female priests should be allowed.

Cardinal Joseph Ratzinger has been in the habit of making derogatory comments about German lay Catholics in recent years. But despite abandoning their allegiance to the institutional Church, the German laity shows abundant signs of a discriminating conscience as well a hunger for change. They are not merely indifferent, nor are they merely "Godless." Catholic organizations like Misereor, Caritas, and Adveniat demonstrate an impressive willingness to provide a wide range of aid programs at home and abroad independent of the auspices of the bishops (in Britain, a similar pattern obtains with Catholic Housing Aid Society, the Catholic Institute for International Relations, the Catholic Fund for Overseas Development, and the Catholic Association for Racial Justice). And while Germans have been opting out of the Church tax system at the rate of 200,000 a year, they donated more than 500 million DM to Catholic charities in 1999.

Lay Catholics in Europe are active, and they care. But such is the current demoralization and distance from official Catholicism that the Church appears to be fragmenting into different models. Within the parish communities there is a dramatic shrinkage and breakup, with churches closing and a declining supply of priests, but with no corresponding strategy to draw the laity into pastoral responsibility. This undermines the continuing attachment to the Catholic sacraments, and the Eucharist in particular. Meanwhile, Catholic professional lay organizations and the official Church are shearing apart, raising questions about the extent to which the lay organizations can be said to be officially "Catholic."

Initiatives such as We Are Church and the various organizations seeking referendums in Europe show that the people are attempting to break down the old divides. Unfortunately, the impetus for change by these means, while aimed at saving the Church, are themselves a force for breakup. For example, recently the bishops in Austria could not agree among themselves whether to include a Church referendum group for reform in the nationwide "Dialogue for Austria," thus pitting bishops against bishops. But one doesn't have to be a conservative Catholic to see the dangers of faith proceeding by ballots and votes. As British religious commentator Michael Walsh remarks: "Catholics are not Congregationalists. We do not decide our faith in parish meetings or diocesan assemblies. We are essentially, an episcopally structured faith, a universal communion, not a loose federation of congregations of like-minded members." Walsh is, of course, right, but that is precisely where the Church appears to be headed unless Rome accepts the importance of bringing the laity systematically and authentically into the governance of the whole Church. Meanwhile, recourse to referendums is surely an expression of rebellion at the failure of the Pope and the bishops to listen.

CHAPTER 12

WOMEN IN THE CHURCH

Nothing has changed. We are still human props of various designs.
—Jackie Hawkins, editor, *The Way*

WHEN DELEGATES MET at the World Conference on Women in Beijing in September 1995, Mother Teresa sent a message expressing her astonishment that "some people are saying that men and women are exactly the same, and are denying the beautiful differences between men and women." She went on to declare that "those who want to make women and men the same are all in favor of abortion."

The certitude with which the late Mother Teresa generalized on the relationship between abortion and feminism infuriated a great many Catholic women. They were no less angered by the way in which Catholic views on contraception and abortion had been hijacked by the Holy See's clerical representatives at the U.N.'s 1994 Cairo conference on population. A similar circumstance occurred at the Beijing conference on women, where the Vatican press official, Joaquin Navarro Valls, stressed on behalf of Catholic women the Holy See's view of "parental responsibility," which was code for a rejection of contraception and abortion.

The role of women in the Catholic Church overlaps at many points with issues of sexual and reproductive ethics (including abortion), marriage, and parenthood, but women are challenging and changing the Church—whether the official leadership likes it or not—both from outside and within and in wide-ranging and profound ways. First and foremost, however, the traditional role of women in the Church has altered forever.

From time immemorial, women who felt called to serve the Church were both drawn and invited to "take the veil." Although there have been examples throughout history of independent, outgoing, and active women religious such as Catherine of Siena and Teresa of Avila, and the great pioneers and founders of many women's religious congregations, the role of nuns, until Vatican II, was essentially one of radical subservience to the male-dominated clergy. The pattern has altered dramatically and permanently. In the world as a whole some 170,000 women discarded the veil in a period of twenty years following Vatican II. The walkout has been most marked in North America and Europe. According to official Vatican figures, between 1983 and 1998 the numbers of women religious in Western countries has continued on a steep decline: in the United States, from 123,579 to 83,624; in France, from 78,996 to 51,311; in Germany, from 63,200 to 41,257; in Britain, from 12,736 to 8,856; and in Italy, from 143,997 to 112,958.

Some sociologists argue that the decline is a result of secularization and social change prompted by better education and job opportunities for women in the world at large. The religious life, according to this explanation, is no longer an attractive avenue for social mobility. Be that as it may, countless personal testimonies bear witness to the persistence of patriarchal attitudes. Apart from the specific issues of reproductive rights, and the barring of women from priestly ministry, there is—in the view of women commentators—the long-running and widespread conflict between two models or metaphors of the Church. On the one hand the traditionalist concept of the Church as a hierarchical male-dominated multinational entity, and on the other the populist, pluralist view of the Church as "the people of God." The split between the two visions is so unbridgeable for some that feminists like Mary Daly have opted to develop their spirituality outside the Church.

Women religious are no longer content to work as teachers, nurses, and domestic helpers—in other words in physical and practical service to a male-dominated Church. Religious sisters nowadays mostly work and live in small groups, typically four or five members, as pastoral assistants in parishes, as chaplains in universities, colleges, and hospitals, and increasingly in the academic world of theology. There has been a remarkable increase in the number of women enrolling in graduate and postgraduate programs to study every area of theology, including pastoral, Scripture, liturgy, and moral. By the early 1990s women accounted for almost a fifth of the more than 1,400 members of the Catholic Theological Society of America (CTSA). There have been four women presidents of CTSA since 1977. More than 15 percent of Catholic seminary faculty staff members in the United States are women. Even in traditionally male-dominated clerical Spain an Association of Spanish Women Theologians (ATE, Asociación de Teólogas Españolas) was founded in 1992 for women holding a degree in theology or a connected discipline.

The Vatican has not been deaf and blind to the aspirations of women. On June 29, 1995, John Paul II published a special letter with a view to the World Conference on Women in Beijing, then in the final stages of preparation. He apologized for the wrongs inflicted on women and made a "heartfelt appeal that everyone, and in a special way states and international institutions, should make every effort to ensure that women regain full respect for their dignity and role." He added: "When one looks at the great process of women's liberation, it has been substantially positive. This journey must go on." But just a year earlier he had definitively and for all time committed the Catholic Church to deny the priesthood to women.

While the overall conflict between what women like Rosemary Ruether characterize as two distinct models is clear enough, it is dangerous to make generalizations or assumptions about women Catholics. Catholic women are not all seeking to alter the status quo within the Church, and whatever their stance, their aims vary enormously. The divisions within the Catholic Church are amply reflected in the divisions among Catholic women. While 60 percent of Catholic women in the United States claimed to be for women priests in 1995, the year in which the dispute over ordination reached its height, some 32 percent were opposed and 8 percent were undecided.

There are, of course, conservative women's groups. Some, like United Women of America, deplore the changes of Vatican II and seek to restore "Marian values" of acquiescence and obedience. Others speak of Catholic feminists as "witches engaged in a diabolic conspiracy to subvert the Church." Helen Hull Hitchcock, who speaks for Women for Faith and Family (founded in 1984) in the United States, collected signatures for a document called *Affirmation for Catholic Women* in 1990, with updates in 1994. One of the articles states: "We accept and affirm the teaching of the Catholic Church on all matters dealing with human reproduction, marriage, family life and roles for men and women in the Church and Society." Hull Hitchock claims that by 1994 some 70,000 women worldwide had signed the affirmation, which had been translated into seven languages. She insists that it is "now impossible" to assert that dissenting feminists speak for all Catholic women. There are conservative Catholic movements for women, led by women, and in Hull Hitchcock's words, with not the slightest hint of irony, they survive "on the refreshment of the apostolic exhortations and encyclicals with which Pope John Paul II has continued to nourish them. . . . They still look with shining, hungry, hopeful eyes toward their courageously orthodox priests and bishops." When Catholic bishops in the United States published a "liberal" draft of a planned pastoral letter on women they were warned by Women for Faith and Family and a women's religious group, Consortium Perfectae Caritatis, that the document could foment divisions. While the bishops had conceded that sexism was a sin, they had not, according to the conservative groups, addressed the "sins of feminism." A leading "feminist" sin, in the eyes of conservative Catholic women, is, naturally, ambiguity on the question of "abortion."

Battling the Patriarchs

The patriarchalism of the Church runs deep and it has been radically challenged not only in the milieu of pastoral work but in the realms of symbolism, liturgy, and theology. In its long history the Church has found little room for women as thinkers, and the prejudice persists. The Church has bestowed the title of "doctor" on thirty-two men and only three women. But women are now entering theology on their own terms and making their own contribution to the altering landscape of the discipline.

Feminist theology, in its fullness, is pluralist since it encompasses many cultures, ethnicities, and religions—Asian, African, Amerindian, Hispanic—while maintaining a steady focus on the struggle for women's rights and liberation. Feminist theology also relates on many levels with minority or disenfranchised groups struggling for liberation from socioeconomic, racial, and class oppression: hence there is a relationship if not an equivalence with liberation theology. In Europe and North America feminist theology has involved, moreover, a dialogue between French and American feminists which has affected both schools of thought and not without antagonism. Julia Kristeva, for example, like many French feminists, has encouraged theologians to consider the patriarchal order that consistently and deeply characterizes women as less than, and other. French feminism, preoccupied with sexuality, desire, aesthetics, and influenced by psychoanalysis and poststructuralist thought, has tended to undermine the more pragmatic and political aims of American feminism. Hence Nancy Hartsock could ask: "Why is it that just at the moment when so many of us who have been silenced begin to demand the right to name ourselves, to act as subjects rather than objects of history, that just then the concept of subjecthood becomes problematic." A more positive critique suggests that the two schools of thought lend depth to each other.

Taken in the round, globally and at the grassroots level, however, the women's movements within the Catholic Church have been compared with the historic challenge of Martin Luther, who repudiated papal power when he burned the corpus of canon law at Lestertor in Germany in 1520. The former editor of the *National Catholic Reporter* declares that "if Catholicism cannot find a way to meet this challenge, it has only modest hopes for survival, at least in its current form." While there is no such thing as an exclusively Catholic feminist theology, Catholic feminists cannot but focus on the traditional exclusions occasioned by an all-male Catholic priesthood. Throughout the Church's history, the male priesthood has ensured that Catholic theology maintained a male center of gravity. Not only were most theologians priests, but the Catholic priest stood at the center of all spiritual power, all binding and loosing, all power over consecrations.

Catholic feminists also see patriarchalism at work in the area of sexual morals, arguing that the Church's teachings on contraception, for example, are designed to sustain male sexist structures. They declare that it will remain impossible to achieve an authentic Catholic ethic until the shackles of male-dominated moral theology are severed. The feminist Christian approach to moral theology is skeptical of absolutes; it favors emphasis on individual conscience and context. Feminist theology avoids a priori reasoning, the application of timeless principles (such as statements about the intrinsic evil of certain acts), favoring the everyday world of experience and mitigating circumstances based on actual situations. Traditional theology is incomplete, say feminists, while it continues to ignore or discard the centuries of women's experience.

Catholic feminist writers like Anne Carr (*Transforming Grace*) point to scriptural passages that see women as being essentially wicked, an occasion of sin for men; as diseased, corrupt, unclean. The Old Testament Book of Leviticus, for example, stigmatizes menstruating women as infectious, a belief sustained by the Early Fathers of the Church. These prejudices have survived until recently in the Catholic Church, and certain clerics used them as rationales for banning women from the sanctuary where the Eucharist was venerated and the sacristy where holy objects and vestments were stored. A new consciousness about women's bodies stimulated feminist critiques of the Adam and Eve story and menstruation myths associated with female impurity. Feminist scholars have exposed in a new, critical light what has long been known: that contempt for women in Judeo-Christian Scripture and early Christian tradition connects with prejudice found in Augustine (in the fourth to fifth centuries) and Aquinas (in the thirteenth century), the great, permanent pillars of Catholic theology.

At the same time, Christian feminists have focused on Mary as a model for women. "Celibatarians strove to create an image of Mary," writes Ute Ranke-Heinemann, "that has nothing in common with that of other women." She goes on: "Everything connected with female sexuality, all that betokens the natural generation and bearing of children, have been denied her. She was not allowed to conceive her son by a man; he had to be sexlessly begotten on her by the Holy Ghost. She was not allowed to give birth to him in the normal way because she had to remain inviolate, nor was she allowed to have any other children because that would have entailed her physical violation."

Anne Carr argues that sin in women is associated with lack of self-assertion, "failure to make choices for themselves." Hence the idea of "sanctifying grace" takes on a new meaning, "the gift of claiming responsibility for one's life, as love for self as well as love of others, as the assumption of healthy power over one's life and circumstances."

Those Catholic feminist scholars who remain within the Church argue that their task is to separate and distinguish authentic Christianity from contemporary prejudice. "Feminist scholars . . . rightly point out," writes Elisabeth Schüssler Fiorenza, "that for all too long the Christian tradition was recorded and studied by the theologians who consciously or unconsciously understood [it] from a patriarchal perspective of male dominance."

Catholic feminist Schüssler Fiorenza has attracted vehement criticism from conservatives for her unorthodox views on abortion. The antagonism goes a long way back. In 1973 she spoke publicly on the *Roe v. Wade* Supreme Court decision, and failed to issue an outright condemnation. The 7 to 2 ruling effectively permitted the termination of pregnancy in the first trimester across the United States. The case had coincided with the widespread influence of feminist thinking on this and other issues: a woman's freedom to control her own body over the rights of the unborn child. The ruling, of course, flew in the face of Catholic moral teaching on abortion and prompted the long-standing campaign of the American hierarchy and pro-life groups in subsequent decades.

Schüssler Fiorenza was not prepared to pronounce on the question as to when human life begins, but she begged an audience at Notre Dame University to consider the issue of "justice, mercy, and faith." Advocating availability of information on birth control, she argued that the absence of information "increases the number of Notre Dame and St. Mary's students who end up in downtown abortion clinics." She went on to list the pressures that led women to contemplate abortion at Notre Dame: expulsion of pregnant women students but not their male partners; advocating adoption as the moral solution to abortion; contempt for women's intellectual gifts; absence of paid pregnancy leave and child care.

In their attempts to work freely and constructively many Catholic women have decided to work outside Catholic institutions. Schüssler Fiorenza eventually left Notre Dame for Harvard; Rosemary Radford Ruether went to the Garrett-Evangelical Theological Seminary in Evanston, Illinois; Uta Ranke-Heinemann, after losing her Catholic teaching license, was awarded the chair in Church history at Essen University; the Catholic theologian Janet Martin Soskice taught in an Anglican seminary before being appointed a senior lecturer in theology at Cambridge University.

Patriarchal Language

The matter of inclusive language is both crucial and fraught for feminists and, of course, for patriarchs. The central issue is that of "false generics" where, for example, "man" is used in Scripture and the liturgy to refer to males and females alike. In the view of Catholic women, the constant use of androcentrist language sustains the patriarchal view that males are dominant and women are inferior within the Church. The women's objections were supported by U.S. bishops in 1990 who endorsed the preference for such obvious inclusive forms as "humanity" rather than "mankind," and "brothers and sisters" rather than "brethren." But the problem runs deeper. When feminists insist that the persons of the Holy Trinity are more correctly described as "Creator, Redeemer, and Sustainer," rather than Father, Son, and Holy Spirit, the Catholic guardians of tradition are outraged. But the thinking stems from the legitimate plea that naming God is a metaphorical pursuit, constrained by culture, society, and history. Regal epithets stem from eras when monarchs were both common and real, whereas today they no longer form part of the everyday experience of most Catholics. Theologians like Sallie McFague of Vanderbilt University reject royal God talk and have no difficulty with images of God that have a distinctly pantheist or New Age ring, as in God, "the Spirit that is the breath, the life of the universe."

Attempts on the part of the Holy See and hierarchies to produce liturgy and catechetical material that avoids exclusive language have been patchy and mostly unsuccessful as far as Catholic feminists are concerned. The harder the advocates of inclusive language worked to satisfy women's objections, the less happy the Vatican was with the results. In the meantime, and especially in the United States, the media, legal, and academic culture was moving inexorably toward inclusive language. An example of language that is exclusive to the point of absurdity is to be seen in the official *Catechism* of the Church which opens with this statement: ". . . at every time and in every place, God draws close to man. He calls man to seek him, to know him, to love him with all his strength. He calls together all men . . ." No longer a case of women's sensitivities, the entire drift of sensibility—men and women—finds such expressions not only unacceptable but ludicrous.

A few months later the Vatican further exacerbated the situation by declaring that the New Revised Standard Version (NRSV), widely in use in Britain and the United States, was not to be used for liturgical and catechetical purposes. Considered by such scholars as Raymond E. Brown to be the best Bible for "study purposes," and sensitively biased toward inclusive language, it had been approved by the U.S. bishops and indeed Vatican liturgists in 1990. But the Congregation for the Doctrine of the Faith in Rome insisted that the translation enfeebled faith.

The issue of exclusive language ensures that women will continue to feel alienated in biblical study, catechetics, and in the liturgy. Meanwhile, the issue of women's priesthood, which is treated elsewhere in this book, alienates women at a much deeper level. But while the issue has emerged more as a contention about papal authority and justice, the feminist view on ordination itself is by no means solid. Although Elisabeth Schüssler Fiorenza originally campaigned vigorously for women's ordination, by the mid-1990s, in view of the Anglican experience, she was arguing against it. Ordination, she now argues, is "subordination" (literally entering into, or under, an "ordo"), which is hardly what women are fighting for. Schüssler Fiorenza and other feminists are now campaigning for the termination of ordination so as to create a Church of equals with a shifting leadership.

The constituency of Catholic women wishing to influence future generations of Catholics is large, powerful, and disaffected. After the Pope's letter to the World Conference on Women in 1995, a number of prominent women, by no means card-carrying feminists, responded in a fashion that is by now both moderate and familiar.

Shirley Williams, professor of electoral politics at Harvard, and former education minister in a British Labour government, went to the heart of the matter as she saw it:

> For too long, women have been stereotyped in the Church, as saintly mothers or wicked temptresses. Their individual humanity has gone unrecognised. For too long the exploitation of women, their disproportionate suffering as victims of poverty, violence and sexual abuse, have been ignored by the Church. And even now, the Pope does not consider access to the priesthood.

For Jackie Hawkins, executive editor of the Jesuit-based journal of spirituality *The Way*, the papal letter was a devious mixture of flattery and a reassertion of patriarchal attitudes:

> Give me a self-confessed, fully-paid-up male chauvinist any day rather than a man who, with however much goodwill, mistakenly believes that he understands women—and feels bound to tell them so.
>
> For a modern woman, the Pope's suit is pressed seductively in the middle section . . . then, presumably when we are meant to be totally disarmed and breathless with anticipation, the manacles snap shut. The final three paragraphs are the usual old story: only men can be icons of Christ, Mary is modelled, unrecognisable as a real woman . . . "in giving themselves to others each day, women fulfil their deepest vocation." Nothing has changed: we are, still, simply human props of various designs. Words of flattery and support have proved hollow.

More in sorrow than in anger, Pia Buxton, a nun, and the British provincial of the Institute of the Blessed Virgin Mary, had this to say:

> I doubt whether Pope John Paul II's words will stem the tide of unease and anger which is developing today among many committed Catholic men and women, clerical and lay, who love the Church and serve it, seek its unity, yet fear a growing division within it.... I appreciate, and am grateful for, the particular gifts that God has given to women and I thank Pope John Paul II for reflecting on these and sharing his reflections with us. But I find that the structures of the Church frequently deny the fulfilment of these gifts and are not always congruent with my experience of praying the Gospel as a woman.

From one purely pragmatic perspective, the growing importance of women to the Catholic Church must be grasped in terms of the plummeting figures of priests and new ordinations, and parishes without priests—especially in western Europe. As the male clergy dwindles, so the role of the laity comes into prominence in the vacuum, and women laity in particular. The Church is becoming rapidly emasculated and desacralized: women are waiting in the wings. But women—and especially those who have stayed—are angry. They are angered by sexism, by exclusions, by inclusive language, and by injustice. In their capacity as lay catechists, Eucharistic ministers, and pastoral assistants in most parts of the world, they have no proper employment rights and can be fired at a moment's notice by a patriarchal pastor.

Disaffected Catholic women will shape the future generations of Catholics. As teachers and mothers they will set the attitudes and values of the next generation of Catholics. An anticlerical generation of mothers is unlikely to encourage their sons to opt for the priesthood. Women will be the last, as a group, to seek to damage the Church, but they are frustrated and increasingly impatient.

It is more than thirty years now since Sister Theresa Kane had the temerity to confront John Paul II on his first visit to the United States. In an unscheduled speech, she told him: "The Church in its struggle to be faithful to its call for reverence and dignity for all persons must respond by providing the possibility of women as persons being included in all ministries of the Church." The Pope did not respond.

CHAPTER 13

THE NEW INQUISITION

There has been of late years a fierce and intolerant temper abroad, which scorns and virtually tramples on the little ones of Christ." The vehemence of this last remark [of John Henry Newman] shows how strongly he felt that people who were engaged in the interpretation of dogmatic statements for the faithful had to be concerned with charity as well as with truth.

—Francis A. Sullivan SJ

ONE AFTERNOON in the summer of 1998, Sister Lavinia Byrne, a small woman with a great halo of frizzy hair, came to have tea with me in my college in Cambridge. She was in such a state of nervous tension that her saucer was rattling against her cup. On the orders of the Vatican, she told me, the remaining 1,300 copies her book *Woman at the Altar*, published in 1994, had been destroyed. This destruction of her book had been perpetrated by her Catholic publisher in the United States, the Liturgical Press of St. John's Abbey, Minnesota (Byrne had originally been told that they were burned in the monastery incinerator, thereby providing heat for the monks—a story that I now take to be apocryphal—but destroyed or taken out of circulation they were). Her crime, it seems, was that she had written about the possibility of ordaining women, and had also stated that contraception was an important step in women's liberation in the twentieth century.

Sister Lavinia Byrne's case is important because it reveals a determination on the part of the Vatican authorities to put a halt to dissident statements presented with an official or quasi-official voice, no matter what the wider consequences. While this may be understandable from the point of view of an anxious centralized bureaucracy, the process is ultimately destructive, violating peer-group discussion, and moral and doctrinal originality and creativity. There are also grave issues of charity and justice.

Those conservatives who applaud the Vatican's stance on matters of orthodoxy claim that the Church is counter the culture and that there is nothing to apologize for, and everything to be proud of—our religion is full of hard sayings, they assert. But most Catholics who enjoy academic status live in pluralist societies and daily reap the benefits of pluralism. Pluralism is a crucial imperative that we, as a Church, offend at our peril. Conservative Catholics are quick to complain when they do not receive the immunity that pluralism accords.

Byrne had for some years inhabited a unique place in the religious life of Britain and not simply as the author of books on women's ministry and sexual morality. She was well known to millions as a regular broadcaster on Radio 4's *Thought for the Day*, an important religious program which goes out during peak drive-time. The Catholic flavor of her utterances constituted a virtually irreplaceable benefit to the Church. Now in her mid-fifties, she had spent her life from the age of seventeen as a member of the Institute of the Blessed Virgin Mary (IBVM), a congregation of sisters exercising a Jesuit spirituality, involved mostly in education. Jokingly referred to as the Cyber-Nun because of her expertise on the Internet (she writes an Internet column for *The Tablet*), she was at that time teaching religious media studies in Cambridge. She spanned many worlds—ecumenical, journalistic, feminist, academic—and she had remained a loyal daughter of her religious order and her Church. As far as many of us were concerned, Byrne was a sign of hope in a world in which Catholic identity was in fast retreat on a broad front. The 1990s, moreover, had seen the gradual erosion and axing of much of religious broadcasting. It seemed a miracle that a Catholic nun had managed to dominate the most important re-

maining religious slot in British broadcasting. This was Catholicism fully integrated into the contemporary media, but capable of
transcending much of the media message. The story she had to
tell me that afternoon, however, belonged more to the Middle
Ages than to a Catholic journalist nun at the turn of the millennium.

Lavinia Byrne had good reason to be tense. In the year
1992–1993—the timing is important—she had been writing her
now notorious book about the ordination of women, a major issue
in the Anglican Church since the Anglicans had decided to say yes
to women priests. Byrne later wrote that she used "Catholic" arguments to advocate ordination for women, and suggested that
the theological and pastoral framework for their ordination was
already in place. There were women, she said, "who talked openly
about their sense of calling to priesthood . . . it would not be an
aberration from the truth but rather a fulfillment of it." When
the book eventually appeared, the dust jacket showed a mosaic of
Mary in the archbishop's chapel in Ravenna. She is Mary the
mother of Jesus at prayer, standing with her arms raised in blessing, dressed for all the world to see as a priest.

The women priesthood issue had been attended by genuine
fears in Rome. In 1993–1994 many Anglican priests and laity had
left their Church to become Catholics following the Anglican decision to allow women's ordination. Might not the sanctioning of
priesthood for women within the Catholic Church prompt a
major traditionalist schism? Once mooted within the Catholic
Church, it was unlikely that Catholic advocates would leave the
subject alone. If the Anglican experience was anything to go by,
the campaign would gather strength on both sides of the divide—
for and against. In time the Catholic Church could find itself dan-
gerously and divisively embroiled. On May 24, 1994, John Paul II
effectively quashed all further argument, and by the same token,
presumably, all threats to Catholic unity. In an Apostolic Letter,
Ordinatio Sacerdotalis, he stated that ordination for women was
out of the question. For many Catholic theologians this attempt

to put a stop to all further discussion was more decisive than the women priest issue. It was seen as an attempt by John Paul II to bind his successors on a question that had not been extensively aired among the world's bishops and theologians, let alone the faithful at large.

According to Byrne, her book was already at the printer when the papal letter was issued. She prevailed on her publisher to add the text of *Ordinatio* as an appendix, and the book was accordingly published the following month, in June 1994.

A year later the Vatican wrote a letter, dated June 21, 1995, to the General Superior of Lavinia Byrne's order, which is based in Rome. It pointed out that Byrne had proposed her thesis "with no recognition of the authority of our Holy Father's pontifical magisterial, and she expresses no acceptance of that magisterium." The author of the letter, Archbishop Francisco Javier Errazuriz, wanted to know whether Byrne had sought permission to publish her book (a requirement of canon law), whether that permission had been granted, and whether the order approved of the thesis advocated by Sister Lavinia. As it happened, Byrne had asked permission of her order to publish, and it had been granted. The order, moreover, following the papal decree on women priests, did not approve of Byrne's thesis.

Byrne says she has evidence that she had been singled out because a group of ultra-conservative women in Britain had been bombarding the Vatican with complaints against her and her book. Be that as it may, the delation process certainly did appear to be the result of bottom-up complaints, rather than top-down vigilance. But the Vatican responded vigorously to the complainants and put pressure on the superior general of Byrne's order in the hope that she would in turn put pressure on Byrne. Byrne remarked: "There was no way the [superior general] could do anything but defend the orthodoxy of the Vatican position and, as it were, capitulate. The work of the other members of the Institute was far more important than mine." Byrne was referring to IBVM work in Hungary, Romania, and the Czech Republic where their sisters were coming out of hiding, and in Macao where they were preparing for missionary work in China. They needed all the material and diplomatic support from the Vatican that they could get.

But Byrne was astonished by the Kafkaesque unreasonableness of the affair. The Vatican wanted nothing less than a "public" declaration of her attachment to the "official" line on women priests and contraception. She told me in 1998, and she has recorded it in her memoir of these events: "I began to feel sick with dread." Matters indeed came to head in April 1998 when an official of the Congregation for the Doctrine of the Faith, of which Cardinal Ratzinger is the head, wrote to Byrne's General Superior asking her "to inform Sister Lavinia Byrne that it will be necessary for her to correct the errors which have been disseminated by her book, by making some form of public assent to the specific teaching of the magisterial documents *Humanae Vitae* and *Ordinatio Sacerdotalis.*"

This was upping the ante in an extraordinary fashion. Byrne was convinced that they wanted her to repudiate the contraceptive pill and her advocacy of a woman priesthood during a BBC broadcast. In her memoir she allows herself an extraordinary understatement: "I think," she writes, "that there is real mismatch between church people and media people."

Byrne has written of her reaction on that day: "I felt as if an icicle had entered my soul. . . . To attempt to reduce the heartbeat of Catholic teaching [to] two pieces of recent papal teaching both of which are indirectly about women and, what a surprise, about sex, seemed to me to trivialise the whole experience of faith. I refused to cooperate. Never at any point did I even entertain the idea of agreeing to his demand." Byrne says that she did not work the whole thing out rationally; it was a "clear imperative inside my being."

At this point Cardinal Basil Hume, who was ill with cancer and had not long to live, wrote a stiff letter to the Vatican dated September 18, 1998. Rarely, I imagine, has a metropolitan cardinal so flatly told a curial official where to get off. Having informed Archbishop Bertone that Byrne was in good faith and good standing and that he, Cardinal Hume, was satisfied that no further action should be taken, he went on to write: "Sister Lavinia is a much respected person in this country, and not only in the Catholic Church. She has done much good, and will continue to do so. I am sure the Congregation will act wisely and with prudence, and now leave the matter to rest. Any other policy will be harmful for the church in this country. Please accept my advice."

Silence descended, but by the end of the following year the accumulation of oppression led Byrne to believe that she could not go on. While staying with friends in New York over the Christmas 1999 holiday, she took the decision to abandon her religious calling after almost forty years as a nun. The decision brought much-needed relief. She is now free, as a private individual, to speak her mind on questions of priesthood for women and on contraception, and one presumes that the Congregation for the Doctrine of the Faith feels that it has won its battle. But it also means that millions of Britons do not hear Lavinia Byrne speaking to them routinely in the morning as a Catholic sister, as someone giving witness to a committed, religious way of life. Had it not been for Cardinal Hume's intervention she would have been hounded out of her order. As it was, she left of her own accord with a heavy heart, and the British listening public is the poorer.

Lavinia Byrne's story raises serious questions not simply about the Church's right to insist that those who speak for it officially should utter orthodox statements and not heresy, but about the manner in which it imposes discipline. This is not just a question of orthodoxy, but of justice, as Cardinal Hume remarked, and also scandal, for punitive disciplining is leading to discouragement of peer-group interaction and discussion which is inhibiting the Church's capacity to engage the intellectual challenges of our time.

Academic Freedom

In August 1990 the Vatican issued a document entitled *From the Heart of the Church* (*Ex Corde Ecclesiae*) which sought to encourage reasonable control of those academics in Catholic universities and colleges in the United States who taught religion in the name of Catholicism. The issue raised, and continues to raise, delicate questions about academic freedom, separation of church and state, academic funding, and the nature of Catholic identity. The directive aimed to clarify the relationship between Catholic universities (which in most cases had been founded by religious orders and had for generations had close links with the hierarchy) and their current identification with orthodox Catholic teaching.

In its determination to draw a clear line between doctrinal orthodoxy and the pluralist freedoms of academe, the Vatican had asked Catholic academic institutions either to opt in or opt out. Because of the evolution of Catholic universities and colleges (nowadays they attract both Catholics and non-Catholics and in some cases they compete with Ivy League institutions), the proposals—which are still largely unresolved—had far-reaching consequences for academic freedom and funding. Putting the argument crudely, could any university or college consider itself free when it took its orders from a bureaucracy in Rome? And could the government, or the state, award funds to an institution which took its orders from a sovereign foreign state, however small?

The issue came to a head after the Vatican had rebuked the long-standing "dissident" Father Charles Curran, a distinguished moral theologian at Catholic University in Washington, D.C.

For some twenty years Curran had been critical of the papal encyclical *Humanae Vitae* (Paul VI's teaching on birth control), claiming that he was not dissenting from dogma but from aspects of the Church's teaching that were not infallible. After a series of investigations by Cardinal Ratzinger's congregation in Rome, the Vatican withdrew Curran's license to teach theology and he was dismissed by Cardinal James Hickey, the university's chancellor. Curran called a press conference to tell the world: "I'm from the United States, and there has been friction between the Vatican and the church in the U.S." He went on to say that he had been targeted as an American, inferring that he was a scapegoat in the Vatican's battle against liberal academics. After a lengthy civil action, in which Curran attempted to sue his university for wrongful dismissal, the trial judge found in favor of Catholic University on February 28, 1989. The episode gave encouragement to those conservatives who wanted a clear line in the sand between what was said in the Church's name, and (who can blame them) what was said by Catholics as individuals, but it sent shivers down the spines of many Catholic academics, widening the gulf between the American hierarchy and Catholic academe.

Twelve years on, at this time of writing, the conflict still smolders, threatening at any point to erupt into a conflagration. In November 2000 it was reported that Catholic bishops in the United States had drafted an affidavit to be signed by all theologians teaching at Catholic colleges and universities stating their doctrinal allegiance. This *mandatum*, or approval to teach, is an aspect of the strategy prompted by the *Ex Corde Ecclesiae* document of 1990. It contains the words: "I am committed to teach authentic Catholic doctrine, and to refrain from putting forward as Catholic teaching anything contrary to the church's magisterium." According to the *Washington Times* the bishops argue that the *mandatum* offers no threat to academic freedom because the bishops and theologians share trust. But is there genuine trust among the Vatican, the bishops of the world, and the theologians?

Faith and Reason

Never was the Catholic Church more in need of intellectual originality, outreach, and resilience than it is today. In the field of genetics and reprotechnology, advances are outstripping our familiar ethical bearings; in the fields of artificial intelligence,

neuroscience, and cognitive science there have been challenges to
notions of human identity and the soul; in the field of Darwinian
biology, sociobiology and evolutionary psychology are undermining traditional notions of human behavior and moral agency; in
cosmology scientists are debating major issues with implications
for the notion of creation.

Nobody could accuse the Catholic Church of being idle in
these fields; nobody could accuse John Paul II of failing to heed
the call for intellectual outreach, especially after his 1998 encyclical, *Fides et Ratio (Faith and Reason)*. And yet, for all his words,
he has encouraged an oppressive intellectual culture, starting in
the area that matters most—moral theology and the study of religious pluralism. Most ominously, Vatican attempts to exert a
strictly orthodox line and to condemn most forms of pluralism as
relativism have acted as a brake on Catholic intellectual outreach
at a time when the Church is in greatest need of peer group intellectual exchange.

The Vatican is a major patron of academic and scholarly
endeavors across a range of ecclesiastical disciplines—theology,
philosophy, Scripture, law, liturgy, music—obviously. Vatican departments involved with culture, other religions, nonbelievers,
and Islam are staffed by scholarly bureaucrats. The Holy See
funds significant international projects in the natural and social
sciences. The Pontifical Academy of Sciences, situated within the
Vatican Gardens in Pirro Ligorio's Casino of Pius IV, holds ple-
nary sessions every two years and a study week attended by two
dozen scientists. On these occasions the Pope announces the win-
ner of the Pius XI medal for a young scientist. The academicians
are appointed for life by the Pope, to a total of seventy. They are
mostly professors from European and American universities, and
include distinguished non-Catholics such as Sir Martin Rees,
Max Perutz, and Charles Townes. In the winter of 1979 Pope John
Paul II paid tribute to Galileo as a Christian, healing a breach with
science that had existed since the mid-seventeenth century. The
Vatican's observatory works closely with Jesuits involved in as-

trophysics. In addition, the Vatican sponsors occasional conferences on science and social science, and there have been notable attempts to focus on issues of immediate interest, such as neuroscience, cosmology, and bioethics. The fact is, however, that these initiatives have little or no impact on the clerical establishment of the Vatican and give the semblance rather than the reality of genuine peer-group interchange.

The true test of the health of the intellectual life of the Catholic Church ultimately depends on the creativity of its theologians, philosophers, historians, and Scripture scholars. Creativity in these fields depends on the exchange of views, academic freedom within and across disciplines, and the capacity to explore Catholic tradition in the light of new knowledge and developments in society.

For some years now it has been well known that scholars of excellence specializing in bioethics, sexual ethics, and ethics of the family are reluctant to take up posts officially linked to the Holy See, or controlled by Catholic bishops. An outstanding example was the decision of one of the world's leading experts on sexual morality, the Jesuit Father John Mahoney, who departed into business ethics, taking up the chair in the subject at King's College, London. And despite the highly publicized Vatican-sponsored international science conferences, there is scant work in progress applying philosophy to neuroscience, cosmology, and genetics, and there is virtually no activity in any key areas where philosophy of religion should engage science. In the year in which I started this book many Catholic scholars I spoke to reported a heightened sense of anxiety and guardedness. Much of that apprehension was occasioned by increased oppression from the Vatican.

Not that there is a lack of intellectual activity in the interests of promoting Vatican orthodoxy. In Rome, the Legionaries of Christ and Opus Dei have been granted pontifical university status for their two seminaries. In many seminaries and Catholic universities around the world, divisions have been widening between conservative students and liberal professors and between conservative professors and liberal professors. A student at the Gregorian University told me that he was the only candidate to offer a paper on the documents of Vatican II. "Everybody," he said, "is running scared."

Inquisition

The Catholic Church has a long history of persecuting its dissidents: under John Paul II's papacy the Vatican has protested its sorrow for the worst of its behavior in the past. But does that regret carry a firm purpose of amendment?

At a glittering Vatican reception attended by cardinals, bishops, and historians on January 22, 1998, Cardinal Joseph Ratzinger proclaimed the opening of the files of the Roman Inquisition, the last of the great persecutions in a 600-year-long campaign against heresy. The significance of this event requires understanding against the background of the historical realities.

The Catholic inquisitions in their entirety killed hundreds of thousands of dissident Catholics, heretics, and alleged witches (some scholars talk of more than a million). Starting in France in the thirteenth century, the inquisitions were a network of courts authorized by the popes to investigate those who had been accused of heresy. Some of these antiheresy courts were permanent features of the great cathedral cities of Europe; others traveled through the countryside setting up temporarily in monasteries and convents. Unorthodox belief was seen as a threat to the integrity of the Church's authority, the source of which resided with the Pope in Rome. The inquisitors were priests who did not scruple to use torture to extort confessions. The violence and executions did not come to an end until the last victim was hanged in Valencia in 1826.

Those who had made a "full confession" of heresy were often—as an act of mercy—strangled before burning; those who refused to confess were burned alive. The act of execution was turned over to the secular arm of the law lest the priesthood stain itself with bloodshed. Giordano Bruno, the Dominican philosopher, was burned alive in Rome's Campo di Fiori in 1600 for refusing to deny that God existed in nature. Galileo, one of the great founders of modern science, was placed under house arrest for nine years in 1633 for asserting that the earth went around the sun. To avoid the stake he renounced what he knew to be the truth. It took the Catholic Church almost 300 years to apologize for Galileo's sentence. Pope John Paul II made an official statement of amends in 1992.

At the glittering self-congratulatory reception for the opening of the Roman archive in 1998, Cardinal Achille Silvestrini declared that the opportunity to study the documents was an "act of self-cleansing." But Cardinal Ratzinger was already on record, in Spain of all places, declaring that the Inquisition "was not as dark as is thought." In fact, "it fought against fanaticism," he said, and its methods were "much more humane" than is generally supposed. That may have been true, up to a point, of the stories told by these newly opened Roman files, which date only from the sixteenth century and which are by no means representative of the history of the earlier persecutions, especially the notorious Spanish Inquisition. The files now available to bona fide scholars in the Vatican give a milder and hence altogether distorted picture of the wider history, with the consequent danger that the Inquisition narrative will be retold for future generations of the faithful around this new material.

I saw them in the bowels of the offices of the Congregation for the Doctrine of the Faith under the guidance of Monsignor Alejandro Cifres Gimenez, the archivist in charge. They slumber on the shelves, squat and overfed, thousands upon thousands of fat, wormy vellum files, disappearing into the vaulted distance of the Vatican basements. In all, there are 4,500 surviving documents. A batch of 225 documents contains "Letters of the Inquisitors," including anonymous tittle-tattle on alleged heretics. Another batch covers the proceedings of the Siena Court of Inquisition, in-

volving allegations against Jews. Yet another fifty volumes deal
with inquisitional crimes in northern Italy, practices such as
usury (lending money at interest), sodomy, witchcraft, and superstition. A later section, of enormous interest for the modern historian, contains documents relating to the Index of Forbidden
Books. Banned books included the works of Voltaire and Balzac,
who attacked the Catholic Church; in more recent times, it included the works of such self-professed atheists as Jean-Paul
Sartre, Simone de Beauvoir, Alberto Moravia, and André Gide, all
banned to Catholics under pain of mortal sin. The Index was not
abolished until 1966.

But scholars would not be allowed to view material relating to
the twentieth-century intellectual persecutions stored within the
same archive. "Nothing can be seen that is dated after 1903,"
Monsignor Gimenez told me. While all other modern Vatican
archival sources are open up to 1922, the 1903 cutoff date therefore excludes scrutiny of the persecution known as the anti-
Modernist campaign, which started in 1904 during the papacy of
Pius X and continued up to the beginning of the First World War.
Its victims were not threatened with the thumbscrews and the
rack, but the psychological and human suffering was no less real
and degrading. Its methods involved anonymous reports known
as "delations" and trials without knowledge of the accuser or the
competence of the judge; its sanctions included dismissal from
teaching posts, instructions not to write, the pulping of books,
even excommunication.

The Modernist crisis and the manner in which it was quashed
is important for it reveals the extent to which John Paul II and
Cardinal Ratzinger, in their attempts to hold the doctrinal line,
have restored a repressive intellectual climate which prevailed at
the beginning of the century. The Pope in St. Peter's chair during the first decade of the twentieth century was Giuseppe Sarto,
Pius X. The son of a postman and a seamstress, Sarto initiated
what some Catholic scholars have called a "Black Terror." Deeply
pious, he loathed intellectual independence within the Church. He

was convinced that he had a divine mission to eliminate what he termed the "poison" of Modernism, by which he meant attempts to reconcile Catholic beliefs with science, democracy, and a proper account of history. Modernism, which was a term of abuse thought up by its Vatican opponents, had an earlier parallel, "Americanism," a term leveled at clerics in the United States who had hinted at establishing democratic principles within the Church. The tendency had been stamped on by Leo XIII in the previous papacy.

To silence the Modernists, Pius X established a worldwide spy and propaganda network. It was directed by a Vatican monsignor called Umberto Benigni. A former journalist and editor, Benigni, used the most up-to-date methods (stringers, telegrams, copying machines) to collect anonymous information on Catholic priests and scholars the world over. He was obsessed with secret codes and nicknames, referring to Pius X in his cables as "Mamma."

At Benigni's suggestion Pius X insisted that Catholic ordinands must take an anti-Modernist oath. This involved assent to all papal teaching, both as to content and as to the "sense" in which the Vatican meant that content to be understood. Such internal assent went beyond anything dreamed up even by Stalin or the worst imaginings of George Orwell. The oath survives to this day in a new but similarly encompassing formula taken by Catholic ordinands, seminary teachers, and Catholic university theologians. The anti-Modernist campaign and all its espionage apparatus was dismantled in 1914 when a wiser Pope, Benedict XV, was elected. But the pernicious result of Pius X's campaign was the shackling of free and imaginative Catholic thinking, discussion, and writing for the next fifty years.

Pietro Gasparri, who was Secretary of State in the Vatican from 1914 to 1930, condemned Pius X when he was called to give evidence in the process to canonize him. "Pope Pius X," Gasparri told the tribunal, "approved, blessed, and encouraged a secret espionage association outside and above the hierarchy, which spied on members of the hierarchy itself, even on their Eminences the

Cardinals; in short, he approved, blessed, and encouraged a sort of Freemasonry in the Church, something unheard of in ecclesiastical history."

After the Second World War, during a period of intellectual aridity, a number of Catholic thinkers attempted to break out of the constraints imposed by Pius X. Known as the New Theology, the movement was mainly composed of French theologians and philosophers of religion. They were eager to place a new emphasis on Catholicism as a social religion, stressing the communitarian and historical aspects of the sacraments and the institutional Church. Pius XII saw this as a threat. In an encyclical entitled *Humani Generis* he declared that once the Pope has pronounced on a topic of faith or morals, all discussion must end, even among competent theologians. New thinking was quashed, the perpetrators—including Chenu, Feret, Congar, de Lubac, Teilhard de Chardin—fired from teaching posts and removed from influence. Yves Congar was ordered to leave France altogether. He was exiled to Jerusalem and then to Cambridge in England. He was forbidden to publish or to speak in public, a punishment he accepted without demur.

Many of these humiliated scholars, whose mission had always been the rediscovery of the true tradition of an undivided Church, had a key influence at the Second Vatican Council, when the decree forbidding discussion of nondogmatic papal teaching was lifted. There followed a period of pluralist creativity in the intellectual life of the Church. But it was short-lived. Under Paul VI, and even more so under John Paul II, the constraints were once again imposed. As he traveled the world, John Paul preached religious freedom and human rights, but within the house of Catholicism he was a narrow authoritarian. The roll call of the suppressed, dismissed, and disciplined theologians, missionaries, and pastors includes some of the most loyal and distinguished servants of the Church. The late Bernard Häring, a moral theologian who was persecuted by the Nazis during the war, and persecuted again by the Vatican for his dissident views on contraception, summed up the pain of the Vatican's contemporary inquisition. "I would prefer Hitler's courts to another papal interrogation. Hitler's trials were certainly more dangerous, but they were not an offence to my honour."

As we have seen, in 1978 the Dutch theologian Edward Schillebeeckx was humiliated and interrogated in Rome for daring to emphasize the humanity of Christ in a scholarly work. The same year, Hans Küng was forbidden to call himself a Catholic theologian because he had raised questions about the scope of papal infallibility. In 1984 Father Leonardo Boff, an exponent of liberation theology in Brazil, was disciplined and later left the priesthood.

Meanwhile, the Vatican was attempting to combat the widespread rejection of the Church's teachings on contraception. Again, as we have seen, the priest and university professor Charles Curran challenged the official teaching on homosexuality, premarital sex, and divorce. Although his nuanced proposals were hardly at variance with Church doctrine, he was forbidden in 1986 to teach at Catholic University. Not long after, the Vatican decreed that all Catholic theologians would have to take an oath swearing their orthodoxy.

In 1993, in his encyclical letter entitled *Veritatis Splendor (Splendor of the Truth)*, John Paul delivered a sermon on the need to abandon relativism and return to absolute truths. The principal thrust of the encyclical was to reiterate papal condemnation of contraception as being in all circumstances wrong. But the message was also evidently about papal primacy and infallibility. As Father Bernard Häring commented: "It is directed, above all, towards one goal: to endorse total assent and submission to all utterances of the Pope."

In May 1994 came the announcement declaring that the Church has no authority to confer priestly ordination on women, and that this judgment was to be held definitively by all the Church's faithful. It spelled trouble for Lavinia Byrne and anybody else who had spoken in favor of women's ordination; but more important it was a crushing blow for the creative freedom of

Catholic theology. It was not so much the women's ordination issue itself that was significant, but the exercise of naked power over the intellectuals and scholars of the Church. Some theologians at first appeared stunned. Bernard Häring suggested that theologians would benefit from "purifying their arguments," adding that "good theology must be watchful against false and dangerous arguments, whether for or against the ordination of women."

A week later Father Francis Sullivan SJ, who had for many years taught the finer points of the magisterium to seminarians at the Gregorian University, informed the readers of *The Tablet* on June 18 that in his view it seemed "at least doubtful" that the Pope's statement was a very weighty one, but it certainly did not constitute an infallible pronouncement.

On November 18, however, Cardinal Ratzinger's Congregation for the Doctrine of the Faith (CDF) issued a statement making it clear that the Pope's teaching on women's ordination "pertained to the deposit of faith" and that it had been "infallibly taught in the ordinary and universal teaching authority." This was telling theologians that they were to shut up once and for all on the issue or face the consequences. Sullivan, who was by now at Boston College in the United States, was not so easily cowed. Known the world over for his book *Magisterium*, he published a new book entitled *Creative Fidelity* in which he undertook to explore yet again the fine shades of authority in papal documents. The volume contained a concluding chapter on the allegedly infallible status of the pronouncement on women priests. The challenge it constituted to the authority of the Pope and the Vatican was devastating. In years to come it will be mulled over and quoted if and when a future Pope decides to overturn the "irreformable" decision of John Paul II on women's ordination. It is the stuff of which schisms are made because it seeks to challenge attempts by popes, or the Vatican, to make up new doctrine as they go along.

Sullivan pointed out that technically the CDF could not claim infallibility for the Pope's pronouncement against women priests unless it could be shown that all the Catholic bishops in the world were in agreement with it: "Unless this is manifestly the case, I do not see how it can be certain that this doctrine has been taught infallibly." Referring back to the dogma of infallibility, dated 1870, Sullivan went on to ask whether the doctrine on women agreed with "the consensus of Catholic theologians," and indeed the "common adherence of Christ's faithful." These two further conditions, according to the First Vatican Council, were essential for an irreformable dogma. Those conditions, according to Sullivan, were not fulfilled.

"One thing, at least, is certain," Sullivan wrote finally. "The statement of the CDF to this effect is not infallible, because, even though published with papal approval, it remains a statement of the Congregation, to which the Pope cannot communicate his prerogative of infallibility."

The split between Jesuit and Vatican experts on the magisterium had only just begun. Meanwhile, the Vatican curbs on theologians were to become more frequent and harsh. In January 1997 a mild-mannered Sri Lankan theologian, Father Tissa Balasuriya, was excommunicated for refusing to disown the alleged heteredoxy contained in his book about the Virgin Mary. Defending Balasuriya, Hans Küng said, "This is really a new step. It means he cannot even participate in the Eucharist as a layperson. It is just horrible." Balasuriya has since been allowed back into communion with the Church after making a qualified assent to papal teaching.

In July 1998 another prominent Catholic priest came under Vatican interdiction. Father Paul Collins is a well-known Australian author and broadcaster. His book *Papal Power*, published in 1997, challenged the current ideology of papal authority as unhistorical. Collins was asked to assent publicly to a number of papal teachings on authority or risk being told that he could no longer write or broadcast. "What they do," he told me in an interview, "is push people into a corner, make them lose their sense of confidence, silence them, separate them from their friends and support systems. Marginalize them."

Collins responded by giving his case maximum publicity. A combative polemicist and former religious editor of the Australian Broadcasting Corporation, Collins refused to engage in private assent to anonymous Vatican judges whom he considers "not even fourth-rate theologians." He immediately set up a worldwide website chat room to expose the persecution of those threatened by Rome. Collins, in consequence, has been left alone.

Religious Pluralism and Orthodoxy

Not so another Jesuit, Father Jacques Dupuis, who in 1997 published a book entitled *Toward a Christian Theology of Religious Pluralism*. Dupuis, who was also of the Gregorian University, and a former colleague of Francis Sullivan, had been working on a theological basis for respect for other religions for several years, until he was disciplined by Ratzinger's Congregation for the Doctrine of the Faith and subjected to a series of cross-examinations and humiliations, including the withdrawal of his right to teach in his own university where he holds a chair.

Religious pluralism has been a controversial and divisive issue in the Catholic Church since the Second Vatican Council and is becoming more so with every passing year. How does the Church profess itself to be the one true Church, and yet respect other religions? Young Catholics who live in pluralist societies and cultures, who have grown up respecting the values and beliefs of others within democratically framed laws, find it right and indeed natural to respect the status of other religions. It is difficult if not impossible for them to proclaim what the official Church appears to be saying: that all other religions, except the Catholic faith, are "gravely deficient." Looking around the world, moreover—at Northern Ireland, the Middle East, North Africa, and in many parts of Asia—it is all too obvious that when intransigent religious attitudes clash or confront each other, violence is all too often the consequence.

The question as to whether the Catholic Church is the only means to salvation is an ancient and vexed one. One might be forgiven for thinking that the Church in recent times has wanted it both ways. In 1953 an American Jesuit priest called Father Leonard Feeney was excommunicated for refusing to withdraw his accusation that Pius XII was a heretic for suggesting that salvation could be achieved outside of the Catholic faith. Feeney had ransacked Church councils and papal documents and settled for the clear statement of the Fourth Lateran Council of 1215 which declared that there is indeed one universal Church of the faithful, "outside which no one at all is saved." Under Pius XII, however, the Vatican seemed to reject this view by making a distinction between those who really belong to the Church by faith and baptism and those who belong to it by a form of unconscious "desire" (*in voto*). But does this mean that other religions can be regarded as parallel means to salvation alongside Christianity? Certainly not. No Pope could afford to go softly on the issue of this level of pluralism without inviting accusations of heresy. And yet the path currently taken by the Vatican seems set to create more divisions than it heals.

Pluralist, multicultural societies are a fact, and Catholics have to live in such societies by according more than mere tolerance for the convictions of their fellow citizens. After all, Catholics expect the same respect of others. Moreover, how can the world avoid destroying itself if its religionists cannot find a way of living together in harmony?

Vatican II had stated in the document *Nostra Aetate* that "the Catholic Church rejects nothing which is true and holy in these religions. She has a sincere respect for those ways of acting and living, those moral and doctrinal teachings which may differ in many respects from what she holds and teaches, but which none the less often reflect the brightness of that Truth, which is the light of all men."

Since then, the Pontifical Council for Interreligious Dialogue in the Vatican has worked on ways of promoting understanding between Christianity and other faiths, and John Paul II has taken some notable initiatives. In 1986 he invited representatives of the world's religions to pray with him at Assisi, a gesture that drew criticism from some Catholic conservatives. In 1991 he again appealed for respect for other religions in his encyclical on the Church's missionary role, *Redemptoris Missio*. But the words and gestures of the past forty years have tended to be mere rhetoric without a deeper philosophical and theological underpinning of religious pluralism.

There have been various attempts to work out a modus vivendi if not an outright solution, both within Catholicism and outside it. Philosophers of religion like W. T. Stace in his *Mysticism and Philosophy* have argued that all religions meet at a high apophatic, wordless point of mysticism that he calls "the One, or the Universal Self." The British theologian John Hick seeks a kind of common denominator God, a theistic layer cake containing elements of God as understood in all the main world religions. But Christian theologians rightly object that theirs is a Trinitarian God, a God that essentially expresses the truths of creation and salvation, and which is profoundly distinct from that of the God of Israel, or of Islam, or the Gods of the Hindus, or Buddhism. All the same, brave attempts have been made by Catholic theologians to find a basis for genuine respect.

Vatican II had insisted on a new pastoral attitude not only toward other Christian denominations, but non-Christian religions as well. One of the leading theologians in the world at the time, the German Jesuit Father Karl Rahner, had been working for some years, as we have seen, on a concept he called the "anonymous Christian." His argument is that any person whose free response to his world includes an act of loving surrender to the "world's Absolute Horizon" makes an act of faith worthy of salvation. By this definition, a Christian might arrive at commitment to the Trinitarian God by means other than the Catholic faith. On this basis, according to him, it was possible to accord respect to the followers of other religions by virtue of the fact that they were in some way subconsciously Christian (a similar rationale, less worked out, had been proposed by Pius XII in his *Mystici Corporis* of 1943).

A major problem with Rahner's idea is that use of the term "anonymous Christian" has been taken to be unacceptably patronizing by most non-Christian religionists who pondered its merits. In fact, its semblance to a kind of religious cultural imperialism made it a nonstarter in religious pluralism forums.

Father Jacques Dupuis's more recent offering in *Toward a Christian Theology of Religious Pluralism*—a book described as "masterly" by Cardinal Franz König, and as "major contribution to present-day interreligious dialogue" by Gerald O'Collins SJ, the professor of Fundamental Theology at the Gregorian University in Rome—takes an altogether more humble approach, that is, a humbling of the Catholic position. He proposes that the fullness of truth is not revealed until the end of the world. So while not denying the uniqueness of Christian revelation he suggests that other religions are traveling, like us, toward that fullness, and we are all united in the humility of our ignorance of full knowledge. He is not saying that all religions are equal, or that the Catholic Church is not the one, true faith, but he is certainly saying that Catholics, like other religions, do not yet enjoy the fullness and completion of revelation. The final vision of God is yet to come. Dupuis and his colleagues insist that theirs is the orthodox view. "It is at our peril," writes O'Collins, "that we fail to follow the lead of John and Paul and acknowledge that in one, very significant, sense we do not yet have the fullness or completion of the divine revelation."

But this has proved most unsatisfactory to Cardinal Ratzinger and the Pope. In fact, it led to the temporary suspension of Father Dupuis's right to teach and a series of hostile cross-examinations in Ratzinger's Vatican offices. At one point, Dupuis was actually accused of asking erroneous questions. When Dupuis learned that the congregation was questioning his theology he was so upset that he had to spend two weeks in hospital.

Then came the public rebuttal. On January 28, 2000, Pope John Paul read out a statement in the presence of Cardinal Ratzinger on a special occasion to celebrate the work of the Congregation for the Doctrine of the Faith. The Revelation of Jesus Christ, he said, is "definitive and complete." Then he went on to insist that all other faiths are deficient compared to "those who have the fullness of the salvic means in the Church." Members of the Jesuit staff at the Gregorian responded by alerting religious journalists to the fact that the Pope's statement was "rank heresy," that it had been written out for the Holy Father by Cardinal Ratzinger's department as part of a campaign to quash the views of Father Dupuis.

The next volley in the unseemly disagreement was a resounding "declaration," dated August 6, and entitled *Dominus Jesus*. It was signed by Cardinal Joseph Ratzinger, but shortly afterward publicly endorsed by the Pope. The subject was the error involved in relativistic theories which seek to justify religious pluralism, but the target was evidently Father Dupuis. The pluralist error is spelled out:

> relativistic attitudes toward truth itself, according to which what is true for some would not be true for others; the radical opposition posited between the logical mentality of the West and the symbolic mentality of the East; the subjectivism which, by regarding reason as the only source of knowledge, becomes incapable of raising its "gaze to the heights, not daring to rise to the truth of being."

At the same time, Ratzinger was making it clear that Christian churches deemed not to be apostolic by having "preserved the valid Episcopate and the genuine and integral substance of the Eucharistic mystery" are not churches in the proper sense. Since Ratzinger had argued often enough that Catholic teaching on the invalidity of Anglican ordination is de facto infallible, this would mean that Anglicanism and Episcopalianism were not churches.

The storm that broke over *Dominus Jesus* was extraordinary, and it was different from most recent reactions to tough doctrinal statements. A Catholic pastor in New York commented to me during the height of the resulting polemic: "This is a Vatican statement that has made ordinary parishioners furious. A lot of the arguments, in their view, involve academics. But *Dominus Jesus* seems to them to insult people they love and with whom they work every day of their lives. They won't put up with it."

That, of course, was just one liberal reaction, and no doubt true of the good Father's parish. It was abundantly clear, however, that it certainly sparked a mainly grassroots protest in a number a Western countries, indicating that the Vatican was running the risk of anger and ridicule. The *National Catholic Reporter* excelled itself in its October 13, 2000, edition by carrying four pages of letters on the topic. There were, to be sure, two letters in support of the declaration, of which this, from a priest, was the most determined:

> Having read *Dominus Jesus*, I wholeheartedly agree with Cardinal Joseph Ratzinger that the "theology of religious pluralism" needs to be nipped in the bud. This new ideology of religious tolerance, begun in 1950, has created a growing confusion in the minds of not only the gullible laity, but also the intelligentsia in theological circles.

No doubt a conservative paper could have rallied many more letters in favor of the declaration, but the rest of the letters in the *National Catholic Reporter* expressed an angst and frustration indicative of what I take to be the pluralist majority of America.

> Such political posturing in a cyber-knit world implies that the Roman church is rushing headlong into the fourteenth century.

> Sounds to me like Jesus is a little more tactful, hopeful and loving than *Dominus Jesus*.

Do dogmatic statements and hierarchical orders help us to love God more and to work passionately to relieve the world's pain? Let us get real!

Cardinal Ratzinger should remove himself from the dense walls that surround him and find out what is going on in our universe.

I am embarrassed and ashamed to have Ratzinger speak for me or the whole church. If "we are the church" it is time to take control of our church in the name of Jesus Christ.

Just when you think ecumenism is making some progress, the Vatican hits you with *Dominus Jesus*. This work is an attempt on the part of Vatican traditionalists to tie up everything in the Church with orthodox ribbons. It is aimed at intimidating those theologians working in interreligious dialogue. Theologians, don't be intimidated. Go on doing what you have been doing. The Catholic laity is behind you. Don't let triumphalism triumph.

This was all very well, but did the authors of these affecting reactions fully understand the genuine anxiety of the men who saw a terrifying gap opening up between orthodox Christianity and "pluralist" notions, especially in Asia, where Ratzinger had pondered despairingly on the spread of what he called a "negative theology"?

The Case of Father Tissa Balasuriya

In the first week of January 1997 the Vatican announced to the world that it had excommunicated the seventy-two-year-old Sri Lankan priest Father Tissa Balasuriya for heresy. This was the first excommunication in the Church for heresy since Father Feeney's brush with the Vatican on the issue of "no salvation outside the Church" in 1953.

Father Balasuriya, who belongs to the order known as Oblates of Mary, had failed to sign a profession of faith which had been drawn up in response to "errors" he had expressed in a book titled *Mary and Human Liberation*. An excommunication can be incurred by failure to make a profession of faith on demand, which Father Balasuriya had done on December 7, 1996. In the Code of Canon Law, it is stated that heresy, deserving excommunication, is "the obstinate post-baptismal denial of some truth which must be believed with divine and Catholic faith, or likewise an obstinate doubt concerning the same."

In his book, Father Balasuriya tells the reader that the divinity of Christ and the inspiration of the Bible are only to be found in Church teaching, "they are not necessarily directly from Jesus." He also expresses doubts about the virginity of Mary: "Due to a desire to affirm a certain perspective of holiness, there has been a trend to attribute perfect and perpetual virginity to Mary even when the scriptural evidence itself is of doubtful import."

He finds original sin open to question "as propounded in traditional theology," and doubts whether "baptism was essential for salvation and the spiritual life." What is more, he argues that the traditional doctrine of original sin is a stumbling block for the people of Asia. "In our countries this idea of human beings born alienated from the creator would seem an abominable concept of the divine. To believe that whole generations of entire continents lived and died with a lesser chance of salvation is repugnant to the notion of a just and loving God." Elsewhere, he states that there is no reason why women should not be priests, and that the doctrine of the Immaculate Conception and the Assumption of Mary deprives her of her human motherhood, thus distancing her from "situations similar to those found by millions of mothers and children even today."

In its statement of Father Balasuriya's errors, the Vatican notes his denial of original sin and all the basic Marian dogmas, and in summary takes him to task for his denial of the Church's doctrinal authority: "Father Balasuriya, in fact, deprives the dogmatic doctrine concerning the Blessed Virgin of every revealed character, thus denying the authority of tradition as a mediation of revealed truth."

Given that Father Balasuriya has worked as a priest all his life in a country where only 8 percent of the population is Catholic (70 percent are Buddhist, 15 percent Hindu, and 7 percent Muslim), the Vatican's interdict on him seems astonishing. What terrible writing did Ratzinger see on the wall in his case? What kind of domino effect did he suspect would occur?

Balasuriya's challenge to the Church is serious. His radical theology arises from a conviction that the Church has condoned colonialism and by its stress on original sin, and personal salvation, has failed to understand the evils that arise from socioeconomic and political structures. The orthodox image of Mary, he believes, is a creation of male-dominant power holders who seek to emphasize her acquiescence and obedience, making her an unacceptable role model for women. She has become a "comforter of the disturbed" instead of a "disturber of the comfortable." But his errors go well beyond the tenets of liberation theology familiar in Latin America. Balasuriya believes that original sin is "offensive to other beliefs." If Christianity is going to survive in Asia, he insists, it must start to communicate with other religions and explain its doctrine of salvation in language and concepts that are not abhorrent to its peoples. "The oriental view of history is more cyclical than linear," he argues. "In Hinduism and Buddhism, this life is only one stage in a vast cycle of birth, death, and re-birth. The cycle continues until all reach ultimate liberation in Nirvana, or Moksha. In the Christian view, this life determines one's ultimate and eternal destiny."

What is curious about the case of Balasuriya is how close his account of Jesus is to that of so many catechetical textbooks (such as the ones used in the series titled Weaving the Web) used in the 1980s and 1990s in Catholic classrooms in the West. The Vatican note focused particularly on the allegation that he had relativized Christological dogma. He had presented Jesus as one showing a path to deliverance from sin and union with God, that he was "one of the greatest spiritual leaders of humanity," but whose divine sonship is never explicitly recognized and whose salvic function is only doubtfully acknowledged. So if this sort of relativized account is already so current in North America and Europe, why pick on an elderly priest in Sri Lanka, an evidently holy man dedicated to the poor in a country where Catholicism is so tiny a minority as to hardly count?

The answer evidently lies on the margins of the anxieties that give Vatican officials sleepless nights: how pluralism slips so easily into relativism. Father Balasuriya may live in a country with scant Catholics, but he is a Third World theologian at a time when the numbers of Catholics on continents stretching from South America to Asia now account for 70 percent of the world's Catholics. In Asia, where so many of the world's religions live side by side, priests like Balasuriya are caught up in social action in defense of the poor and the disadvantaged, as well as in missionary work to spread the word of the Gospel. He believes that this can only be done by aligning the Gospel messages with the cultural pluralism in which he lives and works. But he is an outspoken promulgator of his views, who takes the bother to write and to publish. What are the far-reaching consequences of allowing such "relativism" to thrive and prosper? In the view of the Vatican, just one charismatic, turbulent priest could act like a brushfire in a parched summer.

Was the Vatican right to curb Father Balasuriya's errors? Undoubtedly. But the manner in which he was disciplined may well be remembered long after the shock of his errors evaporates in the general spread of similar relativizations. And it may well do more harm to the Catholic Church than the perceived error. *The Tablet's* editorial tells it from the point of view of a progressive Catholic editorialist:

The heart of the unease which many Catholics will feel lies in the CDF procedures . . . there has been no trial about the facts, no open investigation of them, no discussion of doctrinal points with Fr. Balasuriya, indeed a refusal by the CDF to be drawn into that. What sort of justice is this, which finds a man guilty before he has had a chance to prove his innocence, and denies him his freedom and rights? Where is the due process of law? Without that process, there is tyranny.

Strong, brutal word—tyranny. And here the case of Balasuriya unites with those of Byrne and Dupuis, demonstrating that a separation of love from authority is far more destructive in the long run than the perceived threats to doctrinal orthodoxy.

CHAPTER 14

THE SCIENCE AND POLITICS OF SAINTS

Of all the elements in the making of saints, proof of miracles is the one which most intrigues, perhaps even outrages, the secular mind. It is also the subject of one of the few real debates among the saint-makers.

—Kenneth L. Woodward, *Making Saints*

BY MY BED I keep a relic of Saint Thérèse of Lisieux. It is contained in a reliquary made of metal and glass, with a circumference the size of a ten-cent piece. I owned a similar relic of Thérèse as boy, given to me by a good lady of the parish when I entered the junior seminary. It was a tiny piece of cloth that had touched a preserved piece of bone of the saint. There was a legend: *"Je veux passer mon ciel à faire du bien sur la terre"* [I want to spend my heaven doing good on earth]. I lost that first relic as a result of carelessness, and I obtained the new one from the medieval convent of Santa Lucia in Via Selci in Rome near the Colosseum.

This religious house is the center for the official repository of relics for the Catholic Church, and it is the only place in the world where Catholics may acquire relics that carry an official Vatican stamp of authenticity. Here in 1988 I ordered my relic of Saint Thérèse, patron saint of priests, one of the great exemplars of holiness for the late nineteenth century. It cost 3,000 lira, for the reliquary rather than the relic itself, the sale of which is banned as "simony." On the day of my visit I engaged in some banter with the nun in charge, a pleasant Filipino woman: I had asked her whether she had a feather from the wing of Saint Michael the

Archangel, or a piece of the Virgin Mary's veil, and she took it in good part. The relic of Saint Thérèse arrived at my home in England two months later.

I have ambivalent feelings about the story and personality of Saint Thérèse. As a boy seminarian I was inspired by tales of her courage in small, routine matters of religious life in the provincial convent where she lived her few short years as a nun (she died aged twenty-four). For example, it nowadays makes me cringe to read accounts of how she endured the rattle of a neighboring nun's rosary beads rather than quelling the sound with a sharp look. When I was a boy, it was different. With few opportunities for heroic sanctity in an enclosed community, pious seminarians found such trifles edifying. When I got to know her work better, however, I realized that she represented a heroism of a different kind: an awe-inspiring faith in the face of overwhelming doubt.

> You might imagine [she wrote to her sister] that my soul was as full of consolations as it could hold: that for me, the veil which hides the unseen scarcely existed. And all the time it isn't just a veil, it's a great wall which reaches up to the sky and blots out the stars! No, when I write poems about the happiness of heaven and the eternal possession of God, it strikes no chord of happiness in my own heart—I'm simply talking about what I'd determined to believe. Sometimes, it's true, a tiny ray of light pierces through the darkness, and then, just for a moment, the ordeal is over; but immediately afterwards the memory of it brings me no happiness, it seems to make the darkness thicker than ever.

She looked into the abyss of nihilism, and despite overwhelming doubt, she chose to believe.

A saint, in the view of the Catholic Church, is an individual who is in Heaven, who merits public veneration, and before whom we can place our prayers in confidence that his or her saintly intercession will find favor in the sight of God. There are two levels of sanctity: those pronounced blessed or beatified (worthy of a local following) and those pronounced saints (worthy of a universal following). An individual for whom a cult seeks beatification or sainthood is known as "a servant of God." One who is in the final stages of being raised to blessed is known as a Venerable.

Saints or blesseds are also exemplary. They provide the faithful with examples of how God wishes us to behave: not always a clear notion since some in the past have behaved in a distinctly odd fashion, such as Saint Simeon Stylites, who sat naked for twenty years on top of a pillar sixty feet high; or the aerodynamic Joseph of Cupertino (patron saint of pilots), who used to fly up to church rafters when in ecstasy; or Saint Margaret Mary Alacoque, who would routinely eat cheese to make herself vomit.

John Paul's saint-making has raised individuals and groups of individuals to beatification and sainthood in a way that supposedly reveals Heaven's endorsement of some highly contentious trends on earth. I do not mean by this to say that he is in error, but I simply draw attention to decisions that have political implications for the secular mind. He has proclaimed the holiness, for example, of large numbers of priests and nuns who were killed in the Spanish Civil War; he has beatified the founder of the controversial Spanish group known as Opus Dei, and he has proclaimed the sanctity of Pius IX, the Pope who presided over the dogmatic decrees on papal primacy and papal infallibility in 1870.

But John Paul's enthusiasm for saint-making has been paralleled by a marked lack of enthusiasm for saints among the faithful in north Europe. A senior Vatican official I spoke to recently makes a sweeping observation that he shares, so he tells me, with the Pope: "North European Catholics don't believe in sainthood or miracles in the way they used to. So they don't pray to candidates for sainthood to produce those miracles essential for making more saints." An example of this in Britain, I was assured by my informant, is Cardinal John Henry Newman, the nineteenth-century convert from Anglicanism. The Pope, he told me, has frequently grumbled: "I would like to beatify Cardinal Newman, but he won't do a miracle." And the reason he won't, so the Pope believes, is that Catholics in England aren't praying for one. By the logic of and prevailing official belief in the operation of the supernatural with regard to sainthood, it could be, however, that God will not grant a miracle in Newman's case because the esteemed Cardinal is not, after all, a saint.

The Pope was referring to the rule that beatification and sainthood require the proven miraculous intercession of the candidate. In other words, Vatican officials in the Congregation for the Causes of Saints must find authentic miracles that demonstrate God's approval of the saint, and they must be able to prove that a member of the faithful prayed to that individual and no other for the miraculous performance. Hence we must add to culture, politics, imagination, and divine intervention the perspective of science and medicine in this important activity of official Catholicism.

The Miracle Police

Not long ago, in a parlorlike office in a building overlooking St. Peter's Square in Rome, five senior Italian professors of medicine sat around a table discussing an astonishing physical phenomenon. In 1990, twenty-year-old Jose Branaga Silva of Mexico City jumped headfirst from a fourth-story window onto concrete pavement. As he sailed through the air his mother invoked a candidate for sainthood—Juan Diego, who died 500 years ago. Juan Diego is famous in Hispanic America, for he was the man on whose *tilda* (traditional Amerindian robe) appeared the image of the Virgin now world famous as Our Lady of Guadalupe, or Our Lady of the Americas. Our Lady of Guadalupe is a crucial sociopolitical icon of Catholic Hispanic America: her image outside Mexico City is protected by a bombproof shield.

Silva, as it happened, survived the traumatic landing unharmed. Was this a miracle prompted by his mother's invocation?

Huge red clothbound volumes were handed around the table containing details of the jumper's bowel movements, blood tests, temperature charts, X rays, PET scans (to assess brain damage). The doctors were to decide whether the event defied explanation according to the current laws of medical science. Landing from a height of thirty-six feet with a weight calculated by experts to be the equivalent of 2,000 kgs, his head should have exploded like a ripe melon. Apart from a little grazing, he was completely unharmed. Rushed to the nearest hospital, the young man was pronounced fit and sent home.

The potential miracle, even by the standards of the Vatican medical panel, was unusual: not so much a healing as an extraordinary anomaly in the physics of falling bodies. But it was the only miracle on offer for a pressing candidacy for sainthood in which the Pope had taken an urgent personal interest, and the doctors must scrutinize what they are given. After two hours' deliberation, the professors unanimously gave their official approval, declaring the event *inexplicabile quoad modum*—inexplicable as to how it occurred. The "miracle" was eventually forwarded to a body of theologians and cardinals in support of the claimed sainthood of the sixteenth-century Mexican hermit Juan Diego, on whom Silva's mother called at the precise moment when her boy leaped from the window.

The medical experts had been drawn from a body known as Consulta Medica, seventy specialists who can be called upon to sit in judgment on miracle claims for sainthood. The process of miracle scrutiny does not come cheap. The Congregation for the Causes of Saints spends many hundreds of thousands of dollars of the faithful's money each year, a single process costing up to $700,000 spread over twenty years or so. The torrent of paperwork supporting miracle claims—all those X rays and bowel charts—means that panel members must sacrifice many weekends of their year. They see it, however, as a great privilege. Panel members receive cash from the Vatican, about $400 stuffed into an envelope for each session attended.

In 1998 I interviewed a veteran miracle panelist, Professor Francesco de Rosa, a consultant in internal medicine at the University of Rome's medical school. De Rosa told me that the panelists never speak of miracles during their meetings. "We are simply there," he told me, "to confirm, or deny, that an event is explicable." The underlying theology, as de Rosa puts it, is that God intervenes on request in a direct and specific way to alter the laws of nature so as to show divine approval of the saintly candidacy. Anything that smacks of natural explanation—autosuggestion, hypnosis, psychology (the explicable)—invalidates the miracle potential.

Examples of potential miracles scrutinized by de Rosa in recent years include: a child in southern India whose stunted legs suddenly elongated and grew "normal"; a patient in the United States with a wrist burned to the bone, whose flesh was restored untreated within a day; a nun from northern Italy with inoperable and untreated stomach cancer, whose tumor disappeared in weeks; a young man from Naples who was instantly cured of fatal leukemia without treatment.

All four passed the test. But 99 out of 100 alleged miracles set before the specialists fail to make the grade, de Rosa said. Which puts a strain on the system, for John Paul's papacy has been avid for saints. There are about 11,000 saints in the records of the Church, 10,000 of whom were the subject of established cults before the formal process for saint-making began at the end of the Middle Ages. John Paul had created almost a thousand blesseds and saints by the turn of the millennium. Wherever he travels he likes to beatify and canonize, demonstrating that the Church in its holiness is coextensive with every language and culture. To make more saints faster, he has altered the rules, halving the number of miracles necessary to prove sainthood from two to one. But he will not relent on the "inexplicability" test of the supporting miracles, even though some of his advisers have suggested new criteria that could create more miracles and even more saints.

But how did the Vatican's Congregation for the Causes of Saints know for sure that it was through the posthumous agency of Juan Diego that young Silva was saved? How can even a Catholic believer be so certain that it wasn't through the miraculous intervention of some other saint, or the Virgin Mary, or Jesus? The answer, given by officials, is that Silva's mother had declared under oath that at the very moment her son leaped from the window she uttered a silent prayer to Juan Diego. Had any other saint or candidate for sainthood been invoked at the same time the entire cause would have been thrown out. The invocation problem, however, is not always so easily resolved. With many causes competing, and most of them nowadays enjoying worldwide websites, it is difficult to avoid multiple invocations.

And yet, the future of saint-making is far from happy. The Vatican is finding it increasingly difficult to enlist Catholic doctors and scientists to cooperate in the scrutiny of miracles, because many believe that involvement in the process could damage their careers. At the same time, many holy people with public cults do not get beatified or canonized because the miracle criterion is too tough. In other words, scrupulous medical scientists find it more difficult to state that unexplained cures are literally inexplicable.

I have spoken to officials belonging to religious orders who are involved in the saint-making process (that is, as opposed to Vatican officials) who would like to see a wider variety of responses to prayer accepted as miracles, such as the healing of a broken marriage, cures for alcoholism, and conversions. The appeal for a softer, more inclusive approach to miracles (a wider interpretation of "inexplicability") exposes a split in the politics of saint-making and in Catholic culture at the highest levels in Rome.

The decision to initiate the procedure to make a saint is never taken lightly in the Vatican, and saintly candidacy does not make it onto the fast track without the Pope's personal intervention. John Paul's decision to beatify victims of the Spanish Civil War (which his predecessor, Paul VI, refused to do, not wishing to favor Franco's memory) was as politically loaded as his decision not to sanction the beatification of the left-wing Archbishop Oscar Romero, murdered by a rightist militia assassin while saying Mass in San Salvador in March 1980. Not since Thomas à Becket (the twelfth-century Archbishop of Canterbury) was murdered on the orders of Henry II has there been a comparable case of obvious martyrdom; but the Pope, ever wary of left-wing clerics, especially the ones in South America, remains unenthusiastic about Oscar Romero's potential for sainthood, while honoring him as a brave priest.

The beatification in 1971 of Maximilian Kolbe, who died in a Polish concentration camp in 1941, attracted controversy because of allegations that he had been guilty of anti-Semitism as a journalist before the war. And the beatification in May 1987 of the Dutch Carmelite nun Edith Stein, also killed in a concentration camp, angered Jews, who believe that she died not for her faith but because she was of Jewish origin.

The speedy beatification of Josemaria Escrivá de Balaguer (the founder of Opus Dei) faced fierce opposition from liberals who saw his elevation to blessed as a triumph of traditionalism over reform. He died in 1975 and was beatified in May 1992, whereas processes for beatification normally start only after a candidate has been dead fifty years. Critics of the Opus Dei founder have argued that beatifying him was a significant act of papal approval for the movement and the Church's future direction. These observations do not indicate a dislike, or any criticism whatsoever on my part, of Opus Dei, which, I believe, plays an increasingly important role in traditionalist forms of spirituality in a pluralist Church. But the passions aroused by de Balaguer's beatification are a foretaste of the emotions that a Pope, warm to Opus Dei, would unleash within the Church.

Internal Church politics apart, however, the process of saint-making exposes tensions between science and religion, between the supernatural and scientific explanations, that are set to polarize the Church in years to come. As science continues to penetrate the secrets of the human mind and body, simple explanations, for example, as to why some people get cancer and others do not, recede. Medical scientists are increasingly convinced that sudden remissions of cancer are a result of the baffling complexity of the body's immune system. But they are no closer to precise explanations as to how that system works than they are to a single cure for cancer.

At the same time, philosophers of science argue that all explanations are subject to decay and falsification. How many scientific theories held 100 years ago are still deemed to be valid? They call it the "pessimistic reduction" of scientific theory. And in the case of profound metaphysical questions—the "why" and "ought" as opposed to the "how" questions—explanations are even more elusive. Peter Lipton, professor of the Philosophy of Science at Cambridge University and author of *Inference to the Best Explanation,* speaks of the "infinite why regress": "Once you start asking the large metaphysical questions, it's like a small child finding devastating new questions, one after the other: a process that's unending until mom perhaps loses her cool and ends the infinite regress with an explosion!" In other words, even if one arrives at what seems a feasible explanation, there is always a further explanation to be sought.

I raised these philosophical scruples with Professor de Rosa, the miracle scrutineer, in Rome. In his view, "inexplicability" is a purely practical consideration in the realm of medical science. "As soon as a case comes before us," he says, "I do a Medline search, a worldwide Internet survey of the latest articles on the specific disease or trauma, to establish the prognosis, potential treatment, citations of remission. If the cure clearly defies the explanations of current medical science, and there is no history of remission, then we deem it inexplicable. When the case raises more questions than it answers, we ask for more information."

The professor goes on to describe four other necessary criteria: "It must be a serious problem, obviously," he says, "not something trivial. And we have to be satisfied that effective treatment has not been applied. We have to be convinced that the cure is sudden, or at least a matter of a few days or weeks rather than months or years. Finally, we have to know that the cure is permanent: that there has been no relapse."

Visiting the Congregation for the Causes of Saints, I viewed the cases of thirty or so miracles. Did any of them strike me as ultimately inexplicable? To this layperson, they all appeared unusual, and in some cases, yes, even inexplicable in the general, imprecise way in which the word is commonly employed. But I constantly encountered a problem that dogged all my inquiries among the "miracle police." When I pleaded with de Rosa to show me tangible proof of the "before" and the "after," he retreated behind a fence of confidentiality.

While a canonization or beatification process is still in progress, all the evidence is strictly secret. Evidence relating to cases already through the process, on the other hand, has disappeared into the bottomless archives of the Vatican, or been irretrievably returned to some remote hospital. In a great many completed cases, moreover, the miracles happened so many years ago that the patient and the medical attendants are long dead. So the empirical evidence for each miracle might well have been plentiful and impressive to the Vatican panels, but it remains tantalizingly inaccessible to the contemporary outside investigator.

An example of this was the file I was shown on the case of Joseph Pennaparampil, a six-year-old child in the diocese of Kerala in India. Joseph was born in 1954 with both legs and feet deformed and stunted, a condition judged by local specialists to be permanent. In May 1961 his mother prayed to a candidate for sainthood called Cyril Chavara, dead about ninety years. Within weeks, both legs and feet had allegedly became normal, and the child could walk and run. What could be more decisively miraculous than a case of "no legs—legs"? I pursued this case for several weeks with the assistance of the bluff and friendly Monsignor

Michele di Ruberto, a Vatican official who oversees every bureaucratic aspect of the medical scrutiny of miracles.

"Yes," he told me, "*certo*, it would surely be possible to see the pictures—before and after—of the child, and even the X rays." But as I continued over the days and weeks to ask for this documentation, he repeatedly found reasons for not producing it.

I am not for one moment suggesting that the Vatican is in the business of manufacturing evidence; but all too frequently I found a gap between the claims and the evidence.

One such miracle claim describes a curious journey from Vatican City to a quiet monastery in the Leicestershire countryside in England, to a small township near Onitsha in Nigeria and back to Rome. The file is that of a twentieth-century priest, Father Cyprian Michael Tansi, who was beatified by the Pope on his visit to Nigeria in March 1998. This act of beatification, performed before several hundred thousand of the faithful in a temperature of 104°F, gave notoriety to the miracle that supported Tansi's candidacy. The miracle, as I was first told about it in the Vatican and by many other enthusiastic supporters of Tansi's cult, involved, as they put it, the sudden disappearance of a "large cancerous tumor" in the abdomen of a nineteen-year-old woman called Filomena Omeka.

Born in Nigeria in 1903, Tansi was ordained in 1937 and worked as a pastor in the region of Onitsha, a market town in the southeast of the country. In 1950, on a pilgrimage to Rome, Tansi felt called to become a monk and later settled at the Trappist monastery of Mount Saint Bernard, near Coalville in Leicestershire (the very monastery which rebuked my wife for complaining about the ostracizing of the lay congregation). He died in Leicester Royal Infirmary of an aneurysm in January 1964.

It was a Nigerian Bishop, Francis Arinze, now a highly placed Cardinal in the Vatican, considered a potential Pope, who started the process of sainting Tansi in 1974. The procedure involved the collection of thousands of pages of documents and recorded interviews with those who knew Tansi in Africa and in Leicestershire.

It also involved digging up his remains and transporting them back to Nigeria, where his body is now an important relic.

And now for the miracle. On October 17, 1986, during a Mass at Holy Trinity Church, Onitsha, Filomena Omeka accidentally touched Tansi's coffin, and felt her "tumor sliding away." Almost immediately, her mobility and appetite were restored and she made a rapid return to full health. The story, which continues to be narrated anecdotally, and in Catholic pamphlets on the case, is a continuing tale of wonder. Doctors of all kinds pronounced her inexplicably cured of cancer.

Eventually, after much pestering, I was given access to the entire miracle documentation, including ultrasound reports and biopsies. Sure enough, she had been suffering through the 1980s from an invasive growth, but according to Dr. J. Ojuku, consultant surgeon at the University of Nigeria Teaching Hospital in Enugu, an examination of her abdomen later revealed only "a small solid cystic mass in the retroperitoneal area, 2.5 cm × 2.5 cm." But, far from being within days or weeks of the alleged miracle, the examination took place nearly two and half years later, on January 27, 1989. What is more, the documentation made it clear that Omeka was not suffering from cancer but from retroperitoneal fibrosis—a benign tumor without the fatal outcome of malignant growths.

On June 14, 1995, the miracle medical panel, including de Rosa and three other professors, unanimously declared: "a sudden clinical regression with reduction almost total of the growth. The cure is lasting and inexplicable as to the manner in which it happened." Nowhere has the panel claimed that a malignancy had been cured. Nevertheless, they gave the green light to the pronouncement of a miracle.

The disappearance of Omeka's benign growth, which had clearly caused much discomfort, was, of course, an unusual event, particularly when one takes the cure in conjunction with the coincidence of Omeka coming in contact with Tansi's coffin. But the event is less inexplicable, less miraculous, in the light of the details of the diagnosis and the gap in time between the supposed moment of the miracle and a competent specialist's examination.

The story of the disappearance of Omeka's tumor and its link to beatification in Nigeria tells us much about official Catholicism's cultural productions, and I do not use that term pejoratively. John Paul and the orthodox officials who surround him give weighty credence to the view that God intervenes in direct ways in human affairs; hence the insistence on "inexplicability." At the same time, the notion that science can be pressed into service to make definitive statements about phenomena that defy explanation borders on absurdity. The miracle process involves a hybrid of appropriation (the notion that one can do deals with God, by requesting miracles that can be tested by contemporary science), literalism, and supernaturalism.

For a growing number of Catholics, the scientific scrutiny of ultrasound charts and X rays is an inappropriate way to judge matters of religious faith. A sea change in Catholic attitudes seems set to challenge these appeals to scientific scrutiny in support of the miraculous. But an alteration in the rules is unlikely to occur without a battle.

An example of a more inclusive appeal for saintly status is to be seen in the case of the Blessed Rupert Mayer, a Jesuit persecuted by the Nazis, who died in 1945. For years there were as many as 8,000 visitors to Mayer's tomb in Munich every day of the week. The Vatican, according to a Jesuit involved in the cause for Mayer's sainthood, received up to 30,000 letters a year from the faithful with reports of remarkable alterations in their lives after visiting his shrine: the jobless finding work, the depressed and suicidal returning to psychological health, broken marriages reconciled. But not one of these blessings could count as evidence for his canonization. The Jesuits have been pressing the Vatican to alter its policy to admit these moral and spiritual "miracles." The trouble is, what they are asking runs counter to the Pope's conviction that God performs scientifically verifiable miracles as a result of invocation as palpable proof for sainthood. The Pope, according to insiders, does not want to lose the idea that God intervenes directly, tangibly, and, subject to proof, in answer to prayer. So there matters stay.

The culture that sets store by controlling the supernatural is undoubtedly authoritarian in spirit. Whether it is truly Catholic is less certain. A more "inclusive" Pope is likely to throw out the current process, dismantling the medical panel and embracing the notion of moral and spiritual miracles that appeal to religious imagination rather than exercises of divine power and "proof." A more Catholic, egregiously imaginative notion of miracles would be closer to the significance of miracles in the Gospels which exemplify the story of Christian redemption rather than pseudoscience masquerading as religious power. A more inclusive view of the meaning of miracles and sainthood might accept that it is more difficult to change human hearts than for tumors to disappear.

Fatima and the Third Secret

Two beatifications, very close to the heart of John Paul II, occurred during the great Jubilee Year of 2000. On May 13, Feast of Our Lady of Fatima, he declared the Portuguese peasant children Francisco Marto and his sister Jacinta blessed. They had been dead eighty years. Together with the still surviving seer, Sister Lucia dos Santos, they had witnessed a series of apparitions of the Virgin at Fatima in Portugal between May 13, 1917, and October 13, 1917. The apparitions had included apocalyptic visions of Hell, intimations of terrible wars, and a solar phenomenon in which the sun spun and changed color, reportedly witnessed by 10,000 people. A crucial feature of the Fatima messages, which Sister Lucia continued to deliver to the Pope until 1940, was the warning that unless people prayed to Mary and turned to God, communism would spread its errors, and there would be global chastisements. The chastisements were linked with three secrets. The first two were associated with the prophecy of the end of the First World War, and the second with the coming of the Second World War. The third secret—due to be opened in 1960—was associated with the advent of a Third World War more terrible than the previous two.

The Fatima cult and its anniversary, May 13, became especially significant for John Paul, for on that day in 1981 he was shot down in St. Peter's Square by the Turkish terrorist Mehmet Ali Agca. A year later he placed the bullet that nearly killed him in the crown of the Virgin's statue at the shrine of Fatima. He told the faithful that one hand guided the gun, but it was another hand, "a motherly hand," which guided the bullet millimeters away from vital blood vessels, and so halted him "at the threshold of death."

John Paul's long-held conviction about the interventionist role of the Virgin Mary in the history of the world thus became evident to him in a personal, revelatory way. She had intervened to save his life that day in St. Peter's Square. He gives the impression that he is inclined to believe that he was saved for a divine purpose.

John Paul was soon to be instrumental in prompting a powerful mediation between earth and Heaven by recourse to a rite that had been suggested by Mary to the child seers at Fatima. In 1940 Sister Lucia wrote to Pius XII requesting him, as the Virgin had commanded, to consecrate the Soviet Union to the Immaculate Heart of Mary. Pacelli left it until December 8, 1942, to respond to the Virgin's request, although not strictly to the letter. Gathering forty cardinals around him in St. Peter's Basilica, he consecrated not the USSR but the whole world to the Immaculate Heart of Mary (the fact that he had not carried out the Virgin's instructions to the letter was later deemed by Fatima devotees a reason for the expanding power of the Soviet Union during the Cold War). Later, in 1944, Sister Lucia entrusted to Pius XII the famous Third Secret of Fatima, rumored to contain the date of the Third World War, and to be opened by the reigning Pope in 1960.

Pius XII nourished a keen devotion to the Fatima cult. He

claimed that he had witnessed the spinning of the sun associated with the visions in the Vatican gardens, although his accompanying chauffeur had seen nothing. He kept the unopened third secret in a locked cabinet in his office, but died in October 1958 before the due time for its publication.

John XXIII, Pius XII's successor, read the third secret but decided—for reasons best known to himself—not to publish it. While he was as devoted as any Catholic to the Virgin Mary, he was influential in pruning Mariolatrous excesses. Vatican II advocated the generous fostering of the cult of the Blessed Virgin, but recommended a middle way between indifference and exaggeration (*Lumen Gentium*). Paul VI, like John, also decided not to publish the third secret; while he acknowledged the cult of Fatima and visited the shrine, he appeared to treat the surviving seer, Lucia, with a certain coolness.

It was left to John Paul, in the aftermath of the attempt against his life, to fulfill to the letter the Virgin's request, which he did on March 25, 1984. This time he dedicated the world, but also, specifically and separately, the Soviet Union, to the Immaculate Heart of Mary, a circumstance that was to be remembered by devotees of Fatima when the Soviet Union and Soviet communism collapsed at the end of the decade. But there was more to come: revelations that would unite John Paul in a unique way to Fatima and its secrets.

Devotion to Mary shaped the youthful Polish piety of John Paul II. He has been responsible for encouraging a robust renewal of enthusiasm for her cult. His motto *"Totus Tuus,"* "All Yours," is in homage to the obedience and acquiescence of the Virgin to God's will. It is an abbreviation of the formula of consecration found in the writings of Saint Louis-Marie Grignion de Montfort: "I am totally yours and all that I possess is yours. I accept you in all that is mine. Give me your heart, O Mary." John Paul rejected the notion, widespread among some progressives, that Vatican II sanctioned a retreat from old-style Marian veneration. What is more, he pondered in his heart a special, apocalyptic place for Mary. In a series of homilies preached before Paul VI when he was still a Cardinal, John Paul spoke of the Second Coming of Christ and of the Virgin Mary, "clothed with the sun." He referred to her as the "Second Eve" and accorded her a special role in foiling Satan in a Second Fall of man which he believed would be taking place in our times. In a key encyclical, *Redemptoris Mater (Mother of the Redeemer,* 1987), he spoke of her apparitions across the world as if she were making a pilgrimage through time and space toward the Second Coming. It is known that he favors the controversial shrine of Medjugorje in Yugoslavia where the Virgin allegedly appeared to six young people almost every day for several years during the last two decades of the twentieth century.

More recently, however, John Paul, backed by his closest theological and diplomatic Vatican officials, has endowed the Fatima cult with the highest approval, and put himself personally and individually at the center of its supposed prophecies. So extraordinary is this personal involvement that it raises crucial questions about the dominant spirituality and theology of the final years of this papacy.

In the minds of most of the popes of the twentieth century, Fatima was associated with the growth and fate of communism. It was, as Eamon Duffy puts it, "a focus of the fierce anxieties and atavisms of the religious and political Right." It was a rallying call for the fascistic regimes of Salazar and Franco; during the Cold War period many thought that the mysterious "third secret" predicted nuclear war, the avoidance of which depended on Marian intercession.

The Fatima cult became inextricably associated with the exercise of centralized papal authority, the lonely pontifical figure defending Holy Mother Church from the pinnacle. Ever since Pius IX defined, without mention of episcopal approbation, the dogma of the Immaculate Conception of the Blessed Virgin Mary in 1854, there has been a close link in the minds of modern popes and the faithful between Marian apparitions and papal authority.

Cults surrounding new Marian apparitions grew in outreach with the coming of modern travel and communications. Marian shrines became a focus for global cults as modern pilgrims traveled in their hundreds of thousands, and eventually their millions, to new sites of veneration. But a cult only became "official" when the Pope gave his assent, as with Lourdes and Fatima. Hence there was an indissoluble link between Mary's alleged appearances and the papal power that either endorsed or rejected them. Few could have guessed that John Paul II not only would endow Fatima with the seal of highest approval but place himself personally at the center of the cult's prophecies.

On the Feast of Our Lady of Fatima, 2000, as the two seers were beatified, Cardinal Sodano, Secretary of State, formally revealed the "third secret" of Fatima to a congregation of a million pilgrims. He told the world that it contained "a prophetic vision" similar to those found in Scripture. It concerned the war waged by atheist systems against the Church and Christians. It related to the "immense suffering endured by witnesses to the faith in the last century of the second millennium." In part of the vision, he said, "a bishop, clothed in white, makes his way with great effort towards the Cross amid the corpses of martyred bishops, priests, men and women religious and many lay people. He, too, falls to the ground, apparently dead under a burst of gunfire." The "bishop in white" of the third secret, according to a later clarification by Cardinal Ratzinger, refers to the attempt on John Paul's life in 1981, and to his providential survival.

What does this tale tell us? These apparitions, secrets, apocalyptic chastisements, and a "martyred" Pope saved quite literally from a death-dealing bullet by the Mother of God herself? It smacks quite emphatically of making public revelation of private revelation. According to strict theological orthodoxy, "public" revelation, meaning those truths revealed to the inspired writers of the New Testament, had a definitive completion date. That date, by common consent of all Christian theologians, was the death of the last Apostle. There was no new revelation to come, which means that revelations to individuals (be they popes or peasants) through apparitions of Christ, or the Virgin, or the saints, or other supernatural avenues, are purely "private." That is to say, their purpose is to confirm the faith or spirituality of the individual involved or to confirm for the wider faithful what is already the subject of "public" revelation.

By suggesting that the prophetic and visionary nature of the third secret was parallel to Scripture, Cardinal Sodano came perilously close to blurring the distinction between private and public revelation. And while, theologically speaking, it is not incumbent on Catholics to actually believe in private revelation, the fact that the Pope, his Secretary of State, and the head of the Congregation of the Doctrine of the Faith dignified the apparitions and the secrets by beatifying the two deceased seers, indicates that this is what the Pope and the official Church believes and would have the rest of us believe.

Quite apart from the lurid visions of Hell, which Catholics on the whole have rejected from our iconography, the Fatima phenomenon tells a story that is at odds with the transformed attitudes and understandings that followed Vatican II. Fatima tells the world that what happens in human history does not depend on communitarian and societal action and responsibility but upon miraculous interventions mediated by Mary and endorsed by the papacy. Conflict and war, the rise and fall of ideologies and regimes (it is noticeable that the scourge of communism, but not Nazism, is singled out by the Virgin), are a direct result of the neglect of Marian devotion. Avoidance of these dire eventualities will be achieved by Mary's intercession, but that intercession is dependent on the prayers of the faithful, and finally, it must have the papal seal of approval.

Witnessing as a young man in Poland the devastation and genocide of the Second World War, John Paul spent much of his life pondering the nature of evil. As he entered middle age, he was increasingly convinced that the world's wickedness was beyond human responsibility and understanding. "The evil which exists in the world," he said in a sermon, "seems to be greater than ever, much greater than the evil for which each of us feels personally responsible." Such sentiments indicated his profound belief, even before he became Pope, in the otherworldly conflict between the powers of darkness and the powers of light. And while there is no suggestion that he is a strict body-soul dualist, there are strong indications here of classical gnosticism: the notion that what happens in this world is dependent on mighty struggles beyond the veil of appearances, and that the frustration of the power of evil depends on forms of appeasement or intercession.

The high-level approval of this form of gnosticism and Manichaeism bestows legitimacy on those segments of Catholicism (sample one of the many Fatima websites to get a taste) which advocate Marian intercession as the answer to the "apostasy and chaos" which currently beset the Church. Even more worrying for the relationship between the papacy and the faithful is the idea that the third secret is about John Paul personally. The underlying significance of the tale it tells, in consequence, is that the Virgin Mary took time out of eternity to tell the world that John Paul is to be regarded a quasi-martyr of the twentieth century. His virtual martyrdom, moreover, as with all the others in the vision, is a direct result of the consequences of "atheism" (so much for the post–Vatican II efforts to grant nonbelievers respect), and he enjoys the spiritual honor that accrues to martyrdom even before death. But there is something else. The fact that he has been spared from the assassin's bullet indicates that he has a divinely ordained mission to fulfill; that his personal survival is sustained by extraordinary, miraculous providence; that the nonstop flow of interventions, instructions, meditations, rebukes, and exhortations drowning out all the other voices in the Church carry a special seal of divine endorsement. In my view the third secret sees the apotheosis of the papal narcissism and egotism of a Pope who has gone beyond the fatal twenty years after which, in the words of John Henry Newman, popes become deranged and dangerous. "It is not good for a Pope to live twenty years," wrote Newman. "It is anomaly and bears no good fruit; he becomes a god, has no one to contradict him, does not know facts, and does cruel things without meaning it."

Following the revelation of the bizarre personal apotheosis suggested in the third secret, a large segment of the Catholic world fell mysteriously quiet. For the progressives it was the silence of sheer shock and alarm. The cult of Fatima is a peculiar cultural product, promoted and sustained by the modern media, and hence more akin to an ideology than a devotion, especially in view of its association with anticommunism. Most progressive Catholic theologians I have spoken to on the issue feel that there is little point in making a fuss. But the writer of the following letter to *The Tablet* was not alone in wondering whether the third secret was not a harbinger of things to come:

> Cardinal Sodano announced that the Congregation for the Doctrine of the Faith had been set the task of preparing a commentary on [the announcement of the third secret] so that the faithful might better understand it. That seems to come close to equating the secret with the status of a gospel text. Secondly, he proceeded to identify the figure "clothed in white" who is gunned down as Pope John Paul II, thus elevating what can never be more than mere interpretation to the status of a fact.
>
> In so doing he is by implication proclaiming the validity of the other "secrets" of Fatima. One of these, we are told, was a vision of hell, an experience which, it is said, the seven- , nine- and ten-year-old visionaries could never forget, so raw in its savagery was the imagery.
>
> Buttressed by such implicit approval, what is to prevent those already dissatisfied by the weak brew of Religious Education programmes from updating the slides of hell I was shown as a teenager, with all the technological expertise available today.

CHAPTER 15

HIERARCHY

Without the support of a strong papacy the Christian hierarchy would have long ago degenerated into a feudal, semi-clerical, semi-secular caste, endowed with hereditary benefices and more and more a slave to civil authority.

—John Henry Newman

ENTERING THE VAST BASILICA of St. Peter's in Rome one is drawn inexorably to the space beneath the dome and the site of the tomb of Saint Peter. Pilgrims over many centuries journeyed to the Eternal City, not so much to see the Pope as to pray at the site of the buried relics of the first Apostle. But every born Catholic, from childhood, knows that the Holy Father inherits the guarantee made to Peter, the first Apostle. It is etched around the perimeter of the dome, in huge letters: TU ES PETRUS ET SUPER HANC PETRAM AEDIFICABO ECCLESIAM MEAM (Thou art Peter and upon this rock I will build my Church).

The office of Pope is to watch over the Church "like a sentinel," as John Paul II has put it, so that the voice of truth can be heard throughout Christendom. His task is to serve the interests of unity and to admonish individuals or groups of individuals who are sacrificing the common good of the Church to their own interests.

Arguments about papal power and authority have raged down the centuries. A constant focus of disagreement has been the rival claims of those who believe that the great councils, composed of all the bishops, take precedence over the Pope's authority, and those who argue the reverse. More recently the precise terms in which the Pope acts as final arbiter of truth have been subjected to increasing scrutiny—not so much from outside the Church, but from within—by certain bishops, although by no means all, who insist that they share in the authority bestowed by the Petrine guarantee, no less than do priests, religious, theologians, and the laity.

The history of papal authority can be told in several different ways. The simplest version is that the Pope, as the direct successor of Saint Peter, the first Apostle, is ultimately and unquestionably in charge and that's the end of the matter. But the dogmas of papal infallibility and primacy date only from 1870. Why so late in the day? Can it be that the history is more complex than the simple version?

There is no doubt that the tradition of supreme papal authority is ancient, but the precise manner in which that authority has been exercised has developed and expanded down the ages. In the early Christian period the local churches were virtually autonomous. It was not until the beginning of the third century that the Church of Rome became, according to Eamon Duffy, an "acknowledged point of reference for Christians throughout the Mediterranean world." Even so, this meant little more, in terms of jurisdiction, than Rome's potential as an occasional court of appeal. Other bishops and their churches were engaged in teaching, exhorting, and excluding heretical communities.

Early in the second millennium, we see for the first time a Pope dominating the Western Church beyond Italy. Pope Leo IX, installed as pontiff in 1048, initiated a series of reforms to combat corruption. "In one week," writes Duffy, "Leo had asserted papal authority as it had never been asserted before. Bishops had been excommunicated and deposed, a powerful and prestigious archbishop was summoned to explain himself in Rome, and the whole system of payments for promotion within the Church had been earth-shakingly challenged." This gathering of the reins of power, principally in acts of reform, continued under Gregory VII, but not without resistance and criticism. In 1076 the German bishops at the Synod of Worms accused Gregory of abrogating the power of binding and loosing from the bishops. Harsh censure of papal power is reflected in the art of Fra Angelico, who depicts popes condemned to Hell, and Dante, who consigns such figures as Nicholas II, Boniface VIII, and Clement V to the eternal fires of his Inferno.

During the Middle Ages, despite the flourishing of a papal monarchism, the Church's authority was necessarily distributed through countless webs of local discretion in a complex "space" of interconnections reflected in the "Gothic" relatedness of medieval society. As in a medieval cathedral, there were many thrusting spires of authority. Certainly the tallest of these was the papacy, but Roman primacy for much of the period, given the difficulties of travel and communication, was as a final court of appeal rather than a constantly initiating executive.

But the early modern period saw the growth of a new kind of papal power in response to hostile pressures on many fronts. Following the Reformation, the papacy had been reluctantly readjusting to the realities of a fragmented Christendom amid the challenge of Enlightenment ideas and new ways of looking at the world. In response to the political and social changes that gathered pace in the aftermath of the French Revolution, the papacy had struggled to survive and exert an influence in a climate of antagonistic Protestantism, political revolution, and humanism. Then came the Industrial Revolution, secularism, science, industrialization, and the evolving nation-state. Modern popes were fighting on two fronts—as primates of an embattled Church and as monarchs of a tottering papal kingdom, the sovereign territories of the Papal States that dominated the midriff of Italy. Caught in a bewildering series of confrontations with the new masters of Europe, the popes found themselves attempting to protect the Church universal while defending the integrity of its collapsing temporal power.

Through the turmoil of these eras, the Church was riven internally by an issue fraught with consequences for the modern papacy. Broadly, the struggle was between those who urged an absolutist papal primacy from the Roman center and those who argued for the restoration of authority among the bishops (indeed, those who even argued for the formation of national churches independent of Rome). In time, these tensions deepened against the background of modern conflict between the Church and the world. The Catholic Church became an object of oppression in Europe through much of the nineteenth century: its property and wealth systematically plundered; religious orders and clergy deprived of their scope for action; schools confiscated by the state or shut down. The papacy itself was repeatedly humiliated and the papal territories were in constant danger of dismemberment and annexation as the forces for Italian unity and modernization gathered strength.

The triumph of the modern centralizers of Church power, or "ultramontanists" (a phrase coined in France, indicating papal power from "beyond the mountains," or the Alps), was sealed at the First Vatican Council of 1870 coinciding with the final loss of the Pope's temporal dominions. At that Council, the Pope was declared infallible in matters of faith and morals as well as the undisputed "primate" or chief—supreme spiritual and administrative head of the Church. In some respects, this definition satisfied even those who had felt it inopportune: it was, after all, a statement about the limits of infallibility and primacy as much as their amplitude.

The historic decree of papal infallibility was passed on July 18, 1870, by 433 bishops, with only two against, and read as follows:

> The Roman Pontiff, when he speaks ex cathedra, that is, when, exercising the office of pastor and teacher of all Christians, he defines . . . a doctrine concerning faith and morals to be held by the whole Church, through the divine assistance promised to him in St. Peter, is possessed of that infallibility with which the Divine Redeemer wished His Church to be endowed . . . and therefore such definitions of the Roman Pontiff are ir-

reformable of themselves, and not from the consent of the Church.

An additional decree endowed the Pope with supreme jurisdiction over his bishops, individually and collectively. The Pope, in effect, was ultimately in authority. During the hour of these great decisions, a storm broke over St. Peter's dome and a thunderclap shattered a pane of glass in the tall windows. According to *The Times* (London), while the anti-infallibilists saw in the event a portent of divine disapproval, Cardinal Henry Manning, the Archbishop of Westminster and an enthusiastic lobbyist for Pope Pius IX, the Pope of the Council, responded disdainfully: "They forgot Sinai and the Ten Commandments."

The endorsement of a radical form of papal primacy coincided with the gathering speed of modern communications and travel. The advent of telegraph wires, undersea cables, and steamship travel transformed the potential of the Petrine office—an outreach that has extended immeasurably in our era of e-mails, televisions, and jet airplanes. Rome became a center of mass modern pilgrimage, the Eternal City being now a distance of just two or three days from much of Europe. At the same time the Pope became the object of universal adulation enhanced by mass publication of colored pictures of his personage. The modern cult of the papacy, amplified by the media and modern travel, expanded in the reign of Leo XIII (1878–1903), and so did the great taboo—the inadmissibility of criticism. Loyalty to the popes of the twentieth century, whatever their shortcomings, can still unite Catholics across every divide in the Church.

Papal centrism emerged as an ideology, however, in the reign of Pope Pius X (1903–1914), when canon lawyers (under the leadership of Eugenio Pacelli, the future Pius XII, and his mentor Cardinal Secretary of State Pietro Gasparri) were instructed to codify the laws of the Church in the manner of the Napoleonic code: all the faithful, by this Code, would be equal in the eyes of Church

law. It was arguably the most important event in the history of
the Catholic Church in the twentieth century. The fruit of thirteen years' work and 2,000 scholars, the Code was published in
1917. This book of law, published in its single-volume popular
edition without historical or social context, reached every
Catholic priest in the world, crossing all cultural and language
frontiers, its timelessness and universality lending eternity to un-
ambiguous decrees concerning papal authority. According to Ulrich Stutz, a distinguished Protestant canon lawyer of the period,
the ideological significance loomed enormous for the future of the
Catholic Church. "Now that infallibility in the area of faith and
morals has been attributed to the papacy," he wrote in 1917, with
a frankness denied his Catholic counterparts, "it has completed
the work in the legal sphere and given the Church a comprehen-
sive law book that exhaustively regulates conditions within the
Church, a *unicus et authenticus fons* [a unique and authentic
source] for administration, jurisdiction, and legal instruction—
unlike anything the Church has previously possessed in its two-
thousand-year existence."

The Code described the Pope as possessing "the supreme and
most complete jurisdiction throughout the church, both in matters of faith and morals and in those that affect discipline and
Church government throughout the world." In matters of doctrinal and moral infallibility, it opened the way for suggesting that
papal encyclicals were irreformable: "It is not enough to avoid
heresy but one must also carefully shun all errors."

It is significant that the two creators of the 1917 Code of
Canon Law exerted immense influence over the Church for a period of forty-four years. Pietro Gasparri was appointed Cardinal
Secretary of State in 1914 and served until he was succeeded by
Eugenio Pacelli in 1930, who reigned as Pope from 1939 to his
death in 1958. There is no doubt that the Catholic Church
through this era enjoyed unprecedented discipline and unity: the
bishops, the clergy, religious, and the laity all appeared to march

in step to the one drumbeat of the popes. During this period, the papacy and the Church came to resemble a multinational company run by the chief executive in Rome. The role of the Pope was to teach and correct as the single voice of the Vicar of Christ on earth. His departments—the various congregations, tribunals, and offices—neither advised nor consulted with the Pontiff; they interpreted his mind and will and obeyed his explicit instructions.

As I have argued in my account of the life of Eugenio Pacelli, that growth in apparent unity and discipline came at a price. It is arguable that by drawing all authority to the center, the local churches were weakened and demoralized. By signing a concordat with Hitler in the summer of 1933, Pacelli, on behalf of Pius XI, substituted grassroots reaction to Hitler with Vatican-Berlin summitry. Hitler used the concordat to separate Catholic worship and Catholic political action in Germany. The Catholic Center Party, a pawn in the negotiations, went into voluntary liquidation. The Church, led by Pacelli and Pius XI, was seen to be dignifying and taking benefits from the regime, especially in the area of Catholic education. Meanwhile, from April 1933, the educational rights of Jews were being withdrawn—teachers dismissed and pupils and students subjected to quotas. Catholic dissidents were thus demoralized, and the fence-sitters were discouraged, while decisive signals were broadcast to Germany and the international community: the Catholic Church, at its very heart, could do business with Hitler. It is difficult not to see this as fellow-traveling, and in this instance fellow-traveling proved far more dangerous and damaging than the action of the handful of bishops who openly sympathized with the regime.

In the postwar period Pius XII emerged as a hero of the war and a resister of the Holocaust. His defenders, who included Jews, calculated that he had saved the lives of some 860,000 Jews. The fellow-traveling of the early 1930s was forgotten. The 1950s saw the apotheosis of papal power as Pacelli presided over a monolithic, triumphalist Church in antagonistic confrontation with communism both in Italy and beyond the Iron Curtain.

But it could not hold. The internal structures and morale of the Catholic Church began to show signs of fragmentation and decay in the final years of Pius XII, leading to a yearning for reassessment and renewal. The Second Vatican Council was opened in 1962 by John XXIII, who succeeded Pacelli in 1958, precisely to reject the monolithic, centralized Church model of his predecessors, in preference to a collegial, decentralized human community on the move. In the two key documents, *The Constitution on the Church* (*Lumen Gentium*) and *The Constitution on the Church in the Modern World* (*Gaudium et Spes*), there was a new emphasis on history, accessible liturgy, community, the Holy Spirit, and love. Expectations ran high, and there was no lack of contention and anxiety—old habits and disciplines died hard. In the view of those described as liberals and progressives the single most important decision for change was the call for "collegiality"—the recognition of the need for a sharing of authority between the bishops and the Pope. In their view, the long-term spirit and success of the Council depended upon this. It involved a belief in the presence of the Holy Spirit in the wider community of the Church, locally and at large, not just at the center. There were indications from the very outset that papal Vatican centrism would not acquiesce easily.

Collegiality, in the progressive view, was challenged and resisted at the Vatican power center. There is no doubt that the Holy Office (the keepers of doctrinal orthodoxy) resisted, but it has also been argued that the Council suffered from the continuing effects of the suppression of creative theology, the rigid intellectual and institutional conformism that went back to the days of Pius X. It had been unrealistic to imagine that the permafrost of sixty years could thaw in the span of a decade. The bishops and their advisers entered the Council inhibited by years of caution.

Pope John XXIII did much to prevent the Council falling into the hands of the reactionaries, but he died on June 3, 1963, and was succeeded on June 21 by Paul VI, Pacelli's former undersecretary Giovanni Battista Montini. Paul VI presided over the third and fourth sessions of the Council and was Pope in the critical postconciliar era. That period saw the growth of the tension between progressives, who believed that a profound transfer of authority had been affirmed but not applied, and the traditionalists, who were insistent that no such thing should or would occur.

The Council fathers did not dismantle the structures that underpinned the ideology of papal power. No reform of the Curia was sanctioned (the progressive wing of the Church insists that the Vatican bureaucracy actually became more powerful); there was no attempt to repeal the provisions protecting centralized power in the 1917 Code which were endorsed in the Code's 1983 revision. In the progressive view, there was a moral obligation on popes to apply collegiality, but no institutional mechanism. The popes who followed John were unwilling to let go.

Decentralizing the Church

The problem of the centralization of Church authority has not gone away. In the meantime the faithful as whole, while remaining loyal to the Pope, have grown less and less accepting of the power structure. In 1996 the Gallup organization conducted a survey which revealed that 65 percent of Catholic respondents in the U.S. said they hoped for a Pope who would permit the laity to choose their own bishops, and 78 percent supported the idea of a Pope who would choose some of his advisers from ordinary laypeople. It is not so very surprising that Catholics in the United States should seek a measure of democracy in the Church, but for such a large proportion to challenge the authority of the Pope is remarkable. In many other countries of the world, however, the proportion of Catholics questioning the authority of the Pope is even larger. In the year 2000 in Germany, for example, 85 percent of the Catholic population questioned the infallibility of the Pope and 81 percent said they did not accept the Pope's official teachings as ultimate. Nor is the challenge to the Pope restricted to the laity. Theologians, bishops, and even cardinals have expressed dissatisfaction with the highly centralized structure whereby the man in the white robe rules, doctrinally and administratively, from the loneliness of the pinnacle in a vastly unequal authority relationship.

While there have been challenges to papal and centralized authority since the twelfth century, the circumstances of papal power—aided by communications from the late nineteenth century onward—have been at an unprecedented zenith in the modern period. Critics of the papacy routinely call for reform in terms that employ not just aspirations for greater empowerment and emancipation of the faithful but nuanced doctrinal arguments that appeal to historic councils and papal documents. An example of this is the scrutiny of John Paul II's directive on the ordination of women by Professor Francis Sullivan SJ, a leading authority on the technical circumstances of infallible papal statements (as I discussed it in chapter 13, "The New Inquisition"). These sorts of critiques are not aimed at undermining the papacy, which the vast majority of Catholics wish to see survive as a symbol of unity, but in exploring the complexities of authority in a global Church of a billion souls.

Calls for a reform of the hierarchical structure of the Church have been made by senior churchmen. In a surprisingly outspoken document published in March 1999 Cardinal Franz König, emeritus primate of Austria, called on the Vatican to decentralize and to involve the world's bishops in government. The task of decentralization, he writes, is all the more urgent since the Church "is no longer Europe-centred. . . . How to govern a Church of such diversity? We must decentralise." Appealing to Vatican II, he said that the Church was "a communion of local Churches," and he described the present style of leadership in the Roman Curia as "defective."

"Because of the difficulties in Europe," he continues, "it was always a case of preserving Church unity which, almost exclusively, took precedence. Accordingly, the possibility of diversity within this unity—the necessity, indeed, for such diversity—was given little consideration." The bishops synods, he noted, were not allowed to do the job prescribed for them by Paul VI, and he went on to say that "the procedure for appointing bishops also needs to come under scrutiny, for there have been difficulties when the bishops conference concerned was not adequately consulted, or was not consulted at all."

Cardinal König was referring to the instance at Chur in Switzerland when parishioners lay down in front of the cathedral to prevent the new Vatican-appointed Bishop from entering. But he also had in mind a deep and systemic consequence of papal nomination of bishops. The ancient process of selecting bishops with a large measure of local discretion—including the local clergy and laity—once ensured diversity and a pluralist basis for selection of leadership and teaching authority.

Like all pluralist processes, the selection of bishops, and even of popes, was from time to time attended by scandal and corruption. The Conclave that followed the death of Leo XIII in 1903 saw the interference of the Emperor Franz Josef, who attempted to veto the candidacy of Cardinal Rampolla. Pius X altered the rules of the Conclave to ensure that such secular meddling would never again be repeated; Pius was also instrumental in putting a stop to lay and political interference in the nomination of French bishops. But there is widespread fear among bishops, theologians, and laypeople that under John Paul II the insistence on papal domination of the nomination process has created a monoculture of bishops. In other words, by strictly controlling the episcopal selection process he is dictating the shape of the Church for the future, leaving little latitude for corrections that might be made by the pluralist diversity of his successors.

The papal practice of nominating all bishops in the Latin Church throughout the world is surprisingly recent. As we have seen, the decree under which the Pope assumes that right dates back a little over eighty years to the 1917 Code of Canon Law. Throughout much of the Church's history, however, popes inherited the right to nominate bishops only within the Papal States and areas in the East where dioceses owed direct allegiance to the

Pope. The late Garrett Sweeney, in *Bishops and Writers,* his study on the question, has a powerful image to illustrate the effects of the regulation: "If 'The Church' is conceptualised as a single machine, with divine assistance concentrated at the top, and nothing more is required of bishops than that they should operate the machine efficiently, it is entirely appropriate that they should be appointed from Rome."

The nomination of bishops, moreover, was to have important implications for the exercise of infallible or definitive teaching by all the Catholic bishops when they teach in union with one another and the Pope. Clarified six decades later, in a revised version of the Code of Canon Law (1983), this idea of infallibility currently assumes collegial pluralism. And yet as critics of the status quo point out, collegiality is a difficult ideal to attain when the Pope selects every bishop in the college after his own views and prejudices.

That They May Be One

No one in the Catholic Church is more acutely conscious of the centrifugal forces that threaten to tear the Church apart than the Pope. It goes without saying, moreover, that popes in the modern era are not motivated by lust for power or self-aggrandizement. The role of Vicar of Christ is overwhelming in its obligations to preserve the Church from error, schism, and disintegration, as Pope Paul VI confided in this private note to himself that might have been penned by any of the popes of the twentieth century:

> I was solitary before, but now my solitariness becomes complete and awesome. Hence the dizziness, the vertigo. Like a statue on a plinth—that is how I live now. Jesus was also alone on the cross. I should not seek outside help to absolve me from my duty; my duty is too plain: decide, assume every responsibility for guiding others, even when it seems illogical and perhaps absurd. And to suffer alone. . . . Me and God. The colloquy must be full and endless.

It is a solitude that is attended, however, by certain dangers—not least the perils of increasing egotism and despotism. The longer the papacy, the more entrenched the papal consciousness.

But how necessary is this solitary superhuman effort at the Church's pinnacle in the maintenance of unity? Should not the burden be shared by all the bishops? By all the clergy and the faithful—men and women? And while the benefits of centralization are obvious, what are the dangers?

John Paul II is all too conscious of the dangers. In 1995 he issued an encyclical entitled *Ut Unum Sint* (*That They Might Be One*), which called for a discussion by all Christians to explore ways of making the papacy "more a service of love than of domination." He was inviting study and critiques on the issues of unity between the separated churches, and "collegiality"—the sense in which the Pope is member of the college of bishops. His primacy, he declared, should be exercised in a collective manner. So after reading this document, who could possibly suggest that John Paul was ignoring the call for collegiality when here he was urging it upon the Church. In this instance, however, a courageous senior American prelate, John Quinn (Archbishop of San Francisco until he retired in 1995), took the Pope at his word and in retirement produced a series of hard-hitting suggestions for reform of the papacy at a series of lectures at Campion Hall in Oxford in 1996. A less outspoken version of the lectures was published at the end of 1999 titled *The Reform of the Papacy*.

In the first place, on the issue of the papal claim of primacy over all Christians, Quinn pointed out that "in the first millennium the idea did not exist that the bishop of Rome would intervene in the affairs of other churches on a routine basis or in normal times." The comment sent a signal to those Protestant Churches that might be happy to join forces with the Roman Catholic community provided that they would not be expected to surrender their independence entirely to the Pope. It also raised questions about the sense in which the Pope could currently claim to be patriarch of all the "churches" in Western Catholicism, whether they be in North America, South America, Africa, or India.

Quinn then drew attention to two issues that had prompted criticism of the papacy from within as well as from outside. He noted that following the great Counter-Reformation council, the Council of Trent, a "grim resistance" to criticism of the papal office developed within the Catholic Church, and that by the nineteenth century a "mystique" came to "surround and engulf" the Pope. In consequence, argued the Archbishop, "there is a great reluctance on the part of many Catholics and especially bishops to say anything negative for fear of offending the reverence due to the papal office." Ramming home his message, Quinn declared: "If the Church is in need of continual reform, she is necessarily in need of continual criticism."

Quinn objects to the lack of a major role for the local churches and regional bishops conferences in choosing bishops. But his criticisms are also leveled at more recent and current structures of authority. He quarrels, for example, with the 1998 ruling that regional bishops conferences may not make binding doctrinal declarations unless they obtain a two-thirds majority and obtain approval from Rome. To tie the bishops down in this way, he believes, is a sign of distrust. He is similarly unhappy with the role of the bishops synods, special gatherings of bishops in Rome to discuss matters of major importance to the Church. At present these synods are only consultative, rather than deliberative, and Quinn asserts that the Pope sets the agenda and has invariably made up his mind on the agenda before the bishops even meet. "The synod is called by the pope; its agenda is determined by the pope; preliminary documents of episcopal conferences are not permitted to be shared with other conferences . . . the synod does not have a deliberative vote; its deliberations are secret, and its recommendations to the pope are secret; the pope writes and issues the final document after the synod has concluded and bishops have returned home."

Quinn would also like to see major changes made in the col-

lege of cardinals. He thinks the cardinals are merely a second college within the college of bishops, which should take precedence,
and that popes in future should be elected by presidents of bishops conferences together with other bishops, religious, and even
the laity.

In addition he would like to see a radical reform of the Curia,
the Vatican bureaucracy. He thinks that most issues could be handled by local authorities, as for example supervision of vernacular
translations of Scripture and the liturgy. He believes, moreover,
that to raise Vatican bureaucrats to the level of bishops is an abuse
of the sacrament of Holy Orders. "There is among members of
the Curia," he writes, "a certain proprietary sense over the
Church and, to some degree, over the pope."

Quinn's criticisms were greeted with much enthusiasm by the
liberal wing of the Church, especially as they had come from a
former head of the National Conference of Catholic Bishops in
the United States. But it did not take an "ultra-conservative" to
respond negatively. Writing in *First Things* in the summer of
2000, the distinguished Jesuit theologian Avery Dulles threw out
pretty well every proposal.

"My own impression," he wrote, "is that Rome now plays an
indispensable role in safeguarding the apostolic tradition, in
maintaining the unity of the universal church, and in keeping the
conferences and the diocesan bishops from assuming inordinate
power."

As for the Episcopal conferences being allowed to enact binding doctrinal decisions without any approval from Rome, Dulles
responds: "How could the faithful of one region or nation be
bound to believe doctrines that were not taught in the universal
Church?" He has similar reservations about Quinn's proposals
for the Synod of Bishops, which the progressives make a central
focus of their dissatisfaction on matters collegial. Dulles thinks
they should be no more than "sounding boards" because their assemblies are brief and involve only a small number of bishops. "I
cannot see," he declares, "the advantage in giving such assemblies

the power to issue laws and doctrinal determinations for the universal Church." He adds that while giving the synods more power would make them "more interesting," the result would be "to burden the Catholic people."

The cardinals, he goes on, "function as a corps of highly trusted senior prelates, whose opinions the Pope can occasionally seek out." They know, moreover, "one another's aptitudes and limitations better than do most non-cardinals." As for the appointment of bishops, Dulles sees little wrong with the current centralized system, which "acting with the advice of apostolic nuncios and with the help of confidential consultations, is able to draw on a much larger pool of candidates than would be known in the local church." In other words, those surveying the world from the Vatican pinnacle see more than those down on the plain. Local discretion in choosing bishops, he believes, "would be particularly harmful in dioceses that have a one-sided orientation." He does not by the same token entertain the possibility that centralized authority is equally capable of acting with "one-sided orientation."

In his final comments Dulles reveals the huge gap—precisely on the question of representation within the Church—between the progressive and traditional standpoints: "Quinn seems to present collegiality very much as though the college of bishops were a kind of parliament, designed to offset the dangers of papal monarchy." That indeed is what the progressives believe Vatican II was actually about. But Dulles is having none of it. His peroration, which emphasizes what he terms "the true theological conception," is worth quoting in full to understand where Catholic conservatives are coming from:

There is no conflict between primacy and collegiality. Each needs and serves the other. Nothing requires that the Pope, in exercising his primacy, be bound by the majority opinion of the bishops. He is obliged to exercise the special charisms of his office. If John XXIII had felt bound by the preponderant

views of either his Curia or the world episcopate, Vatican II
would probably not have been convened. Since Quinn relies
heavily on Vatican II, he is also indebted to the relative autonomy of the Pope.

Finally, Dulles drops his dispassionate reviewing style and allows himself a broadside familiar in many polemics across the
right-left divide. Noting that Archbishop Quinn had raised in his
Oxford lecture a shopping list of issues for review in a reformed
Church—the Catechism, contraception, priestly celibacy, ordination of women, general absolution, treatment of divorced and remarried Catholics—Dulles ends by suggesting that Quinn may
have had an ulterior motive in writing his book. The book, he
complains, is "less than forthright" compared with the Oxford
lecture. So he wonders about the "real purpose" of Quinn's proposed structural reforms. Is it "to obtain a reconsideration of such
doctrinal and disciplinary issues? Does this book contain an un-
stated agenda?"

In the January 2001 consistory Father Avery Dulles was made
a Cardinal of the Church, and John Quinn was passed over. It is
unlikely that Quinn's proposed reforms will ever be realized; but
the groundswell of opinion they represent is vast and still growing. A gracious and more generous verdict on Quinn's proposals
would have made more of the Pope's call for help and advice on
reforming the papacy in the interests of Christian unity. It is
worth recording Archbishop Quinn's response to the call in the
conclusion of his book:

> It is immensely significant that in Orthodox, Anglican, or
> Protestant dialogues about Christian unity there is no men-
> tion of abolishing the papacy as a condition for unity. There is,
> in fact, a growing realization of the true service the Petrine
> ministry offers the whole Church. . . . The combination of
> this growing openness and the Pope's prophetic call to probe
> the primacy is one of those unique moments in history. If

there is too much delay, too much diffidence, the time will pass. It is imperative not to lose this moment of grace.

Dulles's questioning of Quinn's motives reveals precisely the corrosive circumstances of the progressive-traditionalist divide, when the motives of any criticism, even when such criticism has been formally invited, are deemed suspect. Nobody, of course, has suggested for one moment that John Paul II had ulterior motives for writing *Ut Unum Sint*.

EPILOGUE

Erotic love is determined by the object; friendship is determined by the object; only love to one's neighbour is determined by love. Since one's neighbour is every man, unconditionally every man, all distinctions are indeed removed from the object.

—Søren Kierkegaard

"CATHOLICISM," as I earlier quoted historian Eamon Duffy, "is a conversation, linking continents and cultures, and reaching backward and forward in time. The luxury of sectarianism, of renouncing whatever in the conversation cannot be squared with the perspective of one's own time and place, is not an option."

Duffy's view favors neither the progressives nor the conservatives; he is pleading for unity, but as an ideal rather than an account of current reality, since instead of "conversation" we nowadays have antagonism. How can the various antagonistic factions in the Catholic Church be encouraged to cease quarreling and return to conversation?

In recent years there has been no lack of partisan recommendations for the future course of the Church. One view has it that John Paul II has already set the course; that he has spent his pontificate winnowing the pure gold of Vatican II from the subsequent liberal chaff, and that the time has now come for discipline and restoration. But calls for a return to greater centralized authority and exclusiveness from the conservatives are invariably calls for the surrender or the self-exclusion of the progressives and hence a recipe for further antagonism. But the same is true of well-meaning calls from the progressives for radical decentralization and inclusiveness. Some years ago the late Peter Hebblethwaite, one of the best-informed Vaticanologists of his day, published a book titled *In the Vatican*. In an epilogue he fantasized an ideal Pope of the future, who would renounce the Vatican and move back to the Lateran Palace, the seat of the bishops of Rome. From thence he would call a new council to organize the reform of the papacy in order to become a humble pastor presiding in charity over disagreements within the Church. I do not think that Hebblethwaite's fantasy is at all realistic. A Pope who suddenly abdicated his authority would surely precipitate a fragmentation such as the Church has not seen in its long history. Like him or hate him, given the structures of centralized power within the Church, Catholics now depend on him to keep in tension the huge forces for breakup. My argument has been, however, that these forces are so strong that they may overcome the determination and the charisma of even a second John Paul II.

So what kind of leadership, or agenda, could at least reduce the anger? What change of heart offers the best prospect for a sense of renewed love in the largest Christian community? Constructive recommendations for resolving the current crisis are thin on the ground, and most have met with intransigent hostility. The Common Ground initiative of the American bishops has borne little fruit, but over the past ten years impressive styles of alternative leadership have been in evidence and positive suggestions for new thinking. None of them alone possesses the answer to the Church's problems; taken together, however, they represent signs for hope.

Several years ago I was fortunate to spend an hour with the Cardinal Archbishop of Milan, Carlo Maria Martini, who was considered eminently *papabile* in the 1980s before he was closely identified with the progressive wing of the Church and thus unacceptable to the conservatives. Martini's words have echoed frequently in my mind while writing this book, for it was the clearest acknowledgment I have heard from a senior Church offi-

cial of the virtual impossibility of keeping the Catholic Church
together without subtle management of the complex forces at
work. He avoided pious nostrums in our conversation and focused
mainly on the realities. From the outset he revealed a distinctive
individual perspective quite remote from the simplistic liberal
image promoted by many of his supporters and his detractors.

"Looking at the conflicts from a contemporary standpoint, the
situation may appear extremely dangerous," he conceded. "My
own opinion is that these differences may be unavoidable, as we
are not all contemporaries in a biographical sense. We are in the
1990s, but some Catholics are still mentally in the 1960s and
some in the 1940s, and some even in the last century; it's inevitable that there will be clashes of mentalities." It was an interesting gloss on Eamon Duffy's view of the Church as so many
conversations between the past and future, a quiet reminder of
the importance of living squarely in the present.

I met Cardinal Martini in his palace to the rear of the Gothic
magnificence of Milan's duomo. Amid the gilded furniture and
lugubrious ecclesiastical oil paintings he sat in a baroque armchair
with the casual ease of an academic rather than a grand prelate. A
world-class biblical scholar, he was formerly rector of two great
Roman academic institutions: the Pontifical Biblical Institute and
the Gregorian University.

He was dressed in a simple black suit and Roman collar; no
pectoral cross, no scarlet sash for the normal business day. He has
a long horse-face, a well-sculpted, haughty nose, and a penetrat-
ing gaze. He speaks English rapidly but eloquently in a gutteral
accent. He was born in 1927, the only son of a bourgeois family in
the Piedmont, the northeast corner of Italy once known as Savoy.
"*Piemontesi falsi ma cortesi!*" quip Italians from the south: "People from the Piedmont are two-faced but well-mannered." His
every gesture and nuance of speech is imbued with northern
courtesy.

He started, very properly, by talking about the divisions of
opinion in his own diocese, but his remarks were clearly relevant

to the Church at large. "They can't all be right. Some are closer to the Gospel and some less so—which is the real danger. We all have the right to express our Christianity in our own way. The problem is when people exclude themselves from the body of the Church, like Archbishop Lefebvre. If that sort of case were to happen repeatedly there would be a real danger; but so long as we can at least keep quarreling peacefully together, I am not anxious."

Any lingering suspicion I might have entertained about Martini's liberalism, or indeed his reluctance to speak his own mind, was dispelled when I asked him whether, had he been Pope, he would have excommunicated Lefebvre.

"The present Pope made a lot of concessions to keep Lefebvre in the Church," said Martini. "I wasn't in favor of those concessions because I don't think Lefebvre was right. On the other hand, I'm in favor of the Pope being conciliatory because the more we can recognize people's right to different viewpoints, the more we can accept all the different traditions and spiritualities. I think variety is a healthy thing."

The comment confirmed a Catholic's right to freedom of expression, while making it clear that self-excluding "liberties" were inadmissible: a careful balancing act between inclusion and exclusion. He would encourage pluralism within the Church, but only up to a point—"they can't all be right." He would come down on heretical forces of reaction, and I assumed, by the same token, heretical forces of innovation.

And what of that other most crucial of divides: the split between official teaching and actual practice in, say, sexual morality?

Martini freewheeled for a while on styles of obedience, and, by inference, styles of authority. "Contraception is something special, to do with special points of moral teaching," he said. "There is a contrast in attitude between northern countries and Latin countries on moral questions. In Italy we believe the ideal is set high so as to attain something. In other countries they think that they must actually achieve the ideal, and they are anxious if they fail."

He had been choosing his words carefully; with reason, for he was about to declare publicly on the most difficult issue in the past century for the Catholic Church, an issue that had marginalized countless millions of the faithful. Yet he was already making a remarkable concession by referring to contraception as a "special point," a "rule" as opposed to a central "infallible" doctrine.

He elaborated. "I don't know what the development will be as regards contraception. But I believe that the Church's teaching has not been expressed so well. The fact is that the problem of contraception is relatively new; it was only really possible with new techniques in the past forty or so years. The Church on the other hand thinks very slowly, so I'm confident we will find some formula to state things better, so that the problem is better understood and more adapted to reality. I admit that there is a gap and this bothers me, but I am confident it can be overcome.

"Let me give you an example: when I was a young student in the seminary there was endless talk about the interpretation of the Bible. That's all over now: little by little we found a formula in the Second Vatican Council that avoided denying the truth of the old position, but managed to express it in an acceptable way. I am sure that the Holy Spirit will guide the Church to overcome the question of contraception as the Church has overcome other moral problems in the past. Usury [lending money at interest] was an almost insurmountable impediment in the fourteenth century, but little by little we began to see the problem in a different light, although it took centuries to resolve it."

As the arguments about contraception are all over, as far as the laity and most pastors are concerned, Martini focuses on bringing teaching in line with the realities of reception and practice. The Church needs to develop a new understanding of the problem to a point where Catholic doctrine on birth control endorses universal practice and belief, listening to the echoes from the faithful at large, but without abandoning entirely the reasons for its original objections. At the same time, the faithful in the north should realize that the Church's objections (which will persist, up to a point) are ideals rather than unyielding rules. Does this sound like a cop-out, or the employment of Jesuitical thinking to resolve a problem largely created by casuistry in the first place? Martini realizes that a solution which involves victory for its own sake—for one side or the other—spells disaster. He wants to come at the issue from a new direction so as to put the highest priority on reducing confrontation and division.

But there are other conflicts, less amenable to subtlety and new thinking. How would he deal with the call for women priests, the rallying cry for most liberals?

He was speaking before the Pope's letter, *Ordinatio Sacerdotalis*, which forbade precisely the sort of comment Martini was about to make, which in itself reveals the brutal nature of Wojtyla's initiative. Despite the constraints of official status, Martini's response revealed a blend of pragmatism, conservatism, and again, intellectual agility. "The problems, the questions raised by women's issues," he said, "should be taken seriously by both sides. Feminism has a tendency to exaggerate its message, to see everything from one point of view, and no doubt there are good reasons for this. The Church is part of society and society develops more rapidly in some sectors than in others. The Church has to develop, too, although it does so more slowly. But the real danger, as far as I see it, is from the opposite side to the pro-women faction. If the Catholic Church were to admit women priests, suddenly we could have divisions a hundred times worse than that of Lefebvre. The Pope has to be concerned with keeping this huge flock with all its different opinions together.

"As for the issue itself, I think we should come to it little by little, to gradual solutions that will satisfy not only the most progressive but the majority, while remaining true to the tradition and within the bounds of common sense. That's my opinion. But I can foresee that we'll have some decades of struggle ahead. When people ask me, and it's usually Americans: 'Will we have women priests?' I answer: 'Not in this millennium!' "

His eyes sparkled with amusement. Since our conversation was still in the twentieth century, only just, he was enjoying the implications of his wordplay.

Turning to another crucial issue that divides Catholics (and would do so with with greater feeling after the Vatican document *Dominus Jesus* in August of 2000), I asked him how he resolved the contradiction between respect for other religions and non-Catholic Christian denominations, and the conviction that only the Catholic Church possesses the fullness of truth.

"In a sense it's nothing short of a miracle, holding these opposites in balance," he said. "I would add another point: the great conquering religions—especially Christianity and Islam—used to believe that some people were saved and others were excluded. But the modern mind repudiates such a notion and this creates a problem. If you believe that every individual, whatever their religion, can achieve salvation, what motive is there to spread the Gospel? But I think that if you believe in something strongly you should want to share it with others. In a healthy, developing humanity, those who are confident in their beliefs should want to share them. If we lose this, humanity will cease to seek for truth and cease to develop. The alternative is sectarianism: being shut up and withering away."

Martini did not pretend to know how to hold "these opposites in balance," but his admission that there was a deep contradiction involved suggested that the question should be approached with care and with fresh thinking. His response to direct questions about the conflict between progressives and conservatives was similarly diplomatic. He avoided commenting on the issue in the universal Church and focused instead on the priorities within his own diocese.

"In my pastoral work," he said, "I insist on a prayerful approach to the body of Scripture to encourage a Christian mentality. I think two things—Scripture and the Eucharist—contain everything we need." He appeared to be saying that the Church's divisions stemmed from a tendency to lose oneself in the complexities of ecclesiastical politics, theology, and sexual morality; that only a return to the fundamentals of Christian worship could bring Catholics together.

Father Andrew Greeley, priest and sociologist, has similarly and for some years been advocating a Catholic regeneration through a return to the Catholic sacraments and "sacramentals." Greeley believes that what differentiates Catholicism from its separated Christian brethren, and, at the same time, makes a "unique contribution to the human condition," is the "Catholic imagination": the quest for God in Catholic ritual, Catholic images, and sacrament—visible signs and symbols of God's presence in the world. Greeley's passionate focus on sacramentals and sacraments connects with arguments for a relationship between God's real presence and the continued existence of the artistic imagination urged, for example, by George Steiner in his remarkable book *Real Presences*.

But a perspective that honors "unique contributions" requires an authentic philosophy and theology of pluralism that is not confused with relativism (the idea that one set of beliefs and values is as good, or as worthless, as any other). In this conclusion, therefore, I want to make a defense of pluralism as a profoundly Christian principle that has the power to unite both Catholic traditionalists and advocates of aggiornamento in the spirit of John XXIII.

The question is implicit, for example, in John Rawls's *A Theory of Justice*, as to whether it is preferable for goodness to prosper in society by the imposition of sets of monopoly values from above, top-down, or whether individuals or groups of individuals should be free to choose and pursue their own sets of precepts, principles, and beliefs. The choice adequately describes the difference between fundamentalist and pluralist societies, totalitarian and democratic societies. In our more or less democratic Western institutions and societies we tend to favor the latter rather than the former, and we accept, either explicitly or implicitly, that the operation of such toleration is based on universal human respect.

Recent popes, moreover, have emphasized that such freedom is central to Catholic social teaching. John XXIII, for example: "The dignity of the human person . . . requires that every person enjoy the right to act freely and responsibly. . . . Each one acts on his or her own decision . . . without being moved by the force or pressure brought to bear externally."

Apart from the difficult but not insoluble question as to how tolerant sects deal with intolerant ones in pluralist societies (the right to issue fatwas, for example), on what basis do individuals accord one another the respect that underpins such universal tolerance? The question is urgent among those political scientists who ask whether a decline in Christian belief could destroy the basis of democracy and pluralist principles in this late modern period. I want to argue here that the notion of common humanity and universal respect, which inhabits the political consciousness of Western democracies, requires a more profound underpinning than the largely discredited ideals of Enlightenment humanism, or the philosophies of ancient Greece and Rome (the sentimental values, for example, of Marcus Aurelius).

It is by now a familiar argument, although not so familiar or well endorsed among Catholics, that the basis of both political and religious pluralism is nothing other than the special love known to Christians as agape. Agape is different from friendship and erotic love in that it is universal and nonjudgmental. It is based on the notion that we are all without exception children of God, that we are all without exception created for salvation—in other words, destined toward God. This makes every human being exalted, regardless of differences and shortcomings. This makes every human being worthy of our regard and reverence, including their freely chosen values and principles.

In everyday life we are ceaselessly judged, and ceaselessly judging: it is difficult, in fact, to see how societies, families, communities, and businesses could operate without criticism, discrimination, and blame. But it is the radical imperative to love nonjudgmentally that gives agape its unique and dynamic quality, providing the ground for genuine pluralism based on universal respect. Agape is a love that transcends all our deficiencies, moral and physical, and at the same time transcends our injustices. What is more, although agape is to be found in other great world religions, and although it shares its origins in the West within the Judaic tradition, it emerges in its radical and outspoken form with the advent of Christian Scripture and the Eucharist; it is the fundamental Christian tenet: "Thou shalt love the lord thy God with all thy heart, and with all thy soul, and with all thy mind. This is the first and great commandment. And the second is like unto it, thou shalt love thy neighbor as thyself. On these two commandments hang all the law and prophets" (Matthew 22:37–40). And this at a time when Jews thought that they alone were chosen; at a time when the Greeks were convinced that the rest of the world were barbarians.

Henri de Lubac in his study on Catholicism wrote, following Irenaeus, of the "thorough newness" which Christianity represents in history:

> Christianity brought into the world something absolutely new. Its concept of salvation is not only original in relation to that of the religions that surround its birth; it constitutes a unique event in the religious history of humankind. . . . Christianity alone affirms, at once and indissolubly, a transcendent destiny of the human person and for the whole of humankind a common destiny.

We are all exalted by the act of agape, both the lover and the loved. But Christians also subscribe to the extraordinary paradox that despite our exaltedness we are each of us without exception fallen. Original sin, the deep stain in our nature, admits the difficulty of attaining the ideal of agape; original sin establishes the context in which we are forever striving to love selflessly, falling, picking ourselves up again, and falling again. How else could we explain Christian resilience in overcoming our manifest and repeated failures—the Borgias, the Inquisition, the treatment of Jews. Christians expect to fail; expect to pick themselves up and start over. Witness by contrast the catastrophic failure of man-centered projects of the last century—notably fascism and Marxism-Leninism—cast into the dustbin of history along with their hubristic man-centered idealisms.

The God-centeredness of Christianity contrasts in a perfect negative image with the man-God centeredness of Nietzsche's denial of agape. Nietzsche's vision of humankind is based on a devastating rejection, of respect for every individual without exception, a repudiation of universal exaltedness. If Christian love is quenched, Nietzsche believed, then so is the destructive moral authority it exerts within society and culture. Only Christian agape, in his view, inhibited the rise of an exclusive and superior human being.

The Catholic Church has been slow over the past one and a half centuries to trust and rejoice in the political fruits of Christian agape, which are surely no different from its religious fruits. From Pius IX to Pius XI the popes distrusted democracy, and Pius XII came to it only grudgingly in reaction to the Communist threat inside Italy and the greater Communist threat across the Adriatic Sea. Under John XXIII the spirit of agape flourished anew, and the Church was filled for a time with the spirit of its pluralistic outreach. Under John Paul II, however, for all his verbal insistence on freedom of conscience, freedom of religion, we have witnessed the repeated conflation of relativism and pluralism, familiar among the great modern Piuses, and the erection of the anti-Modernist bogey of "indifferentism"—one religion as good or as bad as any other.

The powerful voices at the center of the Church, and those who endorse them at the periphery, distrust and reject the spirit of pluralism, believing that it represents apostasy, dilution, disobedience, secularism, rejection of authentic authority, the coming of a new Dark Age. The response to what many conservatives see as mass apostasy is closure, to draw in and retreat from the world; to create an exclusive and ever more hierarchical, male-oriented, centralized Church based on fear and mistrust. John Paul II throughout his long reign has repeatedly spoken the language of "agape" and of "hope," but his articulation of love has been invariably abstract and ratiocinative: he does not trust the faithful; he does not see providence in their difficulties and doubts; and his optimism has all too often been overshadowed by the apocalyptic darkness of the cult of Fatima.

It may well be, as Cardinal Martini has suggested, that the Church will need a Third Vatican Council, or at least a gathering of all the world's bishops, to rekindle the spirit of agape. Agape and the authentic inclusiveness and hope that it brings is at the very heart of Catholicism, and without it we are nothing but tinkling cymbals.

THE NEXT POPE

Those who like me have experienced the historic change from Pius XII to John XXIII, which was hardly thought possible, or likewise have experienced the collapse of the Soviet empire, can say almost with confidence that a change, indeed a radical revolution, has to come, given the present accumulation of problems. In fact, it is only a matter of time.

—Hans Küng

BY THE TIME this book appears, the Catholic Church could well have a new Pope; although, given his prodigious stamina, John Paul II may be with us, God bless him, for some years to come. When my friend the late Peter Hebblethwaite wrote his book *Next Pope*, announcing that we were already in a "lame duck papacy" and a "pre-Conclave era," it was 1996. Peter Hebblethwaite, God bless him too, has now been dead these five years and John Paul, at this time of writing, has just completed an arduous trip to Greece and Syria. In fact, not so long ago a papal aide told me that His Holiness "ran" down a corridor of the Apostolic Palace to be first to the lift, and it wasn't, he assured me, the alarming, unbalanced "festination" of Parkinson's disease. But inevitably the day will come when some 135 cardinals of the Catholic Church will meet in the Vatican to make a new Pope.

Following Wojtyla's demise there will be nine days of mourning, which will include the lying in state and public viewing of the body, then the funeral, between four and six days after the death. At the end of the Requiem Mass in St. Peter's his body will be placed inside three coffins—pine, oak, and lead—and it is likely that he will be buried in the tombs below the basilica. The prelate responsible for organizing the funeral will be the Cardinal Camerlengo, currently the Spaniard, Eduardo Martinez Somalo. His job is to verify the death (although they no longer do it by striking a silver hammer on the Pope's forehead). He broadcasts the news to the world, then summons the cardinals to the Conclave. He destroys the deceased Pope's seals and ring and locks the papal apartments. All major Vatican business will then cease until a new Pope has been elected.

The election, which takes place in the Sistine Chapel behind locked doors (hence "conclave," meaning "with key"), is preceded by a week or so in which the cardinals ponder the problems of the Church in the world and ask themselves what sort of man will answer the needs of the future. This process takes the form of two retreats, or meditations, within the Vatican, led by priests of high moral reputation. The cardinals pray for guidance in choosing an appropriate Pope. At this time the so-called Grand Electors emerge, senior cardinals, about five in number, who sound out the rest as to their favorite candidates and lobby for their own. "Grand Elector" is not an official title or role, but Vaticanologists are in the habit of identifying them ahead of time. Currently they include Joseph Ratzinger, who oversees the theological orthodoxy of the Church, Godfried Danneels, primate of Belgium; Camillo Ruini, president of the Italian bishops conference; Angelo Sodano, Secretary of State; and Carlo Maria Martini, the Cardinal Archbishop of Milan.

There is a saying in the Vatican: "He who enters the Conclave a Pope, emerges a Cardinal." It is meant as a discouragement to campaigning, lobbying, and media speculation ahead of the final ballot. John Paul himself in 1996 forbade discussion about the possible front-runners for a future papacy. All the same, speculation is human, and favorites have been known to succeed—Paul

VI was an outstanding example, and Pius XI vigorously manipulated the system to tip the scales in favor of his own candidate, Eugenio Pacelli, the future Pius XII.

In the course of a long papacy, those considered *papabili*, potential popes, come and go with the passing of the years. The year Peter Hebblethwaite wrote his book *Next Pope*, the favorites were considered to be Martini, Sodano, and Pio Laghi, then head of the Congregation for Catholic Education. Martini was the bright hope of the progressives, and Sodano and Laghi, both Curial Cardinals (in other words, top Vatican bureaucrats), were considered obvious conservative choices. Other possibles were Roger Etchegaray of France, a middle-of-the-road option, and the Nigerian Francis Arinze, a favored choice for the Third World. Six years on, not one of this list is in with a chance: age, illness, and the circumstances of Vatican politics have undone their prospects.

With the passage of time John Paul has made a profound impression on the composition of the college of cardinals. In his eighth and largest consistory (that is, selection list of new cardinals) he appointed forty-four new cardinals in February 2001. This meant that he had created more cardinals in one go than any other Pope in history, increasing the number of cardinal electors (those under eighty, and eligible to choose a new Pope) to 135, and breaking the limit of 120 established by Paul VI. Wojtyla has now created 125 of the 135 cardinal electors: those who choose his successor are hence men after his own heart. The European cardinals are the largest continental block, sixty-five of them in all, but they no longer outnumber the rest of the world. The other large blocks are: Latin America, twenty-seven; North America, Africa, and Asia, thirteen each. Italy is still the single nation boasting the largest number of cardinals, twenty-four, followed by the United States with eleven and Brazil with seven.

The cardinals are likely to split over whether they wish to see a Curial Pope (like Paul VI), experienced in administration and diplomacy, or a pastoral Pope (like John Paul II), experienced in the day-to-day running of a diocese. Many will be divided over the choice of a progressive or a conservative. Others will ponder their preference for a theologian—an intellectual, or a man of prayer? But the big question, the question that will concentrate the minds of all the elector cardinals, is whether the Church will benefit from a centralizer or a non-centralizer.

John Paul has presided over a bias toward centralized power—strongly identified with Catholic conservatism—unprecedented since the reign of Pius XII. Given the cyclical nature of ancient institutions, the cardinals may wish to see a change. As *The Tablet* puts it: "Conservatives, led by the Vatican Secretary of State, Cardinal Angelo Sodano, have wielded an unusual degree of power, while that of ordinary bishops has been undermined. Their 5-yearly visits to Rome have typically become less a consultation than an instruction of the line to which they must hold. Many want that to change." The key impetus for change, which, the progressives insist, were imperatives at Vatican II, are "collegiality" and "subsidiarity": bishops being allowed greater freedom and authority to run their local churches.

The figurehead of the progressives, Cardinal Carlo Maria Martini of Milan, will be seventy-five in 2001 and has made it clear that he will step down in order to leave Europe and start his retirement in Jerusalem, where he has already bought himself a grave. Apart from Godfried Danneels of Belgium, there is no obvious successor to Martini as the darling of the progressives. Given the strength of the Italian cardinals, and the feeling that it is time for the papacy to return to Italy, it is unlikely this time around to be a foreigner, unless it is one of the Latin Americans in recognition of the importance of the Third World where 70 percent of the Church now lives.

The favored Italian *papabile*, at this time of writing, is Giovanni Battista Re, born in 1934. In the last batch of cardinals he was the first to be announced. Two years ago, the Pope went to visit his hometown in Italy, a mark of great favor. He would be the natural choice of the powerful king-makers, Secretary of State Sodano, and Ruini, who is not only president of the Italian bish-

ops but Vicar for Rome. Re has been number two in the Secretariat of State and was recently made head of the Congregation
for Bishops, a key department.

Vatican observers comment, however, that Re would represent
such a powerful victory for the center that many metropolitan
cardinals, the archbishops of the great dioceses of the world,
would wish to settle for a less obvious bureaucrat. So the name of
Diogini Tettamanzi, aged sixty-seven (in 2001), has emerged. He
is Archbishop of Genoa, a classic middle-of-the-road figure, who
is tipped to go to Milan when and if Martini steps down in 2002.
On the other hand, the Italians might unite behind Darío Castril-
lón Hoyos, a tough and seasoned Vatican bureaucrat from Colom-
bia, in whom they would find a conservative centralizer who
knows the developing world as well the Vatican. Another Latin
American rising star is the man from Honduras, Oscar Rodriguez
Maradiaga from Tegucigalpa, aged fifty-eight. Probably middle-
of-the-road, but an unknown quantity.

A conservative, or even a middle-of-the-road Pope is unlikely
to embark on a reform of the papacy and the Curia, which would
be the essential prelude to breaking the centralizing tendencies of
Wojtyla's pontificate. This, in the view of progressives, would not
bode well for the future of the Church. Failure to rectify over-
centralization would exacerbate the difficulties of maintaining
unity in a world Church of such huge diversity, which, as John R.
Quinn, emeritus Archbishop of San Francisco, comments, "is near
the point of implosion."

Quinn, a powerful American prelate, once president of the
American bishops conference, has usefully drawn a parallel between the need for decentralization in the Catholic Church and
the precedent of international organizations like the International
Red Cross and the United Nations. Central control in such institutions, he argues, gradually becomes counterproductive; the insistence on managing every activity from a central authority
propels the institution toward entropy and disintegration. One

antidote which has succeeded in other world institutions, he points out, is a formula described as "directed autonomy." Members are empowered and encouraged at every level to take responsibility for what they can legitimately contribute in response to boundaries that have been laid down at the center. As Robert H. Waterman, Jr., describes the process in *The Renewal Factor*, "The boss knows that his or her job is to establish those boundaries, then truly get out of the way." The principle, in fact, bears comparison in every way with "subsidiarity," a virtue more honored in the breach in Catholic hierarchy, which is no more than an encouragement of diversity, full participation, and delegation. Subsidiarity, in the view of the progressives, could save the Church from schism and disintegration.

The Catholic Church is not a multinational corporation, however, even though the Pope acts like a CEO; but it has managers, and administration, and responsibilities, and inhabits the real world. It has much to learn, therefore, from the experience, the success, and the failures of other multicultural international institutions. As Quinn reminds us, again: "Directed autonomy simply shows how secular corporations that are international, multicultural, and dealing with complex, diverse, and swiftly changing situations have learned an effective way of avoiding obsolescence, chaos, and fragmentation."

Failure to rectify the current imbalance could accelerate the impetus toward confrontation and breakup; however strong or charismatic a new Pope, it is doubtful whether he could control the rapidly altering events and tensions at the Church's centrifugal and expanding peripheries. Overcontrol at the center is fated to result in loss of control throughout the Church. Failure to initiate reforms in the management of the Church, morever, will bring to a head the theological dispute over centralization, which in turn will lead to a crisis of authority. For the progressives have long urged what the conservatives vociferously deny, that there is a deep contradiction in the growing centralization on the part of the papacy and the Curia on the one hand, and the clear teaching of the Church on collegiality and communion on the other.

The Next Conclave

The next Conclave will take place not earlier than fifteen days after the death of the Pope and not later than twenty days afterward. The cardinals will reside for the first time in a Vatican hotel known as the Santa Marta. In the past they and their secretaries spent the Conclave in uncomfortable cubicles adjacent to the Sistine Chapel where the balloting takes place. Santa Marta has air-conditioning, en suite bathrooms, and room service. But the cardinals will not be able to communicate with the outside world. They will be taken each day by bus to the courtyard known as San Damaso where they will go by elevator to the second loggia of the Apostolic Palace and so to the Sistine Chapel. They will return to Santa Marta's for lunch and a siesta, and do the round trip once again in the early evening.

The cardinals vote secretly on pieces of paper with a pen. The ballots are controlled by three scrutineers who are also chosen by ballot. One is not allowed to abstain. The man who will be Pope must achieve two-thirds of the vote plus one. There are four ballots each day with a day's break after every seven ballots. If the cardinals have not managed to choose a Pope after the subsequent fourteen ballots, following the first sequence of seven, they are allowed by the rules to seek the best of two front-runners, or the candidate with an absolute majority—that is, 50 percent plus one. The cardinal electors will vote on which course of action they will take at the time.

Some believe that in view of the more comfortable lodgings, and with the new rules of election allowing for an absolute majority, the process could take much longer. But Thomas J. Reese, author of *Inside the Vatican*, believes that the cardinals will be at pains to demonstrate to the world that there is no great division or crisis among them. They will get a move on to show the world that the Church is not in crisis.

Given the possibility that the election could be decided finally on a simple majority, the chances are that we will get a conservative Pope since the conservatives represent the clear majority in the current electoral college. In the view of most progressives, a prime task of the new Pope, whatever his leanings, will be to heal the divisions in the Church. This will require a Pope who will strive to mollify the warring factions until the Church can embark on a new council, or at least a meeting of the bishops of the world, that will resolve the current disputes over the intentions of Vatican II.

Many conservatives, however, would be only too happy to see a Pope who carries the Church's divisions to their logical conclusion, forcing the "dissidents" and the "liberals" to toe the line or to exclude themselves. Progressives, by definition, will fight to remain inside the Church, changing it from within, resisting all attempts to identify them as "foreign bodies." But a truly progressive papacy, which refuses to heed the anxieties of the ultra-conservatives, could result in the formation of conservative schismatic factions, similar to the movement of Archbishop Lefebvre.

For a believing Catholic, however, a Conclave transcends the political or corporate elections processes of secular institutions. When the cardinals, and the faithful, have done speculating and calculating the odds, they will be praying for the guidance of the Holy Spirit. Whoever emerges onto the loggia above St. Peter's Square, Catholics will firmly believe, for a time at least, that providence had a crucial part to play in his making.

But in time, inevitably, the consequences of a new papacy will impact, for better or worse, the lives of the faithful—the loyal ones who go to church, the wavering ones who find the practice of their Catholicism oppressive and problematic, the lapsed who miss the Church and would return if they could do so in good conscience. What would a confirmation and continuance of Wojtyla's policies mean for the countless ordinary Catholics who are experiencing special difficulties through no fault of their own?

One could cite the millions in Africa who are forbidden by the official Church to use condoms to combat AIDS; the missionaries who are persecuted for advocating "safe sex"; the countless millions of women who are counseled not to use the contraceptive pill; the pregnant women of Germany who are refused Catholic counseling when they face the difficult choice of abortion; lay Catholics and priests deprived of the freedom to choose their bishops; bishops who are treated like low-grade middle managers; theologians silenced and excluded for daring to voice their opinions in good faith. But I am thinking most of all, as I end this essay, of people who are close to me, deprived of the spiritual sustenance, the liturgy, the sacraments of the Catholic Church, through a new wave of oppression on issues of sexuality and relationships.

Not so long ago, a friend of mine, Celia, asked me this shocking question: "Is it possible that God hates me?" Three years ago at the time of this writing, this young woman—tall, beautiful, resourceful, aged only twenty-five—was married in church. After just eighteen months of marriage, her husband left her to move in with a single mother who was pregnant with his child. Within a year of taking their marriage vows, he had started a secret affair. Celia has had to cope with a combination of destructive, painful emotions: jealousy, solitude, disillusionment. She genuinely loved her erring husband, and has to survive the loss of his affection and companionship, as well as submit to humiliation and failure.

In the eyes of Wojtyla's Church, even though she took her vows of matrimony in good faith, she must now resign herself to a life of sexual abstinence—perpetual "continence." If she marries again, she will be "living in sin," unable to go to Communion in a Catholic church. It will be difficult for her to find a priest willing to baptize the children of a second marriage. There are priests who urge that people in her situation should seek an annulment, but Wojtyla, and, with him an expanding constituency of conservative bishops, has made it clear that the rules for annulment must be tightened rather than relaxed. A more conservative Pope would move to implement and extend the instruction to make annulment more difficult, just as he insists that divorced and remarried Catholics should be denied the sacraments.

Then there is my younger brother. After sixteen years of marriage, his wife left him. An enthusiastic family man, he fought hard to save his marriage, to no avail. His wife divorced him and remarried; the family home was broken up, his children separated. He eventually lost his job, and suffered a serious illness. It took several years for him to recuperate and start a new life. He found a companion, a practicing Christian, but a divorced woman (again, through no fault of her own), and set about rebuilding both their lives. He believed that his faith and his Church had a part to play in mending their broken lives. When they decided to marry, he went to his Catholic parish priest and asked for a simple public blessing on their marriage: this request for a prayer before witnesses in the local Catholic church was refused. So it was that my family—Catholics all of us—gathered in an Anglican church to witness a blessing on his new commitment to married life. The local Catholic priest was doing no more than implementing the harsh centralized rules of Wojtyla's Church: a conservative Pope would confirm that policy and seek to extend it.

And so it goes on: a holy, deeply compassionate priest friend, bullied and harassed by his Bishop for conducting, "without permission," a hugely popular service of general absolution in his parish during Lent; an academic colleague who declined to review a book on women priesthood because she knew that a favorable opinion would adversely affect her future involvement in Catholic tertiary education; an actively gay friend in a long-term partnership, refused Communion at the funeral Mass of his mother; a priest acquaintance who left the ministry without permission in order to marry (permission which, under the present regime, will be denied for many years). This priest and his wife are both faithful Catholics; they now have a child, and are in a state of self-excommunication, denied the sacraments.

These are everyday problems of vast numbers of ordinary Catholics who find themselves discouraged, disillusioned, and marginalized. What is driving them away from the sustenance of Catholic worship and the sacraments, and into communities of faith with more compassion, is a centralized, bullying oppression, aimed at reinstating the sin-cycle of former years. Under a conservative Pope the situation will deteriorate and expand rapidly, pushing greater numbers of Catholics toward antagonism, despair, and mass apostasy.

But what if we had a Pope who genuinely believed that those in trouble, with broken lives, broken relationships, and broken faith, are in the greatest need of inclusion and love? A pastoral Pope for our time would be a Pope who focused his concern on the lost sheep; who ceased to speak of the sinfulness of the faithful, their "culture of death," their "secularism," "indifferentism," and "selfishness." He would recognize that each and every pastor is "father"—the original meaning of the word "pope," *Papa*—within his own faith community. A Pope who would mend the breaking faith of our Church must love all the faithful without exception; he must trust them, in deed as well as in word, and see in the very least of them—the sinners, the marginalized, the dissidents, the discouraged—the continued future of the One, True, Holy, Catholic, and Apostolic Church.

ACKNOWLEDGMENTS

THIS BOOK was made possible by the kindness and, in some cases, unwitting encouragement, of many friends and acquaintances over the years: including Aiden Nichols OP, Leo Chamberlain OSB, Francis Davidson OSB, Ralph Wright OSB, Monsignor Jack Kennedy, Father Vincent Armishaw, the late Denis Hickley, the late Peter Hebblethwaite, Margaret Hebblethwaite, Piers Paul Read, Christian Lady Hesketh, Michael Gilmore, Dan Grisewood, Father Pascal Ryan, Michael Walsh, Nicholas Lash, Timothy Jenkins, Stephen Heath, Catherine Pickstock, Eamon Duffy, John Wilkins, the late Monsignor Francis Davis, the late Father Peter Lawler, the late Philip Caraman SJ, Gerard O'Connell, the late Monsignor Jim Sullivan, Gerry O'Collins SJ, Jonathan Samuel Cornwell, Johanna Gabriella Cornwell, Gabrielle Cornwell, Joanna Cruddas, Maureen Bennett, James Cornwell, and Tobias Wolff.

For information and remoter influences I must thank Roger Birchall, Lavinia Byrne, Paul Collins, Kathy Galvin, the late Adrian Hastings, Clifford Longley, Briege McKenna, John Milbank, Annabel Miller, Robin Morgan, Ben Quash, Tom Reese, the late Gerard Sitwell OSB, Janet Soskice, Peggy Steinfels, Father John Udriss, Dorothy Wade, and Kathy Walsh.

I owe special thanks to Eric Major, Crispin Rope, Clifford J. Corcoran, Birgit Hardt, Barbara Campo, Chuck Antony, my editors Wendy Wolf and Juliet Annan, and my agents Clare Alexander in London and Bob Lescher in the United States.

SOURCE NOTES

Chapter 1: A Catholic Dark Age

John Paul's *Crossing the Threshold of Hope* (Jonathan Cape, London, 1994). Cardinal Ratzinger's comment on the Catholic progressive-traditionalist divide in *Salt of the Earth*, translated by Adrian Walker, interviewer Peter Seewald (Ignatius Press, San Francisco, 1997), p. 54. On modernity and religious values, see Ronald Ingelhart and Wayne E. Baker, "Modernization, Globalization and the Persistence of Traditional Values," in *American Sociological Review* 65 (February 2000), pp. 19–51. Figures on world Catholicism are published annually two years in arrears in the Vatican Secretariat of State's *Annuarium Statisticum Ecclesiae*, hence figures available to me in 2000 were for 1998. The *Annuario Pontificio* (Vatican City) is published every year, containing diocesan information including numbers of active religious and diocesan clergy. Reliable information on the Church in the United States is published by the Center for Applied Research in the Apostolate (CARA). I have based the U.S. figures on CARA's *Catholicism USA* (Orbis Books, New York, 2000), edited by Bryan T. Froehle and Mary L. Gautier. A useful overview of the Church in the Third World to the mid-1990s is Ralph Martin's *The Catholic Church at the End of an Age* (Ignatius Press, San Francisco, 1994). The editorial comment on pluralism and the Church is in *The Tablet*, January 6, 2001, p. 3.

Chapter 2: Divisions

The Detroit meetings are described in *Catholic World Report*, January 1997. Professor Lash's views on conservatives and innovators is in *The Tablet*, October 2, 1999. Also see John R. Quinn, *The Reform of the Papacy* (Herder, New York, 1999). Cardinal Franz König's article on reform is in *The Tablet*, March 29, 1999; König's proposals for the reform of the Congregation for the Doctrine of the Faith is in *The Tablet*, April 7, 2001. Pius X's comments on how to deal with the anti-Modernist sympathizers is cited in Carlo Falconi's *Popes in the Twentieth Century* (Faber, London, 1967), p. 2. The complaint against the "liberals" in *Catholic World Report* by James Hitchcock in "An American Catholic Peace Proposal," April 1998, p. 51. The description of the Church as a black hole can be found in Ratzinger and Seewald, *Salt of the Earth* (Ignatius, San Francisco, 1997), p. 122.

Chapter 3: What Is the Church?

The condemnatory comment on Thomas P. Rausch is in *The Catholic World Report*, April 1998, p. 50. The debate on the role of Pius XI and the future Pius XII in supporting fascism continues; for the latest survey of the documents and historiography see Joseph A. Biesinger, "The Reich Concordat of 1933," in *Controversial Concordats*, ed. Frank J. Coppa (Catholic University of America Press, Washington, D.C., 1999), pp. 133–34. For images of the Church in Vatican II, see *Lumen Gentium* in *Vatican Council II: The Conciliar and Post Conciliar Documents*, volume I (Dominican Publications, Dublin, 1988), p. 345. Karl Rahner, *Hearers of of the Word* (Herder, London, 1969). Teilhard de Chardin's reflection on the Eucharist is in *Hymn of the Universe* (Harper and Row, New York, 1964), p. 318. For Edward Schille-beeckx on negative theology, see *The Understanding of Faith* (Sheed and Ward, New York, 1974) and *Church: The Human Story of God* (Crossroad, New York, 1990). Gustavo Gutiérrez's comment on "the break with an unjust social order" is in *A Theology of Liberation* (Orbis Books, New York, 1972), p. 261. Leonardo Boff, *Church, Charism and Power: Liberation Theology and the Institutional Church* (Crossroad, New York, 1985). Robin Nagle on liberation theology can be found in *Claiming the Virgin* (Routledge, New York, 1997), p. 158. Hans Urs von Balthasar on the external Church is cited in Richard P. McBrien's *Catholicism* (HarperSanFrancisco, 1994), p. 706. Rosemary Radford Ruether's *Women-Church: Theology and Practice of Feminist Liturgical Communities* (Harper and Row, San Francisco, 1985). Mary Douglas at the Catholic Theological Association in *The Tablet*, September 16, 1995.

Chapter 4: The Pope from Poland

Peter Hebblethwaite on the consequences of Vatican II in *The Runaway Church* (Collins, London, 1975), p. 10. De Lubac's view of the conciliar aftermath in *The Motherhood of the Church* (Ignatius, San Francisco, 1982), p. 25. For Wojtyla's association with Dr. Wanda Poltawska, see Jonathan Kwitny, *Man of the Century: The Life and Times of Pope John Paul II* (Little, Brown, London, 1997), pp. 155–56. For the ballot at Wojtyla's election see Michael Walsh, *John Paul II* (Fount, London, 1994), pp. 43–44. For Wojtyla on "ideological compromises," see Kwitny, *Man of the Century*, pp. 466–67. Lefebvre's excommunication is discussed in Tad Szulc, *Pope John Paul II* (Scribner, London, 1995), p. 331. For the Vatican's part in the Ambrosiano Bank scandal see

John Cornwell, *A Thief in the Night* (Viking, London, 1989), p. 126. Bernardin's comment about "altar boys" conveyed by John Wilkins, editor of *The Tablet*, to the author. Archbishop Rembert Weakland on Church models in *The Tablet*, September 9, 1999, p. 1,154. For Cardinal Ratzinger on the Church as dying star, see Ratzinger and Seewald, *Salt of the Earth* (Ignatius, San Francisco, 1997), p. 121. Cardinal Shönborn's comment on the Church of the future, *The Tablet*, March 13, 1999, p. 381.

Chapter 5: A Catholic Personal History

Charles Taylor's comment on the hard choice in *Sources of the Self* (Cambridge University Press, Cambridge, 1992), p. 520. Karl Rahner's more biased view is in *Theological Investigations 4* (Darton, Longman and Todd, London, 1966), p. 58. For the dilemma between humanism and transcendence see also Fergus Kerr's *Immortal Longings* (SPCK, London, 1997), chapter eight passim. "And I have felt a presence . . ." from "Lines Composed a Few Miles above Tintern Abbey," by William Wordsworth, 1798.

Chapter 6: Conversion of Life

Herbert Thurston's *The Physical Phenomena of Mysticism* (Burns and Oates, London, 1952). Coleridge on waterfalls in *Collected Letters*, volume II, edited by E. L. Griggs (Oxford University Press, Oxford, 1956), pp. 853–54. Similarly, in 1805, on a visit to Rome, Coleridge recorded his astonishment at the fountains in St. Peter's Square: "The quiet circle in which Change and Permanence co-exist, not by combination or juxtaposition, but by an absolute annihilation of difference: column of smoke, the fountains before St. Peter's, water-falls, God!—Change without loss—change by perpetual growth, that at once constitutes and annihilates change: the past, and the future included in the Present." *The Notebooks of Samuel Taylor Coleridge*, edited by Kathleen Coburn (Routledge, London, 1961), note 2832.

Chapter 7: The Great Adulteration

The epigraph "These acclamations" is in Fernand Cabrol's long out-of-print book *Liturgical Prayer* (Burns and Oates, London, 1922), p. 53. The adulterations of Catholic "feminists" are recounted by Donna Steichen in *Ungodly Rage: The Hidden Face of Catholic Feminism* (Ignatius Press, San Francisco, 1991), and further developed by Michael W. Cuneo in *Smoke of Satan: Conservative and Traditionalist Dissent in Contemporary American Catholicism* (Johns Hopkins, Baltimore, 1999), p. 29, where Gomar De Pauw's prophecy is cited on p. 23. Catherine Pickstock's critique of liturgical revisions in her thesis *After Writing: On the Liturgical Consummation of Philosophy* (Blackwell, Oxford, 1998), pp. 170–266. See also Eamon Duffy, "Rewriting the Liturgy," in *New Blackfriars*, January 1997. Eamon Duffy's comments on new liturgy are in *Catholicism and Catholicity*, ed. Sarah Beckwith (Blackwell, Oxford, 2000), p. 153; the remark on "I am not worthy" is on p. 156. On irreverence to the Sacred Host, see *The Tablet*, February 10, 2001, p. 10. For the Huron mission see Bruce Trigger, *The Children of the Aataentsic: A History of the Huron People to 1660* (McGill Queens, Montreal, 1976), passim. See also Francis Parkman, *France and England in North America* (Library of America, New York, 1985), passim. A complete edition of the *Relations* is in *The Jesuit Relations and Allied Documents*, edited by Reuben Gold Thwaites (Pageant, New York, 1959). For the mission Jesuits on Hell see Bruce Trigger, *Children of the Aataentsic*, volume II, p. 699. Also see *Popular Catholicism in a World Church: Seven Case Studies in Inculturation*, edited by Thomas Bamat and Jean-Paul Wiest (Orbis, New York, 1999). Father Neuhaus's remarks on "American Shinto" in his Public Square column, *First Things*, March 2000.

Chapter 8: Dilution of Belief

John Fulton's (ed.) project on young Catholics in *Young Catholics at the New Millennium: The Religion and Morality of Young Adults in Western Countries* (University College Dublin Press, Dublin, 2000). John Mahoney SJ's study of Catholic morals in his *The Making of Moral Theology* (Clarendon, Oxford, 1987). Among Greeley's books on Catholic sociology are *American Catholic* (Basic Books, New York, 1977), *The Catholic Myth: The Behavior and Beliefs of American Catholics* (Scribner, New York, 1997), and *The Catholic Imagination* (University of California Press, Los Angeles, 2000). Weaving the Web (Collins Educational, London, 1988–1995). For Greeley's commentary on "weary" Catholics, see *America*, April 10, 1999, p. 9. Ratzinger's comments on German Catholics are in *The Tablet*, April 17, 1999, p. 534. For decline and revival in the Spanish Church see Pedro Belderrain, "What Europeans Believe," in *Misión Abierta* 91, no. 5 (May 1999).

Chapter 9: Catholic "Sexology"

Edward Schillebeeckx has contributed two essays, from which the epigraph is taken, in *Catholic Divorce: The Deception of Annulments*, edited by Pierre Hegy and Joseph Martos (Continuum Publications, London, 2000). For matrimony and chastity, see *Catechism of the Catholic Church* (Geoffrey Chapman, London, 1994), article 7, pp. 358ff. For the Pope on mortal sin and confession, see *The Tablet*, March 27, 1999, p. 448. Father Valerio Paitoni's comment is in *The Tablet*, July 15, 2000, p. 968. Karl Rahner on embryo wastage is cited in Thomas C. Fox, *Sexuality and Catholicism* (George Braziller, New York, 1995), p. 102. Statistics on Catholics who do not think contraception is wrong can be found in, for example, Andrew Greeley, *Sex: The Catholic Experience* (Tabor, Texas, 1994), p. 112. U.S. Catholics on papal authority cited in CNN-*Time* poll conducted by Yakelovich Partners, January 1999. Germans' views on contraception are cited by Forsa Institut, April 2000, based on 1,500 Catholic informants. Catholic Americans on extramarital sex in Greeley, *Sex*, p. 111. Germans on premarital sex cited in Focus INRA opinion survey, 1996. Greeley on single sex in *Sex*, p. 116. John Mahoney on moral theology in *The Making of Moral Theology* (Clarendon, Oxford, 1987), p. 309. John Paul II on the "Gay Pride" Rome march, *The Tablet*, July 15, 2000. John J. McNeill's *The Church and the Homosexual*, 4th edition (Beacon Press, Boston, 1993). Joseph C. Harris on Catholic marriage in the United States in *America*, April 10, 1999. Hegy and Martos (eds.) in *Catholic Divorce*, p. 2; see also the "charade" of annulments, pp. 26ff, 30, and 45. Catholic and non-Catholic abortion figures are in George Gallup, *People's Religion: American Faith in the 90's* (Macmillan, New York, 1989), pp. 176–79. For abortion figures in women using no method see S. K. Henshaw, "Abortion Patients in 1994–1995," in *Family Planning Perspectives 1996* 28, no. 4, pp. 140–47 and 158. Governor Cuomo on Catholic conscience, cited in Thomas Fox's *Sexuality and Catholicism*, pp. 116–17. The declaration on life in *Gaudium et Spes* [*The Church in the Modern World*] in *Vatican Council II: Conciliar and Post Conciliar Documents*, edited by Austin Flannery OP (Dominican Publications, Dublin, 1987). The CCF *New York Times* ad is cited in Michele Dillon's *Catholic Identity* (Cambridge University Press, Cambridge, 1999), p. 106. Ratzinger's threat of excommunication was reported in *Die Welt*, November 20, 2000.

Chapter 10: Priests

Donald B. Cozzens, *The Changing Face of the Priesthood: A Reflection on the Priest's Crisis of Soul* (Liturgical Press, Minnesota, 2000). Information on the percentage of pedophile priests in the United States was supplied by Richard Sipe. CARA figures on seminarian enrollments for 1965–2000 can be found in "Frequently Requested Church Statistics," www.georgetown. edu/research/cara. For projections to 2015, see Lawrence A. Young, "Assessing and Updating the Schoenherr-Young Projections of Clergy Decline in the United States Roman Catholic Church," *Sociology of Religion* (spring 1998). For decline of active priests in Poland, see *Europe Without Priests?* edited by Jan Kerkhofs (SCM Press, London, 1995), p. 2. For age and active ministry of priests in the United States see Bryan T. Froehle and Mary L. Gautier, *Catholicism USA* (Orbis, New York, 2000), p. 111. On deaths and resignations of priests in the United States, see *America*, November 4, 2000, p. 27. On the decline of resident pastors in Europe see Kerkhofs, *Europe Without Priests?* p. 7, and for the decline in France, p. 8. For the decline of resident priests in the United States, see CARA online, "Frequently Asked Questions," www.georgetown.edu/research/cara. Greeley on Sipe is in Andrew Greeley, *Sex: The Catholic Experience* (Tabor, Texas, 1994), p. 119. Cozzens's series of contrasts on changing priesthood is a citation of James J. Bacik in *The Catholic Chronicle* (Toledo), September 29, 1989. For celibacy as deviancy see Thomas Fox, *Sexuality and Catholicism* (George Braziller, New York, 1995), p. 76. Cardinal O'Connor on priestly AIDS in *The Tablet*, October 14, 1995, p. 1,325. For an evenhanded, dispassionate account of the pedophile crisis in the United States, see Philip Jenkins, *Pedophiles and Priests: Anatomy of a Contemporary Crisis* (Oxford University Press, New York, 1996). The comments on Jordan by fellow students were broadcast in the BBC *Panorama* program aired in October 2001. Paul Hendrickson's experience can be found in his book *Seminary: A Search* (Summit Books, New York, 1983), p. 167. William H. Reid's estimate of "sixty offenses for every incident" in *The Psychiatric Times*, April 1988. The NBC report is cited in Tim Unsworth's *The Last Priests in America* (Crossroad, New York, 1991), p. 248. The figure of 48.5 percent for priests and 55.1 percent for seminarians can be found in *Gay Priests*, edited by James G. Wolf (Harper and Row, San Francisco, 1989), pp. 59–60. The view of Father Antonio Mazzi was reported in *The Tablet*, January 13, 2001, p. 56. Cozzens cites Radcliffe in *The Changing Face of the Priesthood*, p. 103. Annabel Miller's citation of seminary rector David Smith is in "This Endangered Species," *The Tablet*, April 24, 1999, pp. 552–54. Monsignor Luca Bonari was quoted in the *Catholic Herald*, February 16, 2001, p. 1. On American Catholics and the next Pope, see Andrew Greeley and Michael Hout, "American Catholics and the Next Pope: A Survey Report, 1996," http://astro.temple.edu/~arcc/grees.htm. On women, WOC, and inclusiveness see Michele Dillon, *Catholic Identity* (Cambridge University Press, Cambridge, 1999), pp. 169–71.

Chapter 11: A Disgruntled Laity

Longley's indignant comment is in *The Tablet*, March 25, 2000, p. 411. Bishop Lehmann's response to the referendum in Germany is in *The Tablet*, September 23, 1995. Pius XI on Catholic Action is quoted in Eamon Duffy's *Saints and Sinners: A History of the Popes* (Yale, New Haven, 1997), p. 258. Vatican II on the laity is usefully described by Kathleen Walsh, "The Apostolate of the Laity," in *Modern Catholicism: Vatican II and After*, edited by

Adrian Hastings (SPCK, London, 1991). Lash's comments on Newman and the "echo" are in *The Tablet*, March 4, 2000, pp. 309–10. On the lay Catholic organizations in Britain, see Mildred Nevile, "The Changing Nature of Catholic Organisations," in *Catholics in England, 1950–2000*, edited by Michael P. Hornsby-Smith (Cassells, London, 1999), pp. 99–121. Michael Walsh on Catholic "congregationalism" can be found in *The Tablet*, February 22, 1997.

Chapter 12: Women in the Church

Figures on the decline in women's vocations based on the Holy See's *Annuarium Statisticum*, 1983–1998. On social mobility and women's vocations, see *The Journal for the Scientific Study of Religion* 35, no. 2 (1996), pp. 171ff. Women in the CTSA in Thomas Fox, *Sexuality and Catholicism* (George Braziller, New York, 1995), p. 217. Women supporting women's ordination in *World Opinion Update* 19, no. 10 (1995); a Gallup poll for 1992 puts the Catholic supporters at two-thirds (cited by Fox in *Sexuality and Catholicism*, p. 207). The comment on "witches in diabolic conspiracy" is cited by John Deedy in *The Catholic Church in the Twentieth Century* (Liturgical Press, Minnesota, 2000), p. 84. Hull Hitchcock's views can be found in *Being Right*, edited by Mary Jo Weaver and R. Scott Appleby (Indiana University Press, Indianapolis, 1995), p. 175. Nancy Hartsock's question is in "Foucault on Power: A Theory for Women?" in *Feminism/Postmodernism*, edited by Linda J. Nicholson (Routledge, New York, 1990), p. 163. A more "positive critique" by Rebecca S. Chopp is in "From Patriarchy into Freedom: A Conversation between American Feminist Theology and French Feminism" in *The Postmodern God*, edited by Graham Ward (Blackwell, Oxford, 1997), p. 237. Uta Ranke-Heinemann on "celibatarians" can be found in *Eunuchs for Heaven* (Andre Deutsch, London), p. 310. Anne Carr, *Transforming Grace: Christian Tradition and Women's Experience* (HarperCollins, San Francisco, 1988), p. 21. Elisabeth Schüssler Fiorenza on patriarchal theologians in *Discipleship of Equals* (Crossroad, New York, 1993), p. 21; on birth control at Notre Dame, ibid., p. 51. The reactions to John Paul II's letter on women from Shirley Williams, Jackie Hawkins, and Sister Pia Buxton in *The Tablet*, July 15, 1995, pp. 920ff.

Chapter 13: The New Inquisition

Francis A. Sullivan's citation of Newman can be found in his *Creative Fidelity: Weighing and Interpreting Documents of the Magisterium* (Gill and Macmillan, Dublin, 1996), pp. 179–80. Lavinia Byrne's story is told in her own words in *The Journey Is My Home* (Hodder, London, 2000). For the American bishops on the *mandatum* see *The Tablet*, December 9, 2000, pp. 1,688–89. Gasparri's view of Pius X is cited in Owen Chadwick, *History of the Popes: 1830–1914* (Oxford University Press, Oxford, 1998), p. 357. Bernhard Haring on ordination of women in *The Tablet*, June 11, 1994, p. 736. Sullivan's discussion of *Ordinatio Sacerdotalis* is in his *Creative Fidelity*, pp. 181–84. Paul Collins on Vatican bullying can be found in John Cornwell, "Burnt Offerings," *Sunday Times Magazine*, August 23, 1998. Mysticism as a basis for religious pluralism is discussed in W. T. Stace, *Mysticism and Philosophy* (Macmillan, London, 1960), p. 326. Karl Rahner's "anonymous Christian" is in *Theological Investigations*, volume VI (Darton, Longman and Todd, London, 1974), pp. 390–91, 393–95. Father Jacques Dupuis SJ's *Toward a Christian Theology of Religious Pluralism* (Orbis, New York, 1997). Gerald O'Collins SJ's review of Dupuis is in *The Tablet*, November 4, 1999. The hospitalization of Dupuis was reported in *The Tablet*, March 21, 1999, p. 448. The citation is from Ratzinger's *Dominus Jesus* (Catholic Truth Society, London), p. 6; the papal quotation within is from *Fides et Ratio* [*Faith and Reason*] in *Acta Apostolicae Sedis* 91 (1999), pp. 5–88.

Chapter 14: The Science and Politics of Saints

Kenneth L. Woodward's *Making Saints: How the Catholic Church Determines Who Becomes a Saint, Who Doesn't, and Why* (Simon & Schuster, New York, 1996). Thérèse of Lisieux on doubt in *Autobiography of a Soul*, translated by Ronald Knox (Fontana Books, London, 1958), p. 202. The correspondent who questioned Sodano and the Congregation for the Doctrine of the Faith wrote in *The Tablet*, May 27, 2000, p. 270.

Chapter 15: Hierarchy

Eamon Duffy on the early Christian period of papacy in his *Saints and Sinners* (Yale University Press, New Haven, 1997), p. 88; on Leo IX, p. 90. The decree of papal infallibility can be found in Denziger and Schönmetzer, *Enchiridion Symbolorum Definitionum et Declarationum* (Rome, 1976), p. 508. Ulrich Stutz, *Der Geist des Codex Juris Canonici* (Stuttgart, 1918), p. 50. For the Gallup poll on laity choosing bishops, see Andrew Greeley and Michael Hout, "American Catholics and the Next Pope: A Survey Report, 1996," available from http://astro.temple.edu/~arcc/grees.htm. German Catholics on papal teaching, Forsa Institut poll, April 2000. Cardinal König's recommendations in *The Tablet*, March 27, 1999, p. 424. Garrett Sweeney's reflection is in *Bishops and Writers* (Anthony Clarke, Cambridge, 1977), p. 208. Paul VI on papal solitude quoted is in P. Hebblethwaite, *Paul VI*

(HarperCollins, London, 1993), p. 339. Newman on papacies beyond twenty years in *Letters and Diaries of John Henry Newman*, volume 22 (London, 1961), pp. 314–15. John Quinn's *The Reform of the Papacy* (Herder, New York, 1999). Avery Dulles, "The Reform of the Papacy," *First Things*, June/July 2000, pp. 62–64.

Epilogue

Interview with Cardinal Martini in the *Sunday Times Magazine*, April 25, 1993. John XXIII on human dignity and freedom is in *Pacem in Terris* (Rome, 1961), paragraph 34. For social scientists on agape and freedom, see, for example, Glenn Tinder, "Can We Be Good Without God?" in *Atlantic Monthly*, December 1989. Father Jacques Dupuis's citation of Henri de Lubac on the newness of Christianity can be found in Dupuis's *Toward a Christian Theology of Religious Pluralism* (Orbis, New York, 1997), p. 137.

INDEX